misbegotten anguish

misbegotten anguish

A Theology and Ethics of Violence

Cheryl Kirk-Duggan

CHALICE PRESS

ST. LOUIS, MISSOURI

Cover art: Detail from untitled pastel drawing by C'babi
Cover design: Geoffrey Connors
Interior design: Elizabeth Wright
Art direction: Michael Domínguez

This book is printed on acid-free, recycled paper.

Visit Chalice Press on the World Wide Web at
www.chalicepress.com

10 9 8 7 6 5 4 3 2 1   01 02 03

Library of Congress Cataloging–in–Publication Data
Kirk-Duggan, Cheryl A.
    Misbegotten anguish : a theology and ethics of violence / Cheryl
Kirk-Duggan.
            p.   cm.
    Includes bibliographical references and index.
    ISBN 0-8272-2327-7
    1. Violence--Religious aspects--Christianity.   2. Womanist theology.
3. Violence–Moral and ethical aspects.   4. Christian ethics.
    I. Title.
    BT736.15 .K57   2001
    241'.697--dc21   00-012059

Printed in the United States of America

To three distinguished gentlemen,
who have lived and embodied Justice,
the lens for me to see the misbegotten anguish before me:

My dad, the late Rudolph V. Kirk,
first African American Deputy Sheriff
in the State of Louisiana since Reconstruction;
in twenty-seven years on the force,
he never fired his gun in the line of duty.

My husband, the Honorable Michael A. Kirk-Duggan,
encyclopedic mind, gigantic heart, and sociopolitical critic
who invites and encourages me to do the monumental;
who helps me not sweat the small stuff;
and who reminds me that it is all small stuff.

My mentor, Dr. Ismael Garcia,
friend and ethicist, who challenged me
in our classes on Justice,
guided me through Central America,
and nurtured my pursuit of critical analysis.

Contents

Preface   ix

Part I: Perceiving and Baptizing Violence

1   Constructing the Kaleidoscope: Introducing Violence
and Justice—A Womanist Reading   3

2   Contemplating the Mimetic Product of Violence:
The Scapegoat   29

Part II: Power, Control, and Loss

3   Contracting Mechanistic Muscles: War and Colonialism   65

4   Cheating, Defaming, and Abusing Eve:
Sexism, Seduction, Gender, and Domestic Violence   95

5   Conjugating Elitism: Classism and Caste-ism   127

Part III: Powers and Pathologies

6   Corrupting the Rainbow: Racism Personified   153

7   Choosing Hypocrisy, Betrayal, and Miseducation:
Our Complicity in Violence   183

Part IV: Prophetic Promises

8   Changing Creation: A Prolegomenon to a Theology
and Ethics of Violence   207

Index   221

The scars
Across her body,
Binding her heart,
Stymieing her mind,
Killing her soul:
Riddled with an agony of deep blue,
Tears like ancient waterfalls
Surged out to whoever looked,
Flooding the distant, yet intimate space,
And screamed:
"Why didn't you see?"

Eyes of perpetrators
Objectified the child,
Those deemed weaker,
Predators hunting prey.
Appetizers of sensual delight
Arousing them to a level of pathological ecstasy
Wet with desire,
Offensive and blasphemous!
Despicable to you?
Pleasant and inviting
To the once victim:
Turned predator.

And, in your politeness,
You kept silent.
You lied, became a hypocrite;
Fancy, neat in your silk;
Cool and comfy in your jeans;
But we lied
When we did not care.
We robbed innocence
When we did not speak.
We participated by consent.

Preface

Violence titillates and terrorizes us. Packaged in celluloid and running for one hundred and twenty minutes, sagas of blood, guts, and gore with fast action, terrific cinematography, a provocative and sultry music score, and actors exhibiting impressive physiques or high-profile careers are the things that make for an Oscar. That same ethos packaged in a forty-ounce bottle, a one hundred-proof flask, or a glassine of nose candy, thrust on our neighbors or the folks down the block, next door, across the street, in the barrio, or in exclusive subdivisions—sometimes right beneath our own noses in our own homes—reeks of dysfunctional behavior, dehumanization, and domination. Such deviant conduct results in domestic abuse, workplace violence, Napoleon Bonapartesque supervisors, depression, addiction, or murder—making violence a number one public health menace. Violence is a public health crisis. Such violence is personal, individual, communal, and systemic. For some persons, violence is orgasmic, leading them to engage in sadomasochism with leather whips and metal chains. An adrenaline rush compels some individuals to kill spirits, minds, and bodies. The adrenaline rush may act as a catalyst to effect sexual arousal. Passion that could be changed to honor the beauty and sacred in all persons becomes evil, as persons created in the image of God become vile perpetrators or demented victims, miscreants of the worst sort. Some active or passive perpetrators are sociopaths and psychopaths: mortal beings who do not have a conscience, who choose to violate other sentient beings at will. Other perpetrators take the childhood abuse vented on them, internalize it, and then project that pain and suffering back on others, with generations of continuous deviant abuse. Conversely, violence has wounded some to such depths that they become paranoid, delusional, paralyzed, and traumatized victims. These broken persons seem to attract individuals who sense their vulnerability. Such hurting, often emotionally immature persons become targets for predators, who then seduce the troubled individual and psychologically coerce the hurting person into compliance. This all-too-frequent scenario creates a *dramatis personae* as victim with a pathology of deep woundedness. The cycle of violence perpetuates itself and becomes generational.

Before we become too self-righteous about our alleged distance from violence, or wonder how in the world violence continues to escalate, we need only realize the amount of violence implicit in many of our world religions, read the violence in our sacred texts, and see the violence common to civil religion. Within the chronicles of Judaism and Christianity, biblical texts celebrate wars, ethnic cleansings, crusades, human sacrifices, and ritualized murders. For some Muslims, to lose one's life in a jihad or holy war is an honorable end. In some countries, to die as a kamikaze pilot or to commit suicide when one can no longer live an honorable life is an honorable thing to do. In these United States, our nationhood is rooted in violence. This union developed on lands taken from native peoples, moistened by their trail of tears. Much of the labor in this country, constructing buildings and railroads, producing goods in factories and through farming, has been accomplished through subjugation and slavery of many peoples, including those of African, Hispanic, and Asian descent. We have civilized some of our violence through professional and amateur sports from boxing, wrestling, soccer, extreme sports, and kickboxing to recreational hunting. We have canonized and ritualized this violence in our national anthem with "bombs bursting in air."

The catalyst for *Misbegotten Anguish* emerged when my husband and I went to see Steven Spielberg's *Saving Private Ryan*. My husband and buddy, Michael, noted, "If you, Cheryl, are going to be against war, then you need to know why." I hesitated about going because of the death and violence in the movie, but for the sake of the cause I agreed. The film both titillated and terrorized me: I was intrigued by the story and the ramifications for the number of lives, military and civilian, lost. I shook my head at the tremendous decimation of natural resources, property, culture, and communities. My heart grieved for all the boys who never really became men because they lied on their enlistment forms out of a need to do something for their country; for certainly the exercise of one's patriotic duty is a noble enterprise. I was captivated by why, in two thousand years plus, humanity has not yet learned to live together. We have not yet "gotten" that war takes too many lives, and most of the wars have been ultimately rooted in economic issues—somebody's greedy need to be in control, to own, to rape the land, to produce more of some commodity. My terror shifted to sadness, amazement, and back to intrigue. I was so hyper after the movie ended that I decided I had to do something about, around, and on violence. Like most teacher-learners, I realized that if I really wanted to delve deeply into this subject, I needed to develop a course and then research, explore, ponder, and teach this material, because my students would help teach me more about the subject matter and about the human spirit than all of my reading could ever teach me.

From that realization, Michael and I brainstormed over film and other narrative genres that feature different kinds of violence. With my musical background, I knew I had to explore opera. Having both studied and performed opera, I was well acquainted with the tragic and violent climaxes of most operas. The heroines often either die of tuberculosis, a.k.a. consumption *(La Boheme)*, go mad *(Lucia di Lammermoor)*, or commit suicide *(Tosca, Madama Butterfly)*. The heroes kill someone or kill someone's character *(Othello)*; they self-destruct because of personal improprieties, and the gods get back at them *(Don Giovanni)*; they are the victims of ritualized homicide *(Billy Budd)*; or they weep over the lifeless body of their murdered heroine *(Carmen)*. With our student constituency being individuals trained to do ministry in the parish, agencies, or educational institutions, I knew we needed to include scripture. Persons in ministry, particularly in the parish, use sacred texts. Problematically, those texts often contain a tremendous amount of violence by the deity and human beings, justifying violence as a tool of salvation and justice. Because our culture is so visually based, I knew that film needed to be another category. With the trauma over the shooting at Columbine and concern about sensational video games and the immediacy of violence in films such as *Pulp Fiction,* we need to look into the short- and long-term effects of such high-tech depiction of violence. Next, I thought through my other conversation partners in philosophy, theology, ethics, and the arts. In the midst of this thinking, the phrase that captured me became the title for this work: *Misbegotten Anguish. Misbegotten Anguish* is the product of a pilgrimage from the viewing of *Saving Private Ryan,* through much reflection and engaging in a seminar with my students as co-teacher-learners, to more reflection and integration.

Misbegotten Anguish explores the theology and ethics of violence, using the genres of scripture, opera, and film. Chapter 1 explores various definitions, images, themes, and metaphors that develop or emerge in studying the concepts, ramifications, and challenges of violence, and the chapter qualifies my understanding of misbegotten anguish. Chapter 2 explores the relationship between psychological activities and epistemological contexts to determine the nature of and catalysts for scapegoating. Chapter 3 examines the attitudes, belief systems, and intricacies of violence amid the civil religious experiences of war and colonialism. Chapter 4 analyzes the function of traditional and cultural mores present in embodied gender oppression or sexism within the context of sociotheological attitudes and the misuse of power. Chapter 5 investigates the impact of individual and systemic attitudes and actions on the experience of classism in the United States. Chapter 6 ponders how human actions and attitudes nurture the sin, the arrogance, and the pathos of racism. Chapter 7 explores individual and communal hypocrisy, betrayal, and miseducation amid our complicity in violence. Chapter 8 concludes the study by offering a constructive framework for transforming misbegotten anguish into sacred encounter of creation, the self, and others. In celebration of all that has transpired on and off the pages of this volume, I take great joy in acknowledging many voices who sang in the choruses that fed my mind, inspired my heart, and brought joy and thanksgiving to my soul.

To Jon L. Berquist, my editor for this project, I owe a debt of thanks. I am deeply appreciative to the president, dean, faculty, and students at the Graduate Theological Union, Berkeley, where I first taught some of these ideas in a course entitled "Misbegotten Anguish." Fourteen brave souls met for a seminar at 8 a.m. on Tuesdays during Fall 1999 to join me on this monumental quest. Not only did we meet but we reached deep within the texts and even deeper within ourselves as we searched for meaning, for wisdom, and ultimately, for healing. Thus, my gratitude to Anna Adams, Marcia Blasi, Brooke Briggance, Stuart Cunningham, Nicola Frail, Kelly Leichsenring, Kimberlee Lekas, Douglas Lubes, Maureen Minihane, Tamae Nakai, Jon Pedigo, Becky Thelen, Mark Throckmorton, and Mary Whited. I hold in deep regard the staff at the Center for Women and Religion, a program unit at the Graduate Theological Union, where I serve as executive director. They celebrated and encouraged each milestone in the completion of this manuscript: Ken Rowe, Joellynn K. Monahan, and Kimberly Whitney. My thanks to the members of WESCOR and the American Academy of Religion, Western Region, for an opportunity to share some of the ideas found in Chapter 7 for my Presidential speech in Spring 2000. To the president, dean, faculty, and students of United

Theological Seminary of the Twin Cities (UTS), and especially the staff of Spencer Library, who were so incredibly supportive, thank you, thank you. My UTS students asked the kinds of questions that kept me pushing the boundaries and during an intense summer session demonstrated to me the embodiment of womanist theology and ethics. Thanks again to Joann Campbell-Sudduth, Jody Furnas-Wright, Grace Hamilton, Arlene Hammond, Ezra-Levi Keefe, Cynthia Kennedy, Mary Kitchell, Shirley Koepsell, Margaret Lovejoy, Barbara Moore, Patricia Nanoff, and Beth Ann Schumacher. During my month at United in Summer 2000, I reconnected with nature in a powerful way, which gave me deeper insights into my self, ever renewing for me the notion that writing is laughing and dancing with God. Deep appreciation to Mary Bednarowski, Carolyn Pressler, Rosetta Ross, and Gloria Roach Thomas for so many words and acts of kindness during the summer term.

As I stand amid a cloud of celestial witnesses, several congregations and prayer partners provide continuous support, no matter how outrageous my path or how incredible the demands I make on myself. I am indebted to the congregations of Phillips Temple CME Church, Berkeley, California, to the Reverends Tony Summers, Paulette Love, and Minister Brenda Houston for their unceasing support, and to Fr. Jason and the wonderful members of St. Columba's Roman Catholic Church, Oakland, California, for always being glad to see me and passing on words of wisdom. For the special spiritual and supportive words of my sister, Dedurie Kirk, and my prayer partners and spiritual soul sisters, Faye Morris, Michele Jackson, Pat Pevoto, Janice Lee, Belinda Richards, Linnie Corey, Salima Swain, Adrian Fowler, and Allison Franzetti, I give thanks. To my beloved husband, who made sure I saw *Saving Private Ryan,* the catalyst for this entire project: for being a terrific house spouse so that I could write, I give my deepest, heartfelt thanks.

Cheryl Kirk-Duggan

PART I

Perceiving
and
Baptizing
Violence

The screams, unsounded,
The pain radiating,
Megawatts of emotional electricity:
These were the causes;
You knew the effect:
Violence, abuse.

Rage internalized;
Rage projected outside:
Found in bottles of 100 proof,
In snorted nose candy,
In obesity and anorexia.
Multiplied, ending in E.R.'s:
Gunshot wounds, stabbings, ODs,
Fleshy pulp, black and blue,
A contorted bleeding mask,
Where once a face resided.

Queens and kings of violence
All wear subtle garb
Coded with colors of gnostic meaning:
Barbed language;
Discriminatory practices;
Psychological and emotional coercion.
Some are psychopaths and sociopaths:
Some wracked with pain,
Hurt so deep—
All catalysts that explode or implode, or both:
An indictment of all,
An invitation to faith communities.
How else shall we save our children?
Our society?

And guess what?
THESE pictures aren't just about *THOSE* people:
Over there, who are poor,
Who live in war-torn countries.
Violence is no respecter of
Class, power, gender, sexual orientation, age, or race.
When we look in the mirror,
Therein lies the potential.
And what is your violence quotient?

1

Constructing the Kaleidoscope

Introducing Violence and Justice—
A Womanist Reading

To read *Misbegotten Anguish* is to confess one's complicity in, denial of, or acceptance of violence. Historical and contemporary documentation abounds regarding the prevalence of violence in the world, both personal and institutional. The proliferation of violence on stage and screen, on canvas and in courtrooms, next door and in our own kitchens has reached mythic proportions. Violence is systemic and often couched in polite language, ingrained by supremacist patriarchy, and, in most subtle, frightening terms, by feminist patriarchy. The first is an experience of male domination; the second is a matter of women who, having been trained in this pathological system, both invoke and embody the tenets of patriarchy while believing firmly that since they are not male, they are per se liberationist. The tragedy of supremacist patriarchy is the loss of a fullness of life in equity for all people. The tragedy of feminist patriarchy is that those women engaged in such patriarchal-like oppression often are unaware of their participation, despite the palpable and blatant appearances. The wounds of feminist patriarchs are so deep, so subconscious, that the women cannot help but operate out of the same ethos they experienced, the very ethos that allowed them to advance to positions of power. This male and female patriarchal malaise is so thick and entrenched that many so-called liberals never see their own prejudices—the veneer of liberalism. These phenomena become apparent when one deemed other, lower in rank, or inferior dares to encroach on the sacred territory of patriarchal privilege, to enter that inner sanctum as a challenge. Then Stalinist tendencies rear their lofty heads, and the once liberal shows her or his real self. The pretenses of empathy, collaboration, and solidarity fall apart like sands trickling through an hourglass. The really sad commentary is that the patriarchal feminist or the good old male liberal will not have a clue as to her or his hypocrisy. Usually, no amount of explaining or providing examples can illumine the particular situation. The saccharine-tinted, supremacist liberalism wafts sweetly in a gentle breeze, but it feels like a fingernail scraping a chalkboard. Their practiced scripts allow the oppressors on a large scale to abuse their power and authority, feigning ignorance of their sins, their scapegoating, and their betrayal of the other.

Consequently, before we can begin to assess our violence quotient, we have to be at a place of integrity. We need to be honest about who we are and where we have been. We must ask what we are doing and at whose expense if we want to know healing and to be community participants who can effect transformation, justice, and peace. Once the openness is there, we can begin the healing process and deal with the pain and hurt of old wounds so that we can get well. There may or may not be visible wounds. We each may need to do an in-depth self-reflection and/or personal inventory, which should be done with a supportive community or at the least a counselor or spiritual director. We must also become acquainted with global and personal history. Sometimes to get to a pervasive issue and visceral veracity such as violence, which often presses one to live in denial, we can best approach the difficult topic through cultural artifacts and media. The Robert Mitchum movie *The Night of the Hunter* [1] makes clear how tedious and labor intensive such a process is, particularly given the ambiguities, similarities, and fine lines between right and wrong, and all the shades of gray in between.

---

[1] This 1955 United Artists film, directed by thespian Charles Laughton, is based on a 1953 novel by Davis Grubb (New York: Harper & Brothers).

This chapter uses *The Night of the Hunter* to uncover some of the critical elements for discerning certain foundational issues about violence and justice from a womanist perspective. After reviewing the plot of the film and my understanding of womanist theological ethics, I then: (1) define various ways of understanding the complex levels of violence, highlighting particular examples from this film; (2) illumine selected acts and types of violence, particularly in the biblical text; (3) offer various ways scholars have viewed the issues of justice; and (4) express the dialogical model of analysis for this volume, weaving together the metaphor of misbegotten anguish, violence, and justice.

The Night of the Hunter: Sugarcoated Anguish

The movie opens with an older woman teaching a Sunday school class by telling a biblical story to a group of young children. As the teacher/guardian continues to speak, the camera pulls our eyes to the faces of children surrounded by a starry night. Shortly thereafter, we meet a murderer who tells his children to hide money just before he is arrested. He was tired of seeing so many children going hungry during the Depression of the 1930s and did not want his children ever to suffer. He stole the money so that he and particularly the children could have a better life. We then meet the Preacher, who shares a jail cell with the children's dad, Ben Harper. The Preacher has been sentenced to thirty days in jail for stealing a road car. This Preacher has the word L-O-V-E tattooed on the fingers of his right hand and H-A-T-E tattooed on his left hand's fingers. He uses his hands as a prop to deliver his homily, saying that Brother Left Hand was the hand Cain used to strike his brother, while L-O-V-E on the right hand is the hand that stretches out to the soul of humanity. We learn many lessons in those few minutes. The Bible story being read to the children signifies the reality and the fruit of false prophets. We see violence subtly and blatantly portrayed. Notions of God, religion, and sexuality merge. The Preacher declares that he detests lace, prostitutes, and female strippers, but at the same time he is drawn toward them.

Robert Mitchum portrays the Preacher, the Reverend Harry Powell, who exacts strong reactions from most people. His persona is manipulative and opportunistic. On the one hand he asserts a trust in God for God's provision, but that provision comes as the result of the Preacher's murdering someone. This man of God sees no contradiction in killing another person to get what he wants. When he arrives in town, he lies and says that he was a chaplain at the prison where Harper was housed before his execution. Preacher Powell plays on the sympathies of the townspeople. Feigning the depths of respectability, he masks a heart of terror and evil. The black-and-white cinematography helps to reveal what appears to be simple and beautiful as vile, rotten, and nauseating. The underlying, sickening evil that fuels self-deception on the part of the Preacher exacerbates and escalates. The nostalgic, idyllic settings simply hide the raging pathology and evil that lie below the surface. The film imparts numerous symbols and uses characters in a manner that demonstrates the historicity of violence, the implications of expulsion from the garden of Eden as generational or original sin, and the stereotypes that our culture has forged regarding the light as good and dark as evil stereotypes. Again the misogynist, sexual tendencies of the Preacher projected onto women are symbolized by his frequent use of his homemade switchblade, an overt phallic symbol. The switchblade serves as his banner of courage, his embodied sexual prowess, for without it, the Preacher might feel himself rendered impotent. He woos, seduces, and marries Willa, the mother of the children whose father has been executed for bank robbery and murder, to gain access to the money her dead husband stole. The Preacher constantly demeans the mother, beating her psychologically into submission, declaring a la Augustine that sexual intercourse is for having babies, not for assuaging sin-filled lust or carnal desires.

Preacher Powell tells Willa that her body is meant for begetting children, not for the lust of men. Willa acquiesces to believe that she is not pure as she travels with Preacher Powell, who rails against desire. Preacher Powell continually taunts the son, John, about the money, and tells him that his mother will believe the preacher over her son. Willa tries to keep peace and harmony between the two, which she sees as a burden. The Preacher also works to separate the daughter, Pearl, from her brother. Finally, one evening in their bedroom, the preacher has so psychologically abused Willa that even when she learns the Preacher married her for the money, she believes that God set it up for him to come and show her the way and the light. As the Preacher rails against her, she lies in bed, folds her arms, closes her eyes, and he stabs her to death. Throughout the film, the Preacher abuses the office of clergy to bargain with God, to rationalize his own criminal activity, and to gain influence over communities wherever he travels. His perverse sensibilities are presented in bas-relief to the simplicity, fragility, and innocence of nature and the children. The L-O-V-E/H-A-T-E tattoos remind us that the extremes of alleged good and evil often parallel each other, and such extreme concepts may be fatal to the well-being of all. Certainly these extremes were not healthy or helpful to the two children, whose father made them promise never to reveal the hiding place of the money within the little girl's doll.

One recoils at what the children in the movie experience; yet every day children are at risk and subject to similar bouts of vulgar and repulsive adult violence. The movie reminds us of the attacks on children today that prostitute and abuse them, that force them to run away and to take drugs or to drink. For example, in the movie the children see the police treat their father as a caged animal. No dignity is accorded him as the police wrestle him to the ground and handcuff him. The children also witness the violence that comes from lying to another adult in the family unit, pitting both adults against the children. Children often receive mixed messages and are taught to "do as I say, not as I do." Their traumas force them to grow up too fast, and to grow old too soon.

In addition to the children's plight and the contrasting use of light and dark, music plays a key feature in *The Night of the Hunter*. The music signifies the romantic pleasantries and joys of small-town life over against the sinister, foreboding presence of evil. After viewing this movie, one cannot listen to the hymn "Leaning on the Everlasting Arms" again in the same way. The Preacher sings the chorus (his perverted theme song, which announces his evil presence) throughout the movie:

Leaning, leaning, safe and secure from all alarms;
leaning, leaning, leaning on the everlasting arms.

The irony of this being the theme song for the diabolical Preacher, who threatens the safety and security of all those he comes in contact with, is not lost on the viewer. The Preacher manipulates, taunts, and plays on the emotions of the townspeople, the widow, and the children. The little girl is mesmerized by the Preacher, but the boy is not. The Preacher works to convince the children that God wants the children to give the money to the Preacher so that the Preacher can build a great cathedral. This payment would atone for the father's sin of murdering two people during the process of robbing the bank and stealing the $10,000. Until the Preacher murders the widow, she too is taken in by the Preacher's charms. He is a predator and taunts the children until he finds out the hiding place for the money. Although the children manage to escape with the doll, the Preacher later tracks them down at a foster home. There the Preacher is arrested after he attempts to retrieve the doll and the foster mother shoots him in the leg. The crowd who sang the praises of the Preacher and saw him as an eligible bachelor is the same crowd who now wishes to lynch him. The movie begins and ends with images of light, with the children hearing Bible stories under a starry sky at the opening and receiving their Christmas presents on a bright, snowy morning at the close. This cinematographic whiteness and lightness does not diminish the grim, menacing brutality of violence.

The Night of the Hunter teaches us about the ambiguities and paradoxes of violence, and cautions us about living on the edge of extremes. Life and matters of violence and evil are not simple, but most complex. Juxtaposing the idyllic and the baneful produces a saccharine-like pathology of destruction. Both extremes are nauseating and sickening, at once drawing us into, then pushing us away from the nostalgic. There is no healthy way to romanticize violence, yet this is often done in popular culture, particularly in action films, be they older Westerns or more recent works of technological wizardry, such as *Star Wars* and *Star Trek.* The many blatant and subtle symbols and images of underlying text call us to question reality, what we believe, see, think, and feel. How is it that beauty can innocently frame an undercurrent of evil? What is the impetus for children and adults to commit violent acts? Theologically and ethically, how do we interrogate and understand questions of generational or original sin, light versus dark, and our other myriad stereotypes? Is there such a thing as generational sin to the point that in most situations, a thief's child will become a thief? That the sins of the mothers and fathers are visited upon the children does not mean that they inherited this capacity through physical DNA, but that they have lived in an environment where crime is committed. Thus, without a great deal of willfulness or the community stepping in, the children also will commit crimes, perhaps even worse ones. Before unmasking and analyzing the theological and ethical dimensions of violence in *The Night of the Hunter,* we turn now to review the methodology that will provide a lens through which to see ambiguity and complexity.

Inviting a Womanist Perspective

A Writ of Protest—
Sound kindled from your being:
An ember, close to death,
An ignited combustion,
That enables us to
Let our lights shine.
For our sacred voices,
Midst time eternal,
Heralding the past,
Speaking transformation
For the present,
Saying, "we shall not be moved."
Oh, beautiful blackness
From the dust of
Africa, America, and the World:
Women of magnificence
Chocolate, sepia, vanilla, mocha hues.
You live, are alive
With the breath of God;
Exposing the oppression,
Championing freedom:
A beauty more radiant than stars,
A strength more indelible than freedom,
A mind and artistry more brilliant than time:
A communal sense that twinkles, and mesmerizes
By Faith, by Grace,
Journeying forward
A Path of Justice.

There are a variety of ways to view, analyze, critique, hear, and understand what goes on in the world in general, and about the dynamics of violence in particular. One of the more inclusive methods or hermeneutics of seeing and hearing is *womanist* theory. *Womanist,* derived by Alice Walker[2] from the term *womanish,* refers to women of African descent who are audacious, outrageous, in charge, and responsible. *Womanist* thought first requires that we engage skills and histories out of the lived experiences of African

---

[2]Alice Walker, *In Search of Our Mothers' Gardens: Womanist Prose* (San Diego: Harcourt Brace Jovanovich, 1983), xi.

American women. We must take a *reality check*–name and talk about the oppression that occurs and how that relates to God talk, or to doing theology, or to God walk, or to ethics. This mode of analysis unfolds in a manner that is inclusive of all persons, particularly embodied in the lives of poor Black women. Their lives are a reservoir where we readily see the results of racism, sexism, classism, homophobia, ageism–and any other categories devised as a weapon against those most easily objectified and forgotten.

Womanist theology is the study or discipline of God talk that emerges out of the rich, yet oppressive experiences of African American women. This theology analyzes and critiques human individual and social behavior in concert with the Divine, considering the ramifications of injustice and malaise due to the triple oppressions of racism, classism, and sexism, and the use of power, moving toward change, balance, and promise. A *womanist* emancipatory theology embraces a message of hope and transformation with the goal of engendering mutuality and community, and honors the *Imago Dei* in all persons. *Womanist* theology builds on the essential goodness of humanity and focuses on liberation amid personal and societal fragmentation in general and theological discourse in particular. With this ground of being, it becomes clear that every person is sacred, made in God's image, which must become a fundamental rubric and operating principle in society if we are ever to stem the tide of violence.

To embrace the sacredness of humanity involves understanding the function and process of theological discourse, and how this discourse, related traditions, and one's tenets of faith shape one's experience of self, of God, and of one's neighbors. Such a stance also moves a person to be keenly aware of the historical oppression of poor women, Black women, and other women of color; their tools of survival or mother wit; and how religion and the church have been a part of the violence, control, and manipulation perpetrated against women, particularly in sermons and shoddy pastoral care.

Womanist theology intentionally creates arenas where African American women's experiences are visible. *Womanists* expose cruelty and are serious about their commitment to the survival, wholeness, and health of all people. I am a Christian *womanist:* I am a *womanist* storyteller and performer who has a faith belief in the Christian story combined with an appreciation for the richness of God's revelation in the world through many faiths, and a theological bent and ethical sensibility toward creating new avenues of possibility and communal solidarity. Consequently, my use of *womanist* theology embodies reformation. Such reformation confronts the many complex issues of individual and communal daily life amid the grace of God and social justice issues with a vision of life that champions immediacy and inclusivity. My *womanist* vision searches for a way to champion the freedom, dignity, and justice of *all* people–a prelude to the praxis of morality, a prelude set not to music, but to the rhythm of words, of poetics.

Womanist theory, with a faith-based curiosity, seeks to discover, analyze, and honor the lives and gifts of Black women to move toward the transformation of themselves, other African Americans, and of society: empowerment instead of denial and destruction. Cloaked in oppression, a Christian *womanist* stance involves first theology (identity, sacrality, subjectivity, spirituality, power). The identity question presses us to ask, Who is God? Who am I? Who really makes up my community? Sacrality holds us accountable for knowing and acting out of a context of a holistic sense of body, mind, and spirit–our total selves, made by God–that we are of God. Subjectivity celebrates the I-amness of each individual, due dignity and respect. Spirituality, or holy vitality, is the experience of living out the sacred, which includes, but is not exclusive to, religion or denominational commitments. Power denotes an influence, permission, and an ability to choose, to make decisions, to responsibly effect change.

Second, a Christian womanist hermeneutics involves the Bible and other sacred texts (authority, characters, language, rituals, history). Authority pertains to giving credence to, the privilege of, and the respect or right to rule, govern, or dictate procedure, process, and protocol. Characters involve the participants and actors in stories or narratives. Language involves the various tools of communication–words, movements, and gestures. Rituals include the formal or informal practices involving patterns of adoration or faith that honor a philosophy, deity, tradition, or way of life. History is the oral or written documented events and stories of the past.

Third, this hermeneutics embraces ethics (value, behavior, visibility, integrity, praxis). Value inheres in something deemed special, important, and significant. Behavior pertains to the complex ways people act, engage, and live. Visibility is the freedom to see and be seen. Integrity comprises principled morality, honor, and honesty. Praxis is the lived, pragmatic, and practical daily reality.

Fourth, a Christian womanist methodology involves context (autobiography, culture, aesthetics, ecology, community). Autobiography involves one's relationship with oneself, in a mode of being and acting that is authentic, with dignity, and without apology. Culture encompasses the various complex systems of knowledge, education, government, art, science, religion, technology, and entertainment. Aesthetics concerns the expression of beauty and elegance. Ecology relates to an appreciation of and respect for all nature and a balanced life within creation from a context of stewardship: the freedom and gift of being responsible for human and other resources. Community incorporates an interrelated body of persons connected by geography, culture, or beliefs.

Womanist theology champions Black women's struggle for freedom, and deals with social and ecclesial oppression in the mandate for silence and submission[3] by unfolding an African American vision of freedom and justice. This impetus springs from the feminist aspects of the Black religious folk expression of mothers to their children. *Womanist* vision creates a way of seeing that is (1) eschatological or goal-oriented; (2) about total health and liberation of individual and communal mind/soul, spirit, and body; (3) about the relational, historical Black experience; (4) based on real feelings, experiences, actions; and (5) a transformational, life-changing process that enhances everyone. Through a liberating, biblical *womanist* vision, identification and healing in communion with a living God intensifies. Thus, people know God as a personal, powerful, compassionate liberator who encompasses masculine and feminine qualities and cares about individuals and communities.

This *God* is "a making a way out of a no-way God," who is a "mother to the motherless and father to the fatherless."[4] Relationship with this God allows one to survive and transcend, and to accept and celebrate the gifts of creation. The *womanist* relational view of God produces intimacy, mercy, love, compassion, and solidarity. This God is real and present. This God creates persons *imago Dei* (in God's image) in a manner that embraces diversity, mutuality, and

---

[3]Womanist theologians, like other groups, do not agree on all issues. Cheryl Sanders argues that Christianity forms the center of ethical and theological identity; that the term *womanist* overemphasizes secularity, lesbian love over heterosexual love, and does not focus on Christianity enough. However, most womanists, myself included, affirm a strong biblical and christological heritage. See Deane William Ferm, *Contemporary American Theologies: A Critical Survey,* rev. ed. (San Francisco: Harper and Row, 1990), 58.

[4]Cheryl Townsend Gilkes, "Mother to the Motherless, Father to the Fatherless: Power, Gender, and Community in an Afrocentric Biblical Tradition," *Semeia: An Experimental Journal for Biblical Criticism* 47 (1989): 57–85.

wholeness. A womanist theology invites an inclusiveness that cares about the "least of these."[5] Such a theology provides identity, and respect for all life. An awareness of the historical and current basis of such a theology calls for a theological, archaeological excavation of past narratives: to learn our origins, see our present reality, and learn how we can hope for the future.

For Delores Williams, womanist theory has several components: the dialogical, liturgical, confessional, ecumenical, and pedagogical.[6] The *dialogical* embarks on honest conversation and ethically based research to expose evils and empower conclusions that require an ethics of accountability and sensible praxis, working toward possible answers that benefit the "least of these." The liturgical dialogue concerns worship. The *liturgical* calls for daily celebrating life as gift, for being responsible enough to make a difference, and to empower, not handle, people. Thus, we are to design worship services that inspire, not tyrannize, from an aesthetics in which salvation concerns all vital human needs[7] and practices a divinely inspired sense of gratitude, which makes it unacceptable to violate humanity or our universe. The liturgical sets the framework for the confessional.

The *confessional* invites us to be unashamed of our bodies, our wants, and needs. The confessional challenges us to identify and testify to the *Imago Dei* within all humanity; to use language carefully; to enjoy an eschatological, holistic life; to not presume anything; and not to take more than we give back. Confessionally, we can avoid continuously measuring progress in dollars and clout, can plant a tree when someone is cruel to us or our loved ones, and can avoid worshiping a God who does not love us.[8] To claim oneself is a confessional act. One can say a person has expressed herself through womanist sensibilities, but ultimately one claims being a womanist. To be womanist is to be Black, although to do womanist analysis, one does not have to be of African descent. A solid confessional base fosters building bridges across ecumenical and interfaith lines.

---

[5]Kelly Brown Douglas, "To Reflect the Image of God," in *Living the Intersection: Womanism and Afrocentrism in Theology,* ed. Cheryl J. Sanders (Minneapolis: Fortress Press, 1995), 76–77.

[6]Delores Williams, "Womanist Theology: Black Women's Voices," in *Weaving the Visions: New Patterns in Feminist Spirituality,* ed. Judith Plaskow and Carol P. Christ (San Francisco: HarperCollins, 1989): 183–85.

[7]See Abraham Maslow, *Motivation and Personality,* 2d ed. (New York: Harper & Row, 1970).

[8]Alice Walker, "The Auburn Lecture: A Day with Alice Walker" (second annual Auburn Lecture at Union Theological Seminary, April 25, 1995.)

The *ecumenical* invites us to affirm stewardship (being responsible and accountable as we hold our lives and blessings in trust) as part of our religious life. The ecumenical (across Christianity) and the interfaith (across all religions) reminds us of the tensions between religions, the frequent ecclesial control of women, and the divisiveness of denominational religious practices that pollute our spiritual environment. Ecumenical communion and community remind us that change cannot occur without modeling or teaching, the role and function of the pedagogical. The *pedagogical* calls us to teach, preach, write, and live in an exemplary manner, aware of who we are, why we are here, and to see and respect our lives and our universe as gift. The *theological* first presents the blueprint for action, that action embodied in the sphere of ethics.

Womanist theology and ethics are conscious of how language can be problematic, particularly religious and political language. Sometimes it appears that the barbed communications from alleged friends are a matter of skewed presence or a corrupted sense of the divine. Particularly dreadful is the use of biblical texts to brainwash and control parishioners, especially using the Suffering Servant image from Isaiah. We must be conscious of language, style of delivery, and interpretative tools as we work toward inclusive discipleship. One must reckon with the class issues, the abuse perpetrated on women who work in service institutions, and see the connection between service and surrogacy.

Womanist theory is a provocation to unmask the threats of oppression, an invitation to see the vast cruelty and coercion that affect "the least of these," and to see the theological, ethical, ontological, and existential realities around this predicament. Womanist ethics invites us to make the invisible visible by applying what we learn about the theological focus of identifying and making sacred the plight of Black women—moving them from object and nobodyness to subject and somebodyness. Such a focus then makes room for truth-telling, the space of assessment, damage control, and accountability. Truth-telling emerges from a call to a new moral vision in dealing with the relational, social, and psychological experiences of the diverse Black communities in America today, being sensitive to the fallout, the rage, the depression, the confusion, and the frustrations from race, sex, and class oppression.

Such oppression calls for the creative and committed use of anger, social witness, and sacred texts. As the late Audre Lorde said, anger does not destroy, but hate does. One can channel anger toward analysis, protest, survival, or justice with an effective use of power, as one experiences that authority. Authority is a vehicle for developing shared power as partnership. Suffering is not God's will or a necessary component for transformation. One can embrace womanist social witness[9] grounded in spirituality to effect communal love and justice. In the process, one explores the realities of the underclass. One also develops a healthy strategy for using scripture. Scripture use, social witness, and the productive use of anger can help one build secular and sacred communities. Creating sacred communities fosters sisterhood as empowered womanist reality—in female circles of friends with mutuality and neighborliness, and in biological and extended kinship groups where women share common character, ancestry, allegiance, or purpose—to contribute to the well-being of others. To discover, designate, and deal with the kinds of oppression in *The Night of the Hunter* amid situations of violence in popular and classical culture, and in our homes, calls for an evocative, engaging paradigm laced by hopeful imagination. Such a paradigm undergirds my understanding of womanist theory and theological ethics as praxis in several ways—it is radical, revolutionary, righteous, revelatory, rhetorical, realizing, risky, representational, relational, rising, restorative, and resilient.

The model is radical in that the methods, processes, and modes of being are original yet rebellious. Revolutionary tactics provide the contest for nonconformist, activist reformation. Righteousness embraces that which is sacred, holy, honorable, faithful, grace-filled, and healthy. Revelation involves the portentous process of discovery, disclosure, and prophetic intent. Rhetoric invites an imagery that is eloquent, values orality and stories, and is sensuous and expressive. Realization allows for a creativity that presses for awareness, understanding, and actualization. The term *risky* creates an insight that this work is dangerous, complex, sensitive, and probably offensive to some. Representational acknowledges the creative process as artistic, functional, and organic. Relational means that the experience embodies love and builds alliances and connections. Rising notes that there is intense movement across a continuum. Restorative depicts a model that nurtures corrections, healing, and visibility to bring about justice. Resilient means that the experience

---

[9]See Emilie M. Townes, *In a Blaze of Glory: Womanist Spirituality as Social Witness* (Nashville: Abingdon Press, 1995).

is buoyant, flexible, and expansive. These twelve R's are ultimately instances of ministerial grace.

Black Christian women have a strong connection with Dr. Jesus, usually steeped in a prayerful faith-based journey amid the Hagar wilderness experience of survival, homelessness, rape, surrogacy, wilderness experience, sexual and socioeconomic oppression. Of import, especially for Delores Williams,[10] is the crucible of atonement available through the ministerial vision of Jesus, which teaches, loves, and empathizes, but does not take advantage of, belittle, or subjugate. Here the call is for a holistic, life-giving, relational God as we move to experience reciprocity, equality, and respect toward the wholeness and survival of extended, communal family. Particularly, it is important to have an inclusive sense of language and to recognize the import of engaging in an appropriate clerical and lay ethical decorum and of exposing that which is inappropriate. When we can name the violence, we can begin to investigate and address the relevant issues.

Illuminating the Reality of Violence

The vocabulary of violence is rife with issues of injustice, pain, suffering, sin, and the wielding of power. The experience of violence is universal and complex. For some, violence is anything that violates or hurts another sentient being or anything in creation. Violence represents an infringement on human rights and the rights of creation. This dehumanizing experience is intrusive, destroys creativity and one's inner essence, is rife with abuse, and prohibits one's freedom. Violence is often self-imposed; it may seem to be defensive or subtle in ways that most people do not label as wrong. Other times the violence is so heinous, so blatant, that it is inconceivable that one human being created by God could commit such acts on another human being created by God. Violence is evolutionary; it seems to escalate with each generation and heightens in intensity and creativity with our increasingly sophisticated technology in software, hardware, and drugs. Violence places everyone and everything in a survival mode, and it thwarts the inherent dignity of the created. Violence displaces the role of holiness and sacrality of God and of humanity. Violence also blurs the lines of reality and is often located in ambiguity. Many scholars have wrestled with this issue of violence

---

[10]Delores Williams, *Sisters of the Wilderness: Womanist God-Talk* (Maryknoll, N.Y.: Orbis Books, 1993).

and its connection with the problem of evil. Here, four scholars help us see violence in the realms of religion, aggression, process theology, and the Lord's Prayer.

Beginning with an understanding of violence arising from the Latin *violare* (to violate), Robert McAfee Brown fleshes out his notion of what it means to violate one's personhood, that is, the totality of an individual, using Dom Helder Camara's concept of a "spiral of violence": injustice, revolt, and repression amid personal and institutional overt physical destruction and covert psychological destruction. Brown identifies seven prominent concerns that affect the levels and propensities of violence. Nuclear weapons, a kind of conventional warfare, allow us to kill millions of people and destroy other life. Terrorism, from plane hijackings and bombings to kidnapping and random murders of innocent people, has escalated and embraces fanatic and unreasonable agendas. The death penalty, state-sponsored murder, perpetuates the very thing society allegedly abhors, denies the prospect of redemption, has probably taken innocent lives, and is not a deterrent. Sexual violence, often a subtler but equally devastating kind of harm, occurs on a personal and systemic level. The drug culture has wreaked havoc on the human body, mind, and spirit, preying on rich and poor alike, breeding greed and hopelessness. Disinformation has caused a credibility gap, particularly as public officials have lied and thus violated the personhood within our society. Revolutions have occurred throughout the world, often with the complicity of organized Christianity and the United States government.[11]

Kathleen Greider approaches the question by analyzing aggression. Greider defines violence as force targeted against people, things, or principles that unintentionally or intentionally harms, damages, or destroys. Connected strongly to violence are vitality, the basic aliveness, and life-affirmation, "to human agency that manifests in passion and capacity to endure."[12] As a counterargument to violence Greider argues for *reckoning with aggression,* where aggression is "significant energy, vigor, agency, enterprise, boldness, and resilience...qualities of immediacy and embodiment, either literal or metaphorical...a form of power, and like power, carries

---

[11]Robert McAfee Brown, *Religion and Violence,* 2d ed. (Philadelphia: Westminster, 1987), viii–xxi, 7–13.

[12]Kathleen Greider, *Reckoning with Aggression: Theology, Violence, and Vitality* (Louisville: Westminster John Knox Press, 1997), 9.

the potential of both positive and negative effects."[13] Greider qualifies her use of aggression in its multiple social and personal dimensions, the particularity of culture, and notes that it is something that we can control. Connected to a relationality of power, aggression allies with stewardship and creation. The stewardship involves an entrustment and dominion within God's creation, where our *being-with-others* affirms a relationship with nature, others, and God. Amid this relationality, Greider reminds us of our own complicity in violence and remarks on the level of naiveté wherein our religious beliefs cannot contain our human interpersonal and systemic physical and psychospiritual forms of violence. Theologically, she sees the power of aggression connected to not only violence but also passivity and vitality.[14] Failing to deal with powerlessness and oppression, or passivity that involves a loss of relationality or self-esteem, or a deep pathological introversion are other kinds of disconnect. A constructive theology of power is an experience of passion, a vitality that involves subjectivity, passion, and power in relation, which transforms, risks, and engages heart and agency.[15]

As Greider builds a theology of aggression, Marjorie Suchocki explores violence in the realm of sin. From a context of process-relational theology, Suchocki[16] views sin as participation through act or intent in superfluous violence that supports the ill-being of any part of creation, which includes violence against God. With reference to Saint Augustine and Reinhold Niebuhr, she argues that sin is not rebellion against God via the sin of pride, but is one's rebellion or insurgence against all creation through gratuitous violence. In her analysis, Suchocki contends that the reality, the beingness of sin is part and parcel of our humanity, as we all inherit from one another's sins. Being in community, therefore, exacerbates the state of sin produced by inherited standards of ill-being that protect the advantage of a minority to the detriment of a majority. Suchocki finds several difficulties with embracing sin as rebellion against God, for the concept ultimately makes God part of the problem, rather than the solution. This notion also helps keep the powerless and the oppressed, powerless and oppressed; is reductionist in distinctions between the gross levels of sin; makes

---

[13]Ibid.

[14]Ibid., 8, 9.

[15]Ibid., 8, 9, 59–67.

[16]Marjorie H. Suchocki, *The Fall to Violence: Original Sin in Relational Theology* (New York: Continuum, 1994), 12, 13, 16–19, 36, 44.

the victims of sin invisible; devalues creation; and supports rather than critiques or illumines the crisis of sin. Further, Suchocki challenges the need to dichotomize pride (nature, men, and the powerful) over against sensuousness (spirit, women, and the marginalized). She sees such discrepancies as distortions and failures resulting from empathy, her second mode of transcendence. Her first mode of transcendence is in the past through memory, and the third is in the future through imagination.

James Poling locates violence in its context of evil amid a familiar prayer. Whether prayed by perpetrators or victims of violence, Jesus' prayer that includes "deliver us from evil" is a call for resistance, a call to avoid violence. Evil is the context and philosophy; violence is the activity of evil. Evil, an abuse of power that destroys lives and spirits given by God, has a personal, social, and religious dimension. Such evil causes individual harm and injury; creates socioeconomic, ideological, and institutional chaos; and denigrates sacred bodies and spirits in community.[17] There are so many levels of violence: the implied and actual; psychological, emotional; physical; economic; religious; cultural; racial; sexual; verbal; and attitudinal—all of which are relational. Violence is relational because it affects the entire way of being as a person in the world. It is individual, communal, and systemic.

Against individuals, violence occurs internally, at home, among so-called friends socially, in faith-based organizations, and in the workplace. Spouses and partners beat up on each other physically (as well as emotionally) through actions such as slapping, kicking, and punching, and they perpetrate forced sexual activity that becomes sexual violence including unwanted fondling, oral intercourse, forced penetration, photographic exploitation and prostitution, and the forced sexual coercion of rape. Domestic violence shelters are bursting at the seams with battered women who have experienced spousal rape.[18] There are not enough shelters to house the women who come forth. These statistics do not include those women who remain silent or those men who happen to be victims of domestic violence. Children are often on the receiving end of domestic conflict. Parents or guardians often spank and beat

---

[17] James Newton Poling, *Deliver Us from Evil: Resisting Racial and Gender Oppression* (Minneapolis: Fortress Press, 1996), xiii, xv.

[18] Information from http://www.divorceinkentucky.com/physicalviolence.html available in July 2001. The Web site has statistics on women in shelters and descriptions of different types of abuse.

children, claiming to do so for the child's own good, when in effect, the beatings are a mechanism for the adult's venting of anger. Such action also teaches that love hurts and gives children excuses to later become perpetrators of violence themselves. Beyond physical violence, the psychological abuse, the denial of love and parental time, and the ignorance of children's realities exact a huge toll on the lives of our families. Unfortunately, such commonplace violence usually does not get our attention or that of the popular press until it occurs in settings where affluence, access, and class are supposed to be the bastions of protection for children, as in the Columbine High School tragedy. The arena of workplace violence, connected to that of familial violence ultimately, spans from foul and offensive language to holding hostages and committing homicide. Assaults, threats, and sabotage occur in circumstances that vary from robbery or violence by disgruntled customers, clients, patients, and so forth to violence by employers, employees, and coworkers. Nonfatal, violent assaults seem to occur mostly in areas of service industries and retail trade. Workplace-related deaths due to homicide also occur in occupations that deal with delivery of goods or services, with money exchange, and with the public. Much workplace violence can only be stemmed when such social issues as poverty, education, and environmental justice are addressed.[19]

Domestic and workplace violence affect the individual, numerous systems, and subsequently the community. Systemic violence largely occurs in government, business, education, and within all kinds of organizational culture at the level of sexism, classism, racism, and heterosexism. The systems buy into and proclaim many ongoing stereotypes and myths about the value that a particular individual or group of individuals can or cannot contribute. Skewed hiring practices and biased pay scales within organizations often guarantee that equity will not occur. Students are tracked by the time they are in the fourth grade. Thus, children deemed inferior or other will not have the opportunity to gain the support they need to have the best education. They will not have an opportunity to take enrichment courses. Often institutional mission and value statements talk a great deal about diversity and outreach, but at the end of the day, who is on the roster and at what level of authority often paints a different picture. Violence within many institutions creates a pathology and exemplifies dysfunctional behavior. Power issues are either so blatant,

---

[19]Information from http://www.cdc.gov/niosh/violpurp.html available in July 2001.

because the firm has the clout and financial backing to get away with being prejudiced, or so subtle that it is almost impossible to accrue enough evidence to make a valid prosecutorial case. Connected to the issues of the abuse of power and psychological and ethical violence within systems are those matters of accountability, closed communication, blurred boundaries, denial, scapegoating, narcissism, selfishness, codependency, and favoritism. The resulting cost of this violence is the loss of our human element. Unfortunately, even when individuals finally make a decision to stop their participation in violence, other factors in the larger community may not support this move. Too many people, for example, have continued domestic violence out of a misreading of biblical or other texts that seem to indicate a man's dominion over a woman and a woman's submission to a man as the head of the house. Many a man has translated the text to mean he has the right—no, the duty—to beat his partner or spouse when he or she has failed to submit. Violence occurs in so many blatant and subtle ways that we must be ever watchful so that we are aware of our own complicity, denial, or blindness to ordinary acts that result in extraordinary harm.

Over the last several months, in numerous conversations with various persons, the depths of violence and the many ways people see this violence have become clear to me. Violence is the destructive intent and unwanted, dysfunctional crossing of boundaries. Violence implies a scapegoating or blaming of someone and a pathological desire around matters of control, communication, and conscience. Some violence is more active and aggressive; others are more passive. Ignoring the rights of another person, desensitizing oneself by observing more violent acts, and the rationalization and justification of personal or systemic use of damaging thoughts, words, or deeds is violent activity. Some violence manifests as one intimidating others for the purpose of domination. The intentional act of seeking to incite or arouse anger and conflict is violence. Helping to cause hostility or invasion, launching attacks, or exacting abuse are the acts of violence. Violence is any oppression, anything that violates and separates us from the truth and the sacred within ourselves, our relationship with Spirit, and community. The unwarranted crossing of boundaries and the collective/institutional perpetration of harm are all violent acts. Violence is a polar opposite of intimacy. Violence is any force that causes injury to any part of creation. Violence involves any acts that are dehumanizing, such as the vulgarity of poverty amidst insatiable wealth, the perennial latch-key child syndrome or any unwanted child, the plight of homelessness, the perpetuation of lies and deceit at the expense of individual and communal health. Violence is awful and complex. Violence denies life. Violence must be viewed in relation to justice.

Registering Notions of Justice

Like violence, justice has been the subject of much study and writing. Justice, a term used in legal, ethical, and philosophical discussions, is necessary because of the confines of human benevolence and the competition concerning scarce goods or resources. Justice, then, has a concern for claims and the rules and standards that litigate those claims, which sets justice apart from generosity, charity, or benevolence. Distributive justice focuses on the allocation of goods; retributive justice focuses on corrective action to reappropriate the goods. According to Aristotle, justice pertains to treating equals equally, and treating unequals unequally, in proportion to their relevant differences. The concept of justice brings to mind whether or not one has a duty to act justly, along with matters of moral reciprocity, functioning under the love command of the gospels. In the gospels, each of us is the neighbor, doing unto others as we would have them do unto us, which relates to impartiality and commutative justice or fair exchange and just pricing. Yet the reciprocity can often focus on *lex talionis,* where one requires a return of evil for evil, just as one returns good for good.[20]

Justice as fairness is the first virtue of social institutions, and justice is a fundamental prerequisite of societies, not simply related to individual property and actions. Emil Brunner and Reinhold Niebuhr argued that legal and social justice are political functions of the law of love, thus the realization of justice. To determine a condition for justice, one must ask two questions: What makes a society unjust or just (that is, what are the criteria of social justice)? What does it mean to say that a society is just or unjust? Answering these questions leads to the conclusion that the dichotomy of the just and the unjust relates to a sense of right and wrong. Even when justice is connected to morality and love, justice must involve a rule of restraint, and morality must involve altruism. When we understand the historicity of justice (that justice principles emerged out of historical experience), we can see the principles that are related to justice: justification,

---

[20]Stanley I. Benn, "Justice," in *The Encyclopedia of Philosophy,* vol. 4, ed. Paul Edwards (New York: Macmillan Company & the Free Press, 1967): 298–99.

entitlement, equality, proportionality, impartiality, rectification, need, reciprocity, and participation. Principles of justification and equality tend to be a part of every type of moral or just relationship.[21]

For Christian ethics, four meanings of justice that are often a part of theological dialogue include (1) a model or standard for human moral agency, rooted in God's being and agency; (2) a moral agent's virtue; (3) a standard for human relationships related to and in comparison with *agape,* unconditional love of neighbor; and (4) the paradigm for the regulation and distribution of social goods and benefits and burdens among the citizens of a state. Human justice is measured in relationship to God's covenantal mercy, love, and justice. Varying across Catholic and Protestant traditions, correspondingly, justice may pertain to human moral action amid God's created order or amid God's biblically revealed saving righteousness. Second, as virtue, justice is a character attribute, a habit of praxis that leads on toward impartiality in decision making and in matters of deserts. Other virtues (theological ones such as faith, hope, love or charity; cardinal virtues such as prudence or practical wisdom, justice, temperance or self-control, and fortitude or courage) empower and move one to act in ways that foster human thriving. Third, justice in some interpretative traditions is more related to impartiality than to the compassion of love. Such justice may pertain to instances related to sin, where one group exercises dominance over another. The question remains as to how justice relates to disinterested love, where one assumes no conflict or excessive self-assertion. Conversely, justice connected with love portends high moral regard and distribution related to need, as one is a child of God. Fourth, as the signature virtue of social institutions, justice focuses on the apt allocation of duties and rights and the benefits of social cooperation to societal participants as equal, free citizens. This stance is different from socialism, which highlights the ideal of social and material equality by overcoming personal privilege, and libertarianism, which prioritizes the protection of uncoerced arrangements.[22]

---

[21]Joseph P. Hester, *Encyclopedia of Values and Ethics* (Santa Barbara, Calif.: ABC-CLIO, 1996), 230–32.

[22]William Werpehowski, "Justice," in *The Westminster Dictionary of Christian Ethics*, rev. ed., ed. James Childress and John Macquarrie (Philadelphia: Westminster Press, 1986), 329–32.

There are numerous theories on justice, and thus, no single way to define these phenomena, and no single theory is substantive enough to satisfy all situations. Several key thinkers on the issue of justice include John Rawls, Robert Nozick, and Michael Walzer. Using the social contract theories of John Locke and Jean-Jacques Rousseau, amid the context of Immanuel Kant's deontology, Rawls offers an alternative model to utilitarianism, where he defines justice as fairness, that is, justice where one chooses the basic tenets of existence for a given community, without domination, or from a context of unfair advantage, a practice of distributive justice. One chooses from an original position, out of a veil of ignorance; those making the decisions lack any knowledge that would predispose a sense of unfairness. Those making the decision must have no essential interest in the goals and purposes of others and must be aware of social organization, economic theory, and human psychology. The desired goal is to secure equitable freedom or liberty and to determine the extent of allowing inequities. Central to Rawls's theory are two principles: equal liberty and difference. The former is a concern to secure each one his or her equal liberty; the latter principle, where some inequalities can occur in the distributive process, only allows those inequalities that improve or protect the position of the "least of these," the least advantaged in the particular society. Rawls follows with his maxim in strategy, in which he claims that the persons in the original position, those in the first decision-making position, make choices that accentuate the minimum. Not knowing what an individual or a society will experience, one protects the least of these and only permits inequalities if they benefit those sorely lacking, connecting the laws of justice and the conditions of the original position. Rawls wants to move from method to principles toward a common ground of justice.[23]

Nozick, like Rawls, offers an alternative to utilitarianism with his entitlement argument. In this argument, Nozick wants to show that no moral ground exists for positing distributive justice, particularly where there is any system or structure of government beyond the smallest state. Only the most minimal-sized state is justifiable, and no activity is allowed that infringes basic human rights. This prohibition on violating others means that the state cannot be the arbiter of justice—the argument of the anarchist. So when a human

---

[23]John Rawls, *A Theory of Justice* (Cambridge, Mass.: Harvard University Press, 1971), 12, 136–38, 152–56, 302; Karen Lebacqz, *Six Theories of Justice* (Minneapolis: Augsburg, 1986), 9–14, 33, 50.

rights conflict develops and there seems to be no way of resolving the matter, persons who are rational, with self-interest, come together to create protective agencies to make sure that everyone's claims are protected and to help adjudicate the conflict. Such an entity is not yet the state, because it does not have a monopoly. When it does occur, then one has a minimal state. When territorial areas are broached, issues arise concerning the crossing of borders, which relates to Nozick's principle of compensation. To permit or prohibit the crossing of borders creates situations that necessitate compensation. The most inexpensive way to offer compensation is to offer protective services. This state is not predisposed to be a welfare state or to intervene. Nozick argues that one should not increase the status of the state for the sake of justice. Distribution occurs through individual decisions, gifts, and exchanges, not distributive justice through a governmental central agency. Justice occurs when one's holdings are just, that is, the process and contexts are justice-based. For Nozick, justice occurs when entitlements are honored. An individual has rights to his or her own goods, but not when that ownership can cause harm to others. Nozick's theory is historical, nonsacrificial, and procedural. Justice occurs based on the origins of the distribution, not on the content of the distribution. No one person's rights can be sacrificed for others. Justice relies on procedural principles or rules under which one acquires and transfers goods and rights in a context of fairness, with private ownership being critical. Karen Lebacqz notes that Nozick fails to take seriously the fact that modern capitalist market societies are not identified by the circumstances that make for causing no-harm and fair exchange, but rather the exact opposite occurs.[24]

Michael Walzer has another perspective on the notion of justice. Walzer begins his preliminary conversation about justice as he talks about equality and egalitarianism, the latter rooted in abolitionist politics, which interrogates supremacy, power, privilege, and capitalist wealth. Within each of these categories, the struggle pertains to an ability of one group of people to dominate another group(s). Domination concerns the distribution of social goods. The goal of political egalitarianism is to be free of domination; to have a society where social goods are not the pawns or devices of domination. Walzer argues for a system of distributive justice as an art, not a

---

[24]Robert Nozick, *Anarchy, State, and Utopia* (New York: Basic Books, 1974), 22–23, 33, 51, 52–53, 56–59, 150, 153; Karen Lebacqz, *Six Theories of Justice* (Minneapolis: Augsburg, 1986), 11, 51–58, 62.

science of differentiation. Distributive justice, a function of production and consumption, of ontology and existentialism, of identity, status, and possessions, cannot be contained within one theory. Social conflict arises out of questions of distribution. Justice is pluralistic, has a particularity, and occurs in spheres. A complex equality paves the way for allowing diversity and particularity within social conflict, as people relate out of their own spheres of control and competence. Following Blaise Pascal and Karl Marx, Walzer contends that social goods and personal qualities exist in their own spheres of operation. These goods have social meanings.[25] "We find our way to distributive justice through an interpretation of those meanings. We search for principles internal to each distributive sphere…the disregard of these principles is tyranny…The regime of complex equality is the opposite of tyranny."[26] Walzer argues for an open-ended distributive justice principle, in which persons who possess one social good have no automatic or privileged claim to any other social good, without consideration of the meaning of the social goods themselves. Under the guidance of that general ethic, Walzer posits three distributive principles. First, free exchange occurs where there are no monopolies or dominant goods and a radically pluralistic market, though the everyday market seems antithetical. Second, desert is based on what one deserves, though there may not always be a connection between persons and goods and often not a sense of urgency of need. Third, need occurs where different people receive different goods for different reasons, under different specifications or procedures. Walzer, among others, notes that money, a measurable medium of exchange, is not neutral and is often a vehicle of dominant good. There are blocked exchanges, as well, where some things– for example, human life–cannot and ought not to be purchased. Thus, exchange is never neutral or as just in a climate of exploitation and dominance.[27]

For our purposes, justice not only involves fairness and reciprocity, but the height of human dignity and respect. If everyone is deemed sacred, everyone must be accorded respect and equality as an operating principle. Justice, then, is not just about the apportionment of goods, but also the given status of humanity as subject rather than object. Thus, any type of violence or oppression is unacceptable. Some may ask if all people must be treated with

---

[25]Michael Walzer, *Spheres of Justice* (New York: Basic Books, 1983), xii–xv, 3, 5, 6, 11, 17.
[26]Ibid., 19.
[27]Ibid., 61, 62.

respect. Is violence never warranted? At this point, such a question is not yet appropriate to tackle. In living through and assessing the various opera, film, and scriptural narratives, I will note the intersection of justice and violence, and in my final chapter make some qualifying remarks about the necessity of violence amid living a just life. For now, it is important to note that violence stands within the philosophical reality of justice and that violence itself is antithetical to justice and is embodied in my notion of Misbegotten Anguish.

Dialogics of Misbegotten Anguish

As noted earlier, the idea for this volume was born out of my experience in viewing Steven Spielberg's movie *Saving Private Ryan*. This viewing stimulated me in ways that I had never imagined. My Sherlock Holmesian mindset began to raise more and more questions. My Dr. Watson became those persons around me who would listen and the various texts themselves. In a moment of divine inspiration the title of this work emerged for me: *Misbegotten Anguish*.

Something that is misbegotten is spurious and deceptive; it is false, bogus, unauthentic. Such a concept is iniquitous, nefarious, and counterfeit. Thus, any such acts are steeped in sin and evil, exacting results that are unfair, unjust, and immoral. Those engaged in such efforts may be deemed despicable and reprehensible. That which is misbegotten is deceitful, fictitious, feigned, and phony. The ultimate deed, then, reeks of dishonesty and artificiality; it feels contrived and dishonest. To experience anguish is to be in distress, agony, and torment, as one knows misery and pain. Essentially, anguish evokes the encounter of wretchedness and despair. The context is one of destruction and suffering. Imagine an individual physically caught up in anguish as one going through paroxysm—tremor, spasm, convulsion, and seizure. Misbegotten anguish is antithetical to beauty, truth, peace, wholeness, and just living. Misbegotten anguish is a sense of destructive, artificial reality, where someone(s) has decided to violate, to do harm under the rational or irrational justification of an alleged higher good, whether for national defense or personal aggrandizement. Misbegotten anguish means the embodied revocation of a just community and state. Misbegotten anguish creates an altar to pain and punishment, amid a liturgy of glory, honor, and righteous indignation. Misbegotten anguish is a pathological praxis of hostile passion and cruelty. Misbegotten anguish is the lens through which we explore, critique, and investigate contemporary personal and systemic violence.

Copied you, copied me
Pantomimed:
Mirrored imagery
Screaming back
When they can't replicate
What we deem important.

And they become *other*
Demonized, signified SCAPEGOAT:
Those to blame, ritually
Sacrificially, politically
Someone, anyone to blame
who thinks, looks, acts, talks differently
Just so we don't have to feel bad.
And we get to stand on the pedestal.
And they get to be—those people.

As we are yet alive,
Must we play the games of annihilation
Just because thousands before have had to tease, taunt, maim?
The good news is
In freedom, we can all model.
We can choose to imitate good news.

2

Contemplating
the Mimetic
Product
of Violence

The Scapegoat

We learn everything from our alphabets to standards of acceptable behavior by mimicking someone else. We imitate; thus, we engage in mimesis. Some of us imitate good, positive paradigms. Some of us model bad paradigms, those that oppress, undermine, destroy, and manipulate. At its worst, this mimetic behavior often emerges in copycat murders and other crimes of passion or in repressed, volcanic rage. At its best, this mimetic behavior occurs when people are moved to be generous because someone or something has inspired them to give to others. Many groups and individuals engage in bad mimesis against a particular person or group in order to blame this person/group for the need to do violence and harm. Such a blameworthy group appears different, thus making them an easy target for discriminatory, abusive practices. There are individuals who thrive by manipulating others and using others for their egotistical, narcissistic purposes. Such calculating behavior can occur on individual, societal, and systemic levels.

This chapter explores the relationship between communal and individual psychological activities and epistemological contexts to determine the nature of and catalysts for scapegoating. That is, how does the way we experience and know in life itself affect the prevalence of scapegoats in the cultures of the United States of America? After reviewing the plot of Puccini's *Madama Butterfly* and the biblical story of the Levite's unnamed secondary wife (translated by many as concubine [Judges 19–21]), I define and analyze *the scapegoat* using Girardian analysis. Both of these texts are ripe for this analysis as they are set in oppressive societies where scapegoating exists. I explore the particular scapegoating mechanism in Judges and *Madama Butterfly*, amid other dynamics of systemic violence and injustice. I conclude by exploring the reality of violence and the need for a scapegoat today.

The Stories: Puccini's *Madama Butterfly* and Judges' Unnamed Secondary Wife

An opera in three acts, with the music by Giacomo Puccini and libretto by Giuseppe Giacosa and Luigi Illica, based on David Belasco's play *Madame Butterfly,* reveals the story of a geisha, Cio-Cio San, also known as Madame Butterfly. This is a story of heartbreaking, doomed love. Butterfly is fragile, loving, in love, and naive. Her husband is reckless, self-centered, self-serving, obnoxious, and cruel. Set at the beginning of the twentieth century in Nagasaki, Japan, the story begins in a beautiful garden, where we meet Goro, an opportunist and marriage broker, and naval officer Lieutenant Benjamin Franklin Pinkerton. Goro has arranged a marriage and a home rental for 999 years for Pinkerton, but both "contracts" can conveniently be dissolved at Pinkerton's whim with a month's notice. The United States Consul, Sharpless, who knows the prospective bride, tries to dissuade Pinkerton from marrying her, knowing that Pinkerton is callous and that his intended, Cio-Cio-San or Madame Butterfly, will take this marriage seriously. And like a butterfly, she is delicate. Pinkerton's arrogance is evident when he makes a toast to the day he "really marries" an American bride from the United States. The day of the wedding, Butterfly and her relatives arrive. She shows Pinkerton several items she has brought with her, including a dagger that her father used to commit suicide at the command of the Mikado and the statues that represent her ancestors' souls. Pinkerton takes all of this very lightly and is most disrespectful. The Imperial Commissioner performs the legal ceremony of marriage, and Butterfly's uncle, a Japanese priest, the Bonze, arrives. Having learned that Butterfly converted to Christianity and renounced her own traditional faith, he curses and shuns her. All her relatives side with the priest and turn on Butterfly. Pinkerton tells them to leave. In a long, beautifully romantic duet, Butterfly forgets about her family; then the couple enter their new home together.

Act 2 begins three years later. Butterfly, maid Suzuki, and Butterfly and Pinkerton's son have spent this time quietly together, for they have not heard from Pinkerton. Suzuki does not believe he will return. Apparently, this kind of behavior was not uncommon. Men married Japanese women and then never returned. This society equated a failure to return with divorce. Butterfly refuses to believe Pinkerton will not return. She shifts from being angry at Suzuki for speaking truth, and perhaps at her self, unconsciously, to sing her most famous aria, "Un bel di," which says one fine day, Pinkerton will sail back into the harbor and come for his beloved wife. Sharpless comes by for a visit with bad news, but Butterfly is so incredibly vulnerable that he cannot read the full contents of the letter from Pinkerton, which reveals that the latter now has an American wife. Goro also stops by with yet another offer of marriage from Prince Yamadori, which Butterfly firmly declines. Sharpless and Butterfly sing the "Letter Duet," but Sharpless still does not make full disclosure. When Sharpless asks what Butterfly would do if Pinkerton did not return, she says the most honorable thing to do would be to commit suicide. Sharpless suggests that Butterfly marry Yamadori. Butterfly says no because of her son, named Sorrow/Trouble, for his name will be Joy when his dad returns. Seeing the impossibility of changing Butterfly's mind, Sharpless leaves. The sound of the cannon signals that Pinkerton's ship, the U.S.S. Abraham Lincoln, has arrived. In ecstasy, Butterfly and Suzuki sing the "Flower Duet," as they decorate the entire house in flower petals from the garden. They wait and wait and wait for Pinkerton to come to the house, as the music from the "Letter Duet" plays in the background, and the famed "Humming Chorus" by an offstage chorus provides a meditative scenario as act 2 closes.

As act 3 opens, Butterfly, Suzuki, and Sorrow/Trouble are still seated where they were when act 2 closed. Butterfly has not slept all night; Suzuki and the child are asleep. Morning dawns, and Butterfly puts the child to bed. Butterfly also lies down to rest. Suzuki looks out and sees Sharpless, accompanied by Lieutenant Pinkerton and an American woman, obviously his American wife. With this realization, Suzuki cannot tell Butterfly what has happened, and Pinkerton is too much of a coward to face Butterfly. Pinkerton sings a farewell song to the place where he and Butterfly once knew happiness and leaves. Butterfly wakes up and sees Kate, the American wife, and understands that tragedy has arrived. With great control and dignity, Butterfly tells Kate not to feel sorry for her and that she can have the child if Pinkerton comes to get him. Sensing that she has no recourse, Butterfly changes from her American clothes to Japanese attire, sings to her son, then blindfolds him and sends him out of the room. Butterfly goes behind the screen and stabs herself with the same dagger her father used to stab himself. She drags herself from behind the screen, and Pinkerton comes running back, calling, "Butterfly! Butterfly!" He is too late. Depending on the stage direction, Butterfly is either crumpled on the floor or collapses in his arms as the orchestra blasts the poignant, fateful melody heard earlier each time her death was foreshadowed.[1] This Italian opera, rife with Mediterranean emotions set within a Japanese context that never fully integrates the work, is the height of ebullience, passion, and gorgeous music that holds innocence, cowardice, arrogance, and misbegotten anguish: the destruction of a family, and the wicked demise of a beautiful, fragile soul.

In Judges 19, another soul is destroyed, her body dismembered, and in the wake of it all, a nation almost comes undone. Judges 19 has parallels not only with *Madama Butterfly* but also with the Sodom and Gomorrah story in Genesis 19 and with contemporary true-life events (the early 1990s case of Jeffrey Dahmer, who dismembered his victims, and also cannibalized them.). The unnamed, secondary wife of a Levite from Ephraim gets upset with her husband and returns to her father's home in Bethlehem, Judah. After about four months, the Levite comes looking for her, with a servant and two donkeys in tow. The woman's father makes the Levite so welcome and offers such generous hospitality that they are unable to leave until the fifth day after the Levite's arrival. Though it is late when

---

[1]See Giacomo Puccini, *Madama Butterfly* (New York: G. Schirmer, 1963); Henry Simon, *100 Great Operas and Their Stories* (New York: Anchor Books, 1957, 1960), 270–74; Giacomo Puccini, *Madama Butterfly,* with the Vienna State Opera Chorus and Vienna Philharmonic Orchestra; Herbert von Karajan, Conductor. London: Musical Heritage Society, CD 533196Z, 1974, 1987, 1994.

they start to leave, the Levite is unwilling to stay another day. The party arrives at Jebus (Jerusalem), but the Levite does not want to stop in what he deems an alien city, so they forge on to Gibeah in Benjaminite territory, but no one offers them hospitality. Finally, an old man from Ephraim who is living in Gibeah makes them welcome. While they are feasting and enjoying themselves, some rude, perverse men from the city pound on the door and demand that the host bring out the man who had just come to his house so that they might know him, that is, have sex with him. The old man refuses, and offers his daughter and the Levite's unnamed secondary wife instead. (To let them have the man is a disgrace, but it is acceptable for the Levite to give his virgin daughter and the Levite's secondary wife to be exploited and gang-raped). The crowd does not listen, so the Levite seizes his secondary wife and puts her out to them. They gang-rape and abuse the unnamed secondary wife all night long. They release her at dawn, and she returns to the home of the host, falling down in the doorway. Her Levite master gets up in the morning and finds her in the doorway. He orders her to get up, but she gives no answer. He puts her on a donkey and leaves for his home. (The text fails to tell us of her condition and shows that the Levite exhibits no concern or compassion for her at all. There is no remorse for her gross exploitation during the night). When the Levite gets home, he takes her body, dismembers her limb by limb into twelve pieces and sends them to all parts of Israel. Chapter 19 has two bookends with pronouncements. The beginning words (Judges 19:1) note that there was no king in Israel. The chapter closes with the pronouncement that such a thing had never occurred since the children of Israel left Egypt. The Deuteronomist then calls for us to consider this issue, take counsel, and then speak out (19:30). Like the unnamed secondary wife, Butterfly is a scapegoat and object, a devalued trinket for the use and whim of men and systemic oppression. With both Judges 19 and *Madama Butterfly* in mind, we shift to explore the meaning and dynamics of scapegoat theory.

Scapegoats in Girardian Theory and Operatic and Biblical Praxis

Conflict in literature, from the Greek tragedies and biblical texts to classical opera and modern-day cinema, usually proceeds through tragedies and ritual sacrifices, which are resolved through the process of scapegoating someone, that is, by identifying and killing a victim. The victim's death provides a catharsis and produces a sense of social camaraderie to such a heightened extent that the crowd or perpetrators begin to understand the experience religiously. With the scapegoat, we see the intersection of religion, violence, and culture. For French literary critic and cultural anthropologist René Girard, the scapegoat is part of a larger matrix he names mimesis, particularly mimetic rivalry. Mimesis, to imitate, is central for our epistemology, the way we know and learn. Mimetic desire is that experience where two or more people desire the same thing, same person, same place, or status. This desire leads to rivalry; several parties want the same object. For Girard, mimetic desire and its ensuing ritualized conflict involves the process of resolving and containing the resulting violence. The scapegoat becomes the culprit, and blaming the scapegoat allows the satiation of lust and thirst for calm, moving the given group of persons from a violent catastrophe into peaceful unification. This shift involves the invoking of a sacred structure, rooted in a sacrificial altar, the locus of creating and recreating communal, social solidarity. The success of the scape-goating process often hinges on the invisibility of the victim. Even when a society understands the experience of victims and the process of scapegoating that usually releases the pressure valves of discontent and internal violence, the violence and need for scapegoating only seem to intensify. For Girard, the gospel turns the whole scapegoating business on its head. Nevertheless, as we see the victim, our rage often blinds us to our own complicity. In media and texts such as opera, film, and scripture, a cautionary tale emerges that warns us of making victims of perpetrators and the accompanying false innocence within ourselves. At issue is how to resolve the conflict.[2] Gil Bailie asks, do we "purge the community of its conflict and violence by assigning all its sin to one figure....[or do we take the second option, where] the community [is] to be made aware of its own complicity in the sinfulness and delusion of the protagonists....[S]in and evil that breeds the crisis...make drama fascinating, and it is the overcoming of sin and evil that resolves dramatic crises."[3] Such crises can be examined in terms of Girard's "Violence and the Sacred" theory.[4]

---

[2]Gil Bailie, "Cinema and Crisis: The Elusive Quest for Catharsis" *Image* 20 (1998): 17–20.

[3]Ibid., 20–21.

[4]René Girard, *Violence and the Sacred* (Baltimore and London: Johns Hopkins University Press, 1977).

For Girard, extensive or collective persecutions of scapegoats are an ordinary kind of violence that can be "legalized," particularly when provoked or supported by public opinion. Individuals and groups need these objects of persecution because they need to define themselves comparatively with one another. The dominant group can define itself and create unity among its members by identifying a susceptible group as "other" or "outside." Those deemed other, because of differences expressed as gender, race, class, age, or sexual orientation, for example, must be vulnerable and visible. Heightened violence results when one cannot name someone other. Girard refers to these conflictual rivals as monstrous doubles. Creating differences, or being aware of the differences themselves creates a definite kind of social order. Anthropologically, Girard argues that human beings imitate the desire of another, because when they come together around the same object, they use one another as models and begin to resemble one another. Human beings learn through imitation or mimesis. Unfortunately, this imitation can also produce pathological greed. Increased similarities create societal confusion. Ultimately, violence erupts as individuals and groups struggle to be different. Yet through their struggles they end up looking and acting more and more like one another. Someone who looks, acts, or thinks different, and is vulnerable, often ends up being the focus of a group's consolidated effort to define itself and those deemed other, by turning their own pursuit of power against those who cannot react. Thus, a group establishes itself by psychologically or physically eliminating or ousting the ones who are different. Lynching (or stoning to death in the ancient world) is the classic act of collective violence.[5]

This group execution or ritual presumes the guilt of the victim and offers the opportunity to kill without guilt to members of the "in" group. Everyone participates, and the execution takes on a festive air. Group unity gives the appearance of being on the "inside," of being "right." Yet this unity itself is a consequence of mimesis or imitation. Everyone in the group imitates everyone else's desire to kill. The murderous activity discharges violence against someone who is powerless to resist. The victim is accused, charged, and executed based on random or fictional evidence, because evidence is irrelevant. The tactics of the crowd or mob, as well as its hidden incentive, is easily transferred to an organization or institution when

---

[5]Conversations with Diana Culbertson, Professor of Literature, Kent State University, summer 1995.

an entire culture yields to mimetic desire and its violent consequences.[6] In review, we learn to desire by seeing what others desire.
If everyone or almost everyone wants or desires the same object,
the object's value increases. On the other hand, if everybody finds
an object irrelevant, worthless, or meaningless, the object, regardless
of its significance, has no value. Sometimes an oppressed group may
mimetically accept majority opinion and devalue themselves. The
psychology of this mimetic desire and nondesire, or imitative
behavior, is contagious. The way a group either values or devalues
can lead to a horrific pathology, mass hysteria, or a group sickness—
an excuse to sin.

The Girardian scapegoat mechanism, then, helps us see, as we
work to rationalize violence through religious practice and myth,
that mimetic rivalry shapes human behavior. In the cinema, the
villain, often the character the story inspires us to despise, is usually
the scapegoat. Some of these characters are ambiguous and complex,
ranging from trickster scoundrels, terrorists, billionaires, criminals,
spies, aliens, or manipulative, misogynist seducers to lustful
courtesans, harlots, and bigots. While Girard argues that the
scapegoat mechanism has been exposed and made ineffectual in
the gospels, the result seems to be that we can no longer rationalize
or make sense of violence. The dismantling of the scapegoat has
produced an infectious appetite for violence, as the resolution of
conflict in film and other narratives is unsatisfying. If we fail to see
our own complicity in the scapegoating, then the problem of violence
remains. If we see our complicity within our Western, postmodern
society, then we can no longer remain ignorant of the innocence of
the victim.[7] Over time, the film industry has had different foci when
it comes to the question of a scapegoat. One could identify the
scapegoat early on in the film industry as the oppressed, the victim
of injustice. Despite the racial scapegoating of the military enemies
of the United States during World War II, one could still see the
innocence of the victim. Some argue that Stanley Kubrick's *Dr.
Strangelove* (1964) was a turning point that focused on human
innocence and powerlessness. During the 1970s, a loss of innocence
accompanied a time of moral chaos and nihilism, where the audience
was turned against itself. The late 1970s and early 1980s brought

---

[6]Ibid.
[7]Ronald Austin, "Sacrificing Images: Violence and the Movies," *Image* 20 (1998): 23–25.

heightened technology and special effects with the fantasy, escapist movies of Steven Spielberg and George Lucas. The 1980s and 1990s brought more commercialized space aliens and disaster films. With the onset of 2000 and the millennium craze, more films have focused on natural disasters. With the "anxious pessimism" during a tremendous time of growing peace and prosperity, the question today is whether such arch-villains continue to function as scapegoats; it has become more and more difficult to sustain even a hint of the sacrality necessary for the scapegoating process to be useful.[8]

> Violence then becomes gratuitous, and however horrendous and shocking, cannot provide genuine catharsis... [Ultimately] the depiction of evil, as with its confrontation in life, is related to our understanding of the sacred. Evil unchallenged by the sacred produces not only fear and pessimism, but confusion. [Film] must continue to play a prophetic role by exposing the scapegoating mechanism.[9]

For Girard, religion is a way of exposing violence. A society tries to sustain differences and to limit rivalry through its myths, taboos, and prohibitions, even though violence and chaos have existed from the foundation, the beginnings of the world. A group finds a victim to lessen internal rivalry and find unity. The collective attempt to prohibit, push out, or murder someone marginal to the group assists the group in obtaining peace. Since murdering the victim holds a group together, the action is symbolically repeated, within the culture, in order to sustain internal peace. That is, rather than always hanging a person, the limbs may be broken or amputated. Hanging terminates life, amputations limit mobility, and both make a statement to the community.

The repeated act of symbolic murders or maiming is ritual sacrifice. Ironically, the victim of the sacrifice and the murder become the savior figure, the cause of the peace, even though the murder occurred because the victim was accused of perpetuating societal chaos. Murdering the victim conceals the truth of the situation: The real root of the violence comes from those who provoked the murder. Group peace requires that the violence always be directed against those unable or unwilling to fight back, because the group will dissolve into murderous rivalry: severe, destructive competition

---

[8]Ibid., 26–27.
[9]Ibid., 28.

among themselves. Girard names the system of ritual murder and expulsion the *sacred.* For Girard, *sacred* equals violence, because when a culture or a religion starts with a sacrifice, a killing, it begins with violence, the worse side of religion. Violence emphasizes the differences within society.[10] How does such violence emerge?

The generating dynamic of the violence or the tool that creates victims is mimetic desire, the desire or want that replicates the desires of others. Rivalry occurs within a group as people imitating one another's desires turn into rivals for the same good. When conflict begins, violence repays violence via imitation or mimesis. Rather than always tearing the group apart by infighting, they find others against whom to focus their aggression. Thus, a dichotomy persists: There remain both institutionalized violence and the personal revolutionary violence of those who seek a new social structure. In this analysis, the oppressed is the scapegoat: Madame Butterfly and the unnamed, secondary wife. Scapegoating, a result of mimetic[11] desire and full-scale violence, is often a vehicle for shaping social order and for stabilizing the relational differences. The conflict, chaos, and confusion of bad mimetic desire sets up a particular social order that concerns power, a tool of violence, that privileges some and hurts others.[12] Widespread violence, deeply rooted within institutions and organizations, has three vectors, like a triangle: Object of desire/Model/Disciple or Imitator. The Object of desire, what one wants, (e.g., position, friend, wisdom) becomes desirable when "'the Model' and 'the Disciple' both want 'the Object'."[13]

Significantly, the desire for the Object produces rivalry. The Disciple imitates, or wants to imitate, the desires of the Model. Desire occurs in everyday human life because we learn through imitation or mimetic desire. On the playgrounds, the game "Simon says" embodies how we learn, by repeating what we see another person

---

[10]Paul Dumochel, ed., *Violence and Truth: On the Work of René Girard* (London: Athlone Press, 1988), 54–55; see also Burton Mack, "Introduction: Religion and Ritual," in *Violent Origins: Walter Burkert, René Girard, and Jonathan Z. Smith on Ritual Killing and Cultural Transformation,* ed. Robert Hammerton-Kelly (Stanford, Calif.: Stanford University Press, 1987), 4, 6.

[11]Critics use "mimesis" to describe relationships between art and nature, art and reality, or the relationship that governs the work of art as nonimitative or pre-Platonic mimesis (ecstatic play), or Platonic mimesis.

[12]Mihai Spariosu, ed., *Mimesis in Contemporary Theory: An Interdisciplinary Approach; The Literary and Philosophical Debate* (Philadelphia: John Benjamins Publishing, 1984), i–iii, 88–100; see Mack, "Introduction," 11.

[13]Dumochel, *Violence and Truth,* 3.

doing that we admire or desire to do. Or the Disciple wants that which someone else has, or wants to be like someone else. When the Object is distant, the Model and Disciple or Imitator are not in conflict. The nearer the Object, the more intense the resulting rivalry. When the Model says to the Disciple, "Imitate me, but not too well," the Disciple becomes paralyzed because of conflicting messages. Uninhibited desire leads to victimization and sacrificial rituals, such as numerous hate crimes and vicious gossip. Such offerings produce both the murder of persons and distorted institutions of oppression. The daily annihilation of personhood that destroys human dignity is the murder for which Girard's model calls. Desire searches for something it imagines to be most clearly other, most unlike itself.[14] With Girardian desire,[15] the tension between Disciple and Model intensifies envy. The Disciple tends to misinterpret the rivalry with the Object, and assigns a meaning to the relationship that does not exist.[16]

The antagonism and blindness of mimesis lead to the "double bind"–another Girardian tool critical for analyzing oppression. The double bind encompasses the desire for an Object by the Other. One values the desired Object because someone else desires it, and one learns desire by imitating the other. Pretty soon, one wants to be like the other. In extreme cases, one wants to become the other. Someone (the Model) desires the object, and soon the Disciple wants to be like the Model. Unknowingly, the closer the Imitator (the Disciple) gets to obtaining the Object, the greater the hostility of and rebuke by the one imitated (the Model). The Imitator assumes that she or he ought to value the Object, but then discovers that the closer one comes to acquiring the Object, the greater the rejection

---

[14]René Girard, *Things Hidden Since the Foundation of the World* (Stanford, Calif.: Stanford University Press, 1987), 283–90, 338. Mimetic rivalry includes anything from eroticism to all types of ambition.

[15]Ibid., 299. My review of Girard and his interpreters finds that other/object/ego, rival/subject/model, and imitator/object/model are interchangeable patterns of correlation representing mimetic triangular desire.

[16]Ruth El Saffar, "Unbinding the Doubles: Reflections on Love and Culture in the Work of René Girard," *Denver Quarterly* 18 (Winter, 1984), 10–11. The rivalry's mimetic character is concealed, but not as the Freudian oedipal secret. El Saffar shows how Girard and Freud are less antithetical than they first appear. She posits that both scholars view culture as irrational forces, have notions of disruptive power (the unconscious or mimesis), and claim that the irrational Other exists in hostile relation to the world of consciousness and of culture. Freud wants to master the object; Girard wants to dissociate from the object. Either the hero, logos, or rationality functions to conquer the forces of darkness.

by, and animosity of the one being imitated.[17] Thus, the rivalry causes what Gregory Bateson describes as the "double bind." The human mind looks for changes and affirms substitution and progress. With the double bind, a subject cannot accurately interpret the double command that comes from the other person: As model, imitate me; but do not imitate me as rival.[18]

Doubling violates differences between people and makes them sensitive to deception and lies.[19] Desire never gets what satisfies it and never builds impartial relationships: Some dominate, others are dominated, and the truth of the situation, the source of relevance (mimetic desire), is concealed. The mutual attraction within their imitative interaction generates the kind of paralysis in which the Disciple wants to be autonomous, but finds himself or herself attracted to the Model-oppressor. He or she wants what the oppressor has: power, status, fullness of being, and so forth. So how is it possible for us to imitate those whom we hate without hating ourselves? This question is complex. First, the Model wants to be Model but defies anyone who imitates too well. The Disciple wants to be autonomous from the Model, wants the Model's independence. The Disciple experiences an external prohibition or double bind from the Model and an internal prohibition or double bind. Studying these two kinds of double binds helps to expose the complex nature of oppression, particularly of scapegoating, and the intricate motives, which include the riddles of self-deception, the gist of power, the source of valuation, and the constant risk of violence when social groups vie for dominance and/or independence.

The amassed violence of systemic, institutional oppression has dehumanized many groups in America, making them the collective, singular "It." Consider, for example, Matt Shepherd or James Byrd in 1998, who appeased the mimetic desire of the persecuting class. Shepherd was killed because of his sexual orientation, Byrd because of his race. Interestingly, the victims in these cases seem to be controlling all by allowing the restoration of order and bringing peace to the community. The ideal victim is the scapegoat. The violence involved during the scapegoating becomes justified because the violence seems to restore order. One such incident is the alleged suicide of honor student Raynard Johnson, a young Black male in a

---

[17]Mack, "Introduction," 8–9.

[18]Girard, *Things Hidden,* 291; see also 294–98, 305.

[19]René Girard, *"To Double Business Bound": Essays on Literature, Mimesis, and Anthropology* (Baltimore: Johns Hopkins, 1978), 46.

small Mississippi town. Calling his death a suicide seems most suspicious, particularly when the belt that was used to hang him did not belong to him, according to his family. Johnson made a perfect scapegoat, because he engaged in interracial dating. The incident, a ritual murder, taught a clear message in that town: Interracial dating could mean the loss of your life. Similarly, in a sleepy West Virginia town, Arthur Carl "J. R." Warren, Jr., an African American, openly gay man, was beaten to death and then run over by a vehicle numerous times to make it look like an accident; three teens have been arrested in this case. Warren's death was another sacrificial ritual that made the statement, "Be openly gay, and we will kill you." Society therefore keeps some group or class as the victim, the object of ridicule, the one to blame, the one to persecute. Below are more details of these two stories of twenty-first century scapegoats:

> On the night of June 16–a moonless night that seemed particularly dark out here in the countryside of southern Mississippi–Jerry Johnson swung his blue pickup truck into the driveway of his rural home. For a stunned moment, he could not comprehend the scene his headlights illuminated.
>
> There was the youngest of his five children, 17-year-old Raynard–a youth who made good grades, grew big collard greens, helped neighbors bale hay free of charge and charmed the girls of the community–hanging from a branch of the small pecan tree on the front lawn.
>
> Johnson tore out of the truck and cut his son down. The body was still warm, he said, but there was no pulse, no heartbeat. Rescue workers and Marion County sheriff's deputies were summoned. But within a couple of hours– before midnight had passed–they were gone, Johnson said, calling Raynard's death a likely suicide, an assumption reportedly backed up by an official autopsy.
>
> But the Johnson family found that conclusion unthinkable. And as word of the tragedy spread, so did many of Raynard's neighbors, his school friends, teachers, fellow church members and civil rights leader Jesse L. Jackson, who is leading two marches here this weekend and describes the case as a racially motivated slaying. Too many things, they said, did not add up.
>
> The mystery of Raynard (pronounced Ra-NARD) Johnson's death has seized this rural community, where

blacks and whites have long lived alongside each other, with rumors and fears. It has drawn a spotlight to what some civil rights activists call "the last taboo" of race relations in America: interracial dating. And it has called national attention once again to troubles in Mississippi, and its brutal past of bombings, lynchings and other hate crimes.

The FBI, the Mississippi Highway Patrol and the county sheriff's department are investigating the death. So far, two autopsies, including one that the family is keeping private, reportedly have found the death consistent with suicide. The official autopsy showed no defensive injuries, such as broken fingernails or bruises, and the only visible mark, on the throat, appeared to match the belt that was looped around the youth's neck.

....

But the Johnsons are not buying it. "There's no doubt in my mind what happened, and it wasn't suicide," said Jerry Johnson, 51, an oil rig worker.

....

"There's a New South today, where blacks and whites live and work together—it's a very different South. And then there's an underbelly of the culture that never moved," Jackson said. "It's not just peculiar to Mississippi. It's a mistake to use Mississippi as a scapegoat again."[20]

And then there is the story of Arthur Carl "J. R." Warren, Jr., made a scapegoat, like Matthew Shepherd, because of his sexual orientation:

Grant Town, West Virginia (CNN)—Funeral services were held Saturday for Arthur Carl "J. R." Warren, Jr., an African-American gay man killed in what some activist groups say was a hate crime.

Authorities said Warren, 26, was beaten to death July 4 by three teenagers. To make the death look as if it were the result of a hit-and-run incident, his body was then run over

---

[20]Sue Anne Pressley, "Dark Questions in a Teen's Death," *The Washington Post,* 8 July 2000. Also available through www.washingtonpost.com in the archives section.

several times by a car before it was dumped by the roadside, officials said.

The accused teenagers, two 17-year-olds and a 16-year-old, confessed to the crime and likely will face murder and conspiracy charges, said Marion County Sheriff Ron Watkins.

The three were scheduled to appear in court Thursday to determine whether they'll be tried as juveniles or adults, Watkins said.[21]

Scapegoats involve not only the categories of race, gender, and sexual orientation but also age and class. For many, 1990s welfare reform is a scapegoat. Allegedly if the United States can reform welfare (1% of the national budget), the national deficit (of trillions of dollars) will disappear. The welfare for the rich—tax shelters such as municipal and mutual bonds—are not questioned; neither are billion-dollar budgets for stealth bombers that do not work. The scapegoat, the victim, is the target of injustice and therefore should be a subject of theological concern, given the socioethical impact.

Desire generates social existence.[22] Culture causes and cures social, inescapable violence. When society does not treat rivalry through rituals intended to ward off evil, tensions will escalate into what Girard calls a sacrificial crisis.[23] The Black-White sacrificial crisis hinges on the White need for control and superiority and the Black need for life without surrender or dying to self. Violence is the process and the symbol of crisis: lynching, subjugation, brutality, annihilation. The depths of depravity, vulgarity, deceit, and disregard for human life produced by such a violent crisis exploded in the life and death of Emmett Till. Till was a 14-year-old African American from Chicago who was abducted, tortured, and killed while visiting relatives in Money, Mississippi, in 1955. The confessed murderers were acquitted by an all-white jury.[24] Only when enough people see the injustices of a system that requires victims in order to sustain the cultural order will that cultural order be ready to suffer the challenge of change. The outrages committed against Emmett Till

---

[21]Account taken from http://www.cnn.com/2000/US/07/08/west.va.hate.crime/index.html in July 2001.

[22]El Saffar, "Unbinding," 12. Also see "Strategies of Madness—Nietzsche, Wagner, and Dostoevski," in Girard, *To Double Business Bound,* 61–83; and Mack, "Introduction," 21. Girard argues that double binds supersede triangular desires when the goal proceeds to share the Object with the rival rather than take the object of love from the rival.

[23]Mack, "Introduction," 9.

[24]The event is remembered in Bob Dylan's song "The Death of Emmett Till" (Warner Bros., 1963).

were conspicuous enough to draw attention to the violence of an entire system. Emmett Till was sacrificed for a system. His sacrifice also worked to destroy that system. His murder was designated by the perpetrators to save a violent system, but it eventually served to create a new social order.[25] To call him a savior is therefore not to exaggerate, for paradoxically, this violence can transform the victim into a savior.

Violence that creates salvation dims and often erases memories of oppression and expulsion, and leaves memories of the beneficial effects of the sacrificial death. Any act of racist annihilation produces a savior, one who saves and keeps society the same. The saving "act" maintains the status quo, soothes the oppressor's psyche, and purges any desire to cause change. The rejection of change cements human situations. The displacement of guilt and the redirected aggression lead to delusion and shape the cultures. Retaining the stereotypes or fictional/mythical versions of reality[26] allows the community to avoid telling the truth about what's going on. When fear is the overarching theme, love is not an option. Only when enough people see the injustices of a system does a movement for transforming culture occur, such as the civil rights movement and her children: Gray Panthers, feminist movement, lesbian-gay movement, and others.[27]

---

[25]Interview with Diana Culbertson in 1995.

[26]D. W. Griffith's film *The Birth of a Nation* (1915) epitomizes the racism in myths of Black inferiority and the negative impact of minstrelsy. See Michael Paul Rogin, *Ronald Reagan, The Movie: And Other Episodes in Political Demonology* (Berkeley, Calif.: University of California Press, 1987), 190–235. Rogin argues that Griffith joined mass appeal to aesthetic invention and set the origins of American movies in a racist epic. In *The Birth of a Nation,* one cannot exegete racism without seeing the place of sexuality; racism and sexuality are inextricably bound. White supremacists create the Black rapist to keep White women in "their place," contrasting Black villainy and blond innocence. As the movie shifts sexuality from White women to Blacks, Blacks are demonized to control them. By projecting White desire, myths are spawned to control Blacks and White women while distancing yet reempowering the southern White male. The White male was the true bearer of historically significant interracial sexuality who portrayed the monstrous double of paternal desire. The final desire in the film is to castrate Black men to prohibit them from penetrating White women. This castration stops the Black seed and redeems the nation. This movie displays the dualities of culture and nature, a system with and without differences. The Ku Klux Klan engenders national unity and molds together human divisions into a sacred brotherhood. Griffith's use of Blackface (White actors using Black makeup) showed how Whiteness protects Black growth and hides Whiteness; this allowed him to place White actors in fantasies he had about Blacks.

[27]See El Saffar, "Unbinding," 6–7. Girard claims that culture *causes* violence, for it expresses humanity's expulsion from God; thus, culture is antithetical to God. Culture cures violence because culture's operative hierarchies and prohibitions can limit, contain, and redirect the powers of toxic behavior. For example, the myths and rituals of all human cultures conceal the original or founding violence—the "creative" or "good" violence toward the sacrificial victim or scapegoat that affords group harmony, solidarity, and human consciousness. "Bad violence" disrupts the balance of differentiation; "good violence" (according to this concept) unifies the many against the one.

While natural human growth processes require imitation, all imitation or mimesis does not lead to rivalry. All rivalry does not begin and end with an actual death. The nonviolent religion of traditional African American Christianity is a kind of mimetic intimacy,[28] and therefore it functions as an alternative to the violent exclusiveness of other cultural systems. Mimetic intimacy transforms mimetic rivalry, satisfies desire, and embraces the other. The victim knows the other as injurer—one who needs mimetic transformation, to experience the *Imitatio Christi*, where to become like Christ is also profound desire. To experience *Imitatio Christi* is to also allow for the transformation of victims and victimizers, particularly in the American context.[29] Such intimacy or closeness incorporated with a quest for justice could break the power of the double binds and model reconciliatory relationships.

The scapegoat is the buffer when two or more have a competing desire for the same object and that intense desire leads to envy, followed by rivalry, then violence. But violence against a scapegoat breaks down differences and makes competing humans more alike. Thus, human beings get involved in an unconscious, communal process of mimetic contagion: groups imitate the desires and actions of violence of others. Many groups focus their violence through a scapegoat, which allows for a venting of violence and a retrieval of stability. Girard argues that New Testament revelation champions the victim and "exposes the scapegoat mechanism as contrary to the will of God...God takes the side of the innocent victim, and, in Jesus, appears as the victim himself...this biblical revelation has been slowly penetrating human consciousness."[30] Girard notes that it is in the resurrection that the Holy Spirit, the Paraclete, reveals Jesus' innocence, the inauguration of Christian grace, to the disciples. For Girard, this grace is for individuals who do not believe in Jesus' guilt. In resurrection experiences of other religions, a previously evil God returns as benevolent. "The Christian resurrection is something which is ultimately hidden from general view and reserved to people who are going to do something with what the Holy Spirit reveals...The witness of the Holy Spirit to Jesus' innocence and the

---

[28]Theophus H. Smith, "King and the Nonviolent Religion of Black America," in *Curing Violence: Religion and the Thought of René Girard*, ed. Mark I. Wallace and Theophus Smith (Sonoma, Calif.: Polebridge Press, 1993), 249.

[29]Ibid., 248–50.

[30]Leo D. Lefebure, "Beyond Scapegoating: A Conversation with René Girard and Ewert Cousins," *Christian Century* 115 (April 1998): 372.

resurrection are essentially connected."[31] Violence, an organizing energy of culture, is universally human.

In Girardian thought, myth disguises violence; myth and rituals conceal a tradition that should be exposed for what it is: ritual murder represented as sacrifice. Myths and rituals sustain the status quo and can be positive or negative, stereotypes or truisms. Spirituals celebrate those myths and rituals that affirm freedom and indict those that support racism. The same fetters that bind the captive bind the captor, and the American people are captives of their own myths, woven so cleverly and so imperceptibly into the fabric of our national experience.[32]

Scapegoating Mechanisms in Judges 19 and *Madama Butterfly*

The Levites are linked with violence in the Hebrew Bible. Levites are complicit in the slaughter of the citizens of Laish (Judges 18), and a bloody war occurs between tribes of related brothers after a Levite sacrifices his unnamed secondary wife (Judges 19–21). Levite violence is often linked with sexual outrage and hatred (Gen. 34; Lev. 25; Judges 19–21). Herein, the secondary wife is a scapegoat. Her death serves as a catalyst for the war that ends with the almost total destruction of the tribe of Benjamin and ultimately leads to Israel's reunification, amid getting Benjamin to own up to its guilt. Members of a society can become united in their hostility against the scapegoat, rather than become one another's rivals. Girardian thought makes it possible, then, to either engage the scapegoat matrix within the text or deny that mechanism by openly acknowledging its sacrificial aspect.[33]

In biblical parlance, a *pilegesh* can be an unmarried woman in a harem with a mistress kind of relationship with a man, and she will probably have a great deal of authority and autonomy. The word is used, for example, to describe Rizpah, a *pilegesh* to King Saul (2 Sam. 21:10–14); David's concubines (2 Sam. 5:13); and the concubines that Absalom violated (2 Sam. 16:22). Another kind of *pilegesh* is a woman who has the status of secondary wife in her marriage to a particular man, as in Judges 19. As a wife, she is property. As a

---

[31]Ibid., 372, 373.

[32]C. Eric Lincoln, *Race, Religion, and the Continuing American Dilemma* (New York: Hill and Wang, 1984), 3.

[33]Stuart Lasine, "Levite Violence, Fratricide, and Sacrifice in the Bible and Later Revolutionary Rhetoric," in *Curing Violence,* ed. Theophus H. Smith and Mark I. Wallace (Sonoma, Calif.: Polebridge Press, 1994), 204–29.

secondary wife, she is property and is expected to act in a subservient manner. As a secondary unnamed wife, she is significantly inferior. For the Deuteronomist, she clearly can have no access to successful independence or autonomy. Her nameless self is often absent and silent within the text, such as when her father urges the Levite to stay longer. Her initial independence in leaving the Levite is totally nullified. From a logical perspective, this text is so problematic. Why does the Levite literally get away with murder? He offers his unnamed secondary wife for the Benjaminites to ravish. If that is all he thought of her, why did he come after her in the first place?[34] Clearly, the unnamed secondary wife is a scapegoat, to be used and mistreated to placate the whims of others: "She is captive to the men who surround her, first her Levite husband, then her Judahite father, and next her Ephraimite host. Finally, she is captive to the Benjaminites, who signal her subservient status within their society by leaving her body ravaged and dead in the midst of their streets."[35] The Gibeahites are inhospitable and do not make the strangers welcome. Instead, they are received by an old man; a stranger, he himself an other. The inhospitality foreshadows the making of other through dismemberment that is about to take place.[36]

The dismemberment of the concubine unleashes a flood of violence. The dismemberment itself is an invitation for Israel to avenge the outrage through punishment of the Gibeahites and a fight with the recalcitrant Benjaminites—men desperate for wives as the other Israelites have made a vow to not give their daughters to the tribe of Benjamin in marriage. Yet the girls from Shiloh are kidnapped to serve as wives. Although Israel practices disobedience and disunity, toward the end of Judges the twelve tribes reconnect in religious, not political, unity.[37]

Thus, themes of self-interest, ambiguity, and betrayal play key roles in the last segment of Judges 17–21. While the Levite is most concerned with his own welfare, we never really learn whether he actually does woo the unnamed secondary wife when he finds her at her father's house. We do not learn why she left him in the first

---

[34]Susan Ackerman, *Warrior, Dancer, Seductress, Queen: Women in Judges and Biblical Israel* (New York: Doubleday, 1998), 236–40.

[35]Ibid., 240.

[36]George F. Moore, *A Critical and Exegetical Commentary on Judges,* The International Critical Commentary (Edinburgh: T & T Clark, 1949), 414.

[37]Ibid., 403–4.

place, though we can imagine some form of abuse, given what happens to her. We do not learn if she wanted to go back with him. The unnamed secondary wife has no voice in the text, but her body speaks volumes to Israel before and after her death. All the men who interact with her betray and abuse her.[38]

The woman in Judges 19 is not only unnamed, thus cloaked in objectified anonymity, but the men of Gibeah gang-rape her. She is the victim of brutal, maniacal control. Her life embodied a "breaking" or "fracturing" with the rape and the later dismemberment. Issues of gender oppression are interwoven with her being a scapegoat. In many translations, she is called a concubine, which is incorrect given that she has a husband and her Levite husband has a father-in-law (19:2–4). Given that the woman does not engage in sexual misconduct, many translations interpret verse 2 as she "became angry with him," instead of saying she played the harlot or that she prostituted herself. Following the next few verses, it seems implausible that the unnamed woman would become a prostitute and then proceed to her father's house. Since ancient women had no divorce rights, perhaps the ancient narrator saw her act of leaving as one of defiance, of harlotry. But given that the unnamed woman did not engage in sexual impropriety, the text is really about the control and ownership of women's sexuality and bodies by men. For the narrator, her independence and defiance becomes sexual wrongdoing. The unnamed woman becomes the scapegoat, the one to be blamed for disrupting the status quo, the one who is thus sexually assaulted, gang-raped, and symbolically sexually mutilated. Extreme violence forged by dismemberment is a way to destroy the unnamed woman's sexuality. By asserting her freedom, thus aping patriarchy, she threatens to dismantle the whole misogynist system. The Levite husband repeats the bodily assault by erasing the rape, and then raping her again with the dismemberment. Any affront to male, misogynistic, patriarchal authority can, and often will, be met by antagonistic repercussion of the most brutal kind. Does anyone mourn for the unnamed woman? There seems to be some guilt, for the narrator admits both that (1) nothing so dastardly has ever occurred (19:30) and (2) there is the question about how such evil ever could occur (20:3). But overall, male violence orchestrates female violation; males' denial of their violence results in their

---

[38]Danna Nolan Fewell, "Judges," in *The Women's Bible Commentary*, ed. Carol A. Newsom and Sharon H. Ringe (Louisville: Westminster/John Knox Press, 1992), 74–75.

patriarchal scapegoating of women.[39] Such scapegoating also emerges in Madame Butterfly's poignant, yet horrific demise, though the story is fraught with ambiguity and different cosmologies and sensibilities from the very beginning.

The agitation of the stringed instruments at the beginning of *Madame Butterfly* indicates movement, marking each entry, signifying magnificent textures layered with more density, heightening the listener's expectations. Pinkerton seems shallow with a one-track mind, narrowly focused on satisfying his own misogynistic, imperialistic, sexual desires. With the backdrop of patriotic themes, he unabashedly portrays the saga of the "ugly American," that is, Yankees who move around from port to port, making love with a girl at every port of call, mixing business and pleasure. Pinkerton's appetites are only curbed by the weather. The Consul Sharpless offers a cautionary tale about his behavior, noting that such behavior leaves the heart cold. While Sharpless and Pinkerton toast America, Goro also moves about, aware of Butterfly's fragile nature and her quiet grace, aware of Pinkerton's "devil-may-care" attitude. Sharpless warns Pinkerton that to break Butterfly, to crush her trusting heart would be a terrible sin, but Pinkerton counters, saying that Sharpless has merely become sentimental. In the first scene, the audience sees that under the lush, beautiful music, something sinister lurks.

Already Butterfly is being set up to be a scapegoat. Neither Consul Sharpless nor Goro, the marriage broker, warns Butterfly or her family about Pinkerton's potential unscrupulousness. When Butterfly and her family arrive for the wedding, they offer Pinkerton respectful greetings of hospitality. Pinkerton acknowledges her compliment, but then sings about the uniqueness of Japanese women, objectifying them all, including Butterfly. Upon Pinkerton's query, Butterfly recounts how her family went from riches to rags, because of a typhoon. This disaster meant that they had to work as geishas, and for this she was not ashamed. Pinkerton's self-centeredness rears again, as he offers no words of consolation, but laughs, because he sees her as a porcelain doll that sets him on fire. Butterfly is but a fifteen-year-old child, yet already considered a spinster in her culture. Even Butterfly's own mother (her father is dead, and she has no siblings) and community are not blameless. Before the ceremony

---

[39]J. Cheryl Exum, "Feminist Criticism: Whose Interests Are Being Served?" in *Judges and Method: New Approaches in Biblical Studies,* ed. Gale Yee (Minneapolis: Fortress Press, 1995), 83–87.

begins, many of the women admit that Goro had also offered them the opportunity to marry Pinkerton. They know impending doom, for they sing about how Butterfly's beauty is already fading in counterpoint with Pinkerton's arrogance as he makes mockery of "the farce" of the procession of his temporary family. Goro tells the community not to be rude. Sharpless sings about Butterfly's incredible beauty and about Pinkerton's incredible luck, warning Pinkerton that this may all be a game to him, but this is deadly serious to Butterfly. As the ceremony begins, Butterfly has already been betrayed and is being set up to take the fall, to be the scapegoat, for maintaining the status quo of Puccini's account of American and Japanese relations at the beginning of the twentieth century. Protocol is more important than Butterfly's life and honor. As the wedding day proceeds, the audience receives more warnings of sacrificial intent as Butterfly, in total delusion about reality, is so laden with denial, so caught up in her fantasy, that she cannot see Pinkerton's farce, making her a perfect victim.

Butterfly and Pinkerton go into the house for final preparations before the ceremony. After he asks her if she likes the house, she tells him about the special items she has brought with her, especially something sacred. Even Goro watches them and then comments that the Mikado gave one particular item to her father and that her father obeyed the Mikado. Here again, the story mentions Butterfly's father's suicide commanded by the Mikado, like the foretelling of Jesus' passion in Mark. This notion of honorable suicide is part of traditional Japanese culture. The samurai ideal of *kenshin,* the ultimate self-sacrifice, is a modern term to describe ancient values.[40] Such a suicide is considered antithetical to that brought on by depression. Emile Durkheim coined the notion of "altruistic suicide" in 1897; it describes an individual's taking his or her life for the alleged greater good of society. Such altruistic suicides include those of World War II kamikaze pilots, Palestinian suicide bombers, and the more contemporaneous self-immolation of Kurdish Nationalists. They were willing to die for their principles and beliefs.[41] Some Japanese people, such as writer Yukio Mishima, have given assent to and performed the suicide ritual of *seppuku,* or self-disembowelment. Obsessed with death, suicide, and a sense of Western culture's

---

[40]http://search.britannica.com/frm_redir.jsp?query="kamikaze" & redir= http://www2.hawaii.edu/~dfukushi/Warrior.html

[41]Information found on http://www.rnw.nl/culture/suicide/html/altruism.html in July 2001.

expunging traditional Japanese values, and in protest against the lack of Japanese nationalism, Mishima performed *seppuku* on May 25, 1970. He argued that "In feudal times we believed that sincerity resided in our entrails, and if we needed to show our insincerity, we had to cut our bellies and take out our visible sincerity. And it was also the symbol of the will of the soldier, the samurai; everybody knew that this was the most painful way to die."[42] Butterfly is aware of this history, even amidst Pinkerton's callousness.

While Butterfly shows him her various keepsakes, Pinkerton asks her what she calls the dolls and she replies that they are her ancestors' souls. He tosses them in the air and then offers his respect. He is totally insensitive and fails to inquire further when Butterfly announces that the day before, she secretly renounced her ancestral religion and has adopted Mr. Pinkerton's God, for this is her destiny. After the Commissioner marries them, they sign the marriage contract, the contract that can be rescinded at Pinkerton's whim. While offering best wishes, Sharpless again reminds Pinkerton to think about Butterfly's feelings. As if the wedding charade has not been dastardly enough, Butterfly's uncle arrives and curses her for going to the mission and for renouncing her ancestral faith. He announces that the whole family will renounce her. Butterfly feels ashamed and alone. She has been scapegoated again. Pinkerton woos her and suggests that she forget her family and declares that Japanese priests are not worth her beautiful tears. The closing scene of act 1 is filled with gorgeous music as Suzuki, Butterfly's maid, helps prepare Butterfly for bed. Pinkerton, on fire with lust, stands in contrast to the graceful Butterfly. In his self-centeredness, he sings of Butterfly as his graceful prize, of her purity and her pale face. He sees the love in Butterfly's eyes and gets her to proclaim her love. She still harbors grief about her uncle. When Butterfly asks Pinkerton if it is true that abroad, a man will capture a butterfly and pin it to a board, he shamelessly parallels her with the butterfly on display. He says not only has he caught her, but she cannot fly away. She belongs to him. Amid the most profound, beautiful music of Puccini, one can almost lose sight of the fact that not only is Butterfly scapegoated, but she is doomed for tragedy.

---

[42]Ibid.

When act 2 opens, three years have passed. Butterfly, her son, and Suzuki are in dire straits, as the money Pinkerton left has almost run out. They go back and forth pondering whether or not Pinkerton will return. So sure that Pinkerton will return, Butterfly sings her most famous aria, or operatic solo, "Un bel di"–"One fine day." Significantly, Butterfly now wears American garb instead of the traditional kimono. Shortly thereafter, they have unexpected visitors, the Consul Sharpless and marriage broker Goro. Goro wants to convince Butterfly to marry the Yamadori. Sharpless has come to read her a "Dear Jane" letter. Butterfly calls Goro evil because he reminds them of her destitute situation and that her family has disowned her. Sharpless senses that he cannot read the entire letter to Butterfly at that time, that she could not bear it. Goro again reminds Butterfly that in Japan, desertion and divorce are the same thing. Butterfly counters by saying that perhaps this is so in Japan, but not in her country, not in America. Butterfly is in complete denial. Feeling somewhat embarrassed and guilty, Sharpless then inflates the sentiments in Pinkerton's letter to Butterfly. He suggests that she accept the Yamadori's proposal, since Pinkerton may never come back. This statement offends Butterfly, but she recovers slightly and contends that Pinkerton might have forgotten her, but not his son. She then sings about the scenario that is her only option other than suicide, and that is of being at the mercy of others, of having to be a geisha, which she vows never to do again.

A geisha is a member of a professional class of women in Japan whose traditional occupation is to entertain men. In modern times, the entertainment usually occurs at businessmen's parties in restaurants or teahouses. The Japanese word *geisha* literally means "art person." Singing, dancing, playing the *samisen* (a lutelike instrument), and the ability to make conversation are vital talents for a geisha. Essentially, the geisha is to provide an ambience of chic and joviality for her wealthy clientele.

> The geisha system is thought to have emerged in the 17th century to provide a class of entertainers set apart from courtesans and prostitutes, who plied their trades respectively among the nobility and samurai. The geisha system was traditionally a form of indentured labour, although some girls…volunteered. Usually, a girl at an early age was given by her parents for a sum of money to a geisha house, which taught, trained, fed, and clothed her for a period of years.

Then she emerged into the society known as *karyukai* (the "flower and willow world") and began earning money to repay her parents' debt and her past keep. The most sought-after geisha could command large sums from their customers. Besides providing entertainment and social companionship, geisha sometimes maintained sexual relationships with their clients.

In the 1920s there were as many as 80,000 geisha in Japan, but by the late 20th century their number had dwindled to only a few thousand, almost all confined to Tokyo and Kyoto, where they were patronized by only the wealthiest businessmen and most influential politicians. This decline in numbers was chiefly due to the easier availability of more casual forms of sex in postwar Japan; bar hostesses have taken over the geisha's role with the ordinary Japanese businessman.

When a geisha marries, she retires from the profession. If she does not marry, she usually retires as a restaurant owner, teacher of music or dance, or trainer of young geisha.[43]

Vowing never to be a geisha again, Butterfly insists that Sharpless tell Pinkerton about his son, which is Butterfly's ploy to ensure that Pinkerton returns. In scene 2, Goro comes back, and Suzuki ridicules him, because he has been spreading rumors about Butterfly, that her son is a bastard and that the father is unknown, which will make the child an outcast. Goro sets up Butterfly to be a scapegoat, the *other* in a country that prizes honor, protocol, and saving face. Butterfly caresses her son and sings that his father is far away. Hearing the cannon from the harbor, she imagines what the harbor is like and that Pinkerton has returned. Puccini places American patriotic musical themes as counterpoint to the melody of "Un bel di." Butterfly is convinced that everyone—Sharpless, Goro, and Suzuki—has lied, and that Pinkerton indeed will return. Now she changes back to Japanese dress. This move signals that at some level, Butterfly must know that if Pinkerton comes back, he will probably not come back to stay. Since hope springs eternal, Butterfly shakes off her premonitions, and she and Suzuki collect flower petals of everything that is in bloom, the results of her tears that watered the soil. As they sing "The Flower Duet," they fill the house with blossoms, in great

---

[43]http://search.britannica.com/eb/article?eu=37012&tocid=0&query=geisha

elation, unaware of what is about to pass. They settle down to wait for Pinkerton's arrival, with no ship in sight. Suzuki and the child fall asleep. Butterfly watches faithfully, intently, as the famed "Humming Chorus," a prayerlike, meditative, angelic chant is sung from offstage, as the curtain closes on act 2.

Act 3 opens as Suzuki finally wakes up, puts the child to bed, and urges Butterfly to go and rest. Butterfly rests, and Sharpless and Pinkerton arrive with an American woman. They are cowards and do not want Suzuki to awaken Butterfly. Suzuki inquires about who the American woman is, and Sharpless tells her she is Pinkerton's wife. Pinkerton sings about the bitter odor of the flowers, projecting the bitterness that he has caused. Pinkerton, Sharpless, and Suzuki sing, each of their own concerns. Suzuki is horrified at their wanting her to ask Butterfly, a mother, to relinquish her child to the Pinkertons. Sharpless asks Suzuki for help in getting the child. Now that he is about to wreak havoc in all their lives, Pinkerton sings that he does not want to stay. Sharpless reminds him of his countless warnings about hurting Butterfly. The egocentric Pinkerton sings about what a terrible torment this will be for him; he plays the coward. Mrs. Kate Pinkerton asks Suzuki to promise to ask Butterfly for the child. In all the commotion, Butterfly wakes up.

Suzuki asks her not to come out, but as Butterfly does so, she sees Sharpless (but not Pinkerton). She excitedly looks everywhere for Pinkerton. Everyone is deadly silent. Suzuki cries. Butterfly learns that Pinkerton is alive, that he is not coming back, and that he is married. Butterfly resolves that her life is over, and agrees to give up her son if Pinkerton will come and get him in a half hour. Even Sharpless argues that it will be better for the boy to go with the Pinkertons. Ever gracious, Butterfly offers Kate Pinkerton best wishes for a happy life and tells Kate not to be sad on her behalf. Suzuki covers everything in the house as they prepare to close it and helps Butterfly dress in a special kimono. Butterfly bows before her altar and reads the inscription on her father's dagger—"Let him die with honor who can no longer stay alive with honor." At that moment, Suzuki pushes the child in the room to see Butterfly, and she drops the dagger. She sings *"Tu? Tu? Piccolo Idio!"*: "You? You? My Little God!" In her song, she prays that her son will never know that his mother died so that he could go across the seas, that he will never regret that his mother was deserted. She continues singing, of how the child was a gift from heaven and admonishing him to remember her face. She ties a scarf around his eyes and sends him out to play with an American flag and a doll in his hands. When Suzuki returns, Butterfly pushes her out the door. Butterfly retrieves the dagger, goes behind the screen, and stabs herself. She drops the knife, comes from behind the screen, and hears Pinkerton calling, "Butterfly, Butterfly." Pinkerton and Sharpless rush into the room, but it is too late. She collapses, and Pinkerton falls on his knees. Some staging has Butterfly die in Pinkerton's arms.

Scapegoating, Systemic Violence, and Injustice

Critical issues of class and gender intersect in Judges 19, highlighting the unequal power dynamics between the Levite and his *pilegesh,* just like the naval lieutenant and his geisha. The unnamed *pilegesh* experiences double oppression in her status as a secondary wife whose role is to provide sexual gratification and/or children for the Levite if his primary wife cannot conceive. Interestingly, the text fails to mention a primary wife. The fascinating discord exacted by the *pilegesh's* leaving the Levite and his subsequent search four months later has been fodder for many scholars. That the *pilegesh* multiplies her husband's shame and humiliation makes sense, given the strictures of patriarchal society. The geisha Butterfly also experiences double, perhaps triple, oppression: Her father committed suicide; she is poor and had to work as a geisha to survive; and she's just another "trophy lay" for a Yankee looking for pleasure. Both patriarchy and traditional Japanese culture place high value on male authority and male privilege, male honor and hospitality, which explains the generosity of the father-in-law to his Levite son-in-law, and the generous hospitality of Butterfly and the reaction of her uncle and other relatives. The double subordination of the *pilegesh* and the *geisha* parallels the double dishonor of the Levite with the abandonment by the *pilegesh* and the shrewd treatment by his father-in-law.[44] Conversely, Pinkerton so successfully dishonors and scapegoats Butterfly, that even at her death, one cannot be sure of his sincerity. The beautiful, soaring music hides the impending tragedy throughout the opera, so even her own music scapegoats Butterfly. In comparing Butterfly and the unnamed secondary wife, it is important to note that the Judges 19 text has a number of parallels with other pericopes in scripture.

---

[44]Gale Yee, "Ideological Criticism: Judges 17–21 and the Dismembered Body," in *Judges and Method: New Approaches in Biblical Studies,* ed. Gale Yee (Minneapolis: Fortress Press, 1995), 161–63.

The travel to Gibeah, the request of the Benjaminites, and the seizing and gang rape of the unnamed secondary wife parallels the Sodom and Gomorrah saga in Genesis 19. Whereas God intercedes in Genesis, no such intervention occurs in the atrocity at Gibeah. The unnamed secondary wife is also a metaphor for every woman, named and unnamed, who has to experience and endure private or public abuse and suffering in the world. So is the plight of Butterfly— the public humiliation of divorce by absence, the earlier need to be a geisha, and the lies that Goro tells, which basically portray this innocent fifteen-year-old as a slut or hustler a la Delilah, or even a Tamar in Genesis 38. In this mix, the exaggerated hospitality of the unnamed secondary wife's father to the Levite stands in juxtaposition to the violent inhospitality the unnamed secondary wife experiences at the hands of all men. Generous hospitality followed by violent inhospitality also occurs earlier in Judges between Jael and Sisera. The gender order is reversed, however, as Jael entertains and then murders Sisera for the sake of Israel's victory over the Canaanites (Judges 4:17–22).[45] Generous hospitality by Butterfly is also followed by violent inhospitality by Pinkerton as he abandons her for three years and marries another, leaving her to do the only honorable thing she can in her culture, kill herself. Can such brutality ever be justified?

These various parallels bring to mind one statement and one question that haunt the Judges 19 text. First comes the introductory "In those days, when there was no king in Israel" (Judges 19:1a). Not only does this statement connote disorder, but for Israel, which as a nation is led by a king, the nation is without divine rule. Prior to the naming of Saul as king, Yahweh was the assumed King of Israel. Thus, the state of chaos is idolatry. Second, "Has such a thing ever happened since the day that the Israelites came up from the land of Egypt?" (Judges 19:30b). For the reader, given that the Levite raises this question, does "such a thing" refer to the inhospitality or the gang rape and dismemberment of the woman? The listener must also ask how such a thing could happen when listening to or viewing a production of *Madama Butterfly*. When the battles actually take place, God uses the Benjaminites as judgment against all Israel in the first two skirmishes. God then allows Israel to be victorious in the third battle to punish the Benjaminites, so much so that Israel

---

[45]Dennis T. Olson, "Judges," in *The New Interpreter's Bible: A Commentary in Twelve Volumes*, vol. 2 (Nashville: Abingdon Press, 1998), 877–79, 886, 888.

almost wipes out the tribe of Benjamin; only six hundred escape. The other Israelites realize what they have done and then set about finding wives for the six hundred survivors. Israel's escalating violence and disobedience create scapegoats, exponentially, from that of the unnamed secondary wife to thousands of people murdered and hundreds of women kidnapped. Group evil becomes mob violence that can only be sated with the making of scapegoats. "Religious idolatry, unholy wars of conquest against a peaceful and defenseless people, abuse of strangers, rape, murder, personal revenge, deception, civil war, and more rape, murder, and kidnapping of young women all combine to portray an Israel in turmoil and near death."[46] Mob violence mixed with human desire for more violence and revenge creates a fertile scenario for scapegoating. Without a king, leader, judge, or guide, the people do what they as a mob deem is right. Interestingly, God is present with them in the chaos, but does allow innocent people to die, as every *man* (gender specific, because they had the power) did what was right in *his* own eyes (Judges 21:25). In *Madama Butterfly*, the place of the American God and the ancestral family religion begs the question and forces one to examine the suicide in the context of tradition and idolatry. (See chapter 5 for further discussion about suicide). Butterfly's mob exercised the violence of recrimination and silence. The silence embodied in the absence of her community, psychologically and spiritually, did to Butterfly what the gang rape and the dismemberment did to the unnamed secondary wife. In both instances, a strong operating force is that of the need to control the woman. Patriarchy has many ways of accomplishing that control.

> Using women's fear of male violence as a means of regulating female behavior is one of patriarchy's most powerful weapons. And it remains effective. If the message to women encoded in the story of Jepthah's daughter was: yield to the paternal word and you will be remembered and celebrated for generations to come; and that of the Samson story was: there are only two kinds of women, and you don't want to be the wrong kind; the message in Judges 19 is a cautionary one: if you do anything that even remotely suggests improper sexual behavior, you invite male aggression.[47]

---

[46]Ibid., 886.
[47]Exum, "Feminist Criticism," 85.

Similarly, the message for Butterfly was: You are but a victim and a pawn at the mercy of tradition, government protocol, and American colonialism (see chapter 3). Forces beyond her control are at work to assure her place as a fragile, gentle, perfect scapegoat.

Butterfly is scapegoated by Pinkerton with his lies of omission and commission. Before their marriage ceremony ever occurs, he knows that he will dissolve the marriage, just as he will dissolve the contractual agreement to rent the house for 999 years. He constantly objectifies Butterfly so that his lust can be fulfilled and he can maintain a perfect record of having a woman at every port. But when he wants a real wife, he will marry an American. Butterfly's uncle, the Bonze, scapegoats Butterfly by publicly denouncing her, thus tying her to all youth who have ever abandoned their religious practices in favor of something different. Goro, the marriage broker, scapegoats Butterfly by false representation. He knows of Pinkerton's character and has tried to lure others into marrying him, but the other women understood the game and knew the offer of marriage was a temporary fantasy. Butterfly's innocence precipitates her death. Sharpless seems to have a good heart in that he continually warns Pinkerton to take this relationship seriously. But even he scapegoats Butterfly with innuendo and pretense by not reading her the full text of the "Dear Jane" letter, by supporting Pinkerton in taking the child from Butterfly, and by bringing Kate Pinkerton to Butterfly's house. And last, the Yamadori on the one hand wants to give Butterfly a way out of her conundrum by divorcing his other wives and offering Butterfly his hand in marriage. But to one so proud and genteel as Butterfly, because she had already given her heart to Pinkerton, for the Yamadori to continue to come around and woo her insulted and thus scapegoated Butterfly. She would probably never have considered marrying anyone who had been married to so many women before.

Sometimes even persecution texts, however, can turn on the perpetrator. Just as the unnamed secondary wife of the Levite is a scapegoat for the maintenance of patriarchal domination, the Deuteronomistic narrator gradually shames and dishonors her Levite husband as he experiences dual humiliation. The possibility of homosexual rape by the Benjaminites symbolically emasculates, dominates, and feminizes the Levite, particularly given that the phallus, as a tool of aggression, creates an area of domination and submission.[48] Earlier in the narrative, the Levite's unnamed

---

[48]Yee, "Ideological Criticism," 164.

secondary wife shames him by leaving him, and her father shames the Levite by his manipulation of generosity and overextension of hospitality so that the Levite initially cannot leave. Butterfly's generosity and love contrasts Pinkerton's callousness.

Neither the Levite nor Pinkerton is innocent. Placing his self-preservation first, the Levite makes his unnamed secondary wife his property; he scapegoats her by giving her to the mob to be gang-raped. Placing his ego and fantasy needs first, Pinkerton objectifies Butterfly and does not protect her from the "mob" of her community, including the wrath of her uncle. The morning after the gang rape of the unnamed secondary wife, when she returns to the house, the text names the Levite her master. The Levite is ready to leave, but her body blocks the doorway. Devoid of compassion and concern, the Levite master commands her to get up. When she fails to answer, he puts her on a donkey and returns to Ephraim. Similarly, Butterfly cannot get up when Pinkerton calls out to her, because she is dead. The biblical text remains ambiguous as to when the Levite's unnamed secondary wife dies. Upon returning to Ephraim, the Levite treats her as he would an animal set aside for ritual sacrifice, dissecting her body into twelve pieces with a knife.[49] The Levite's actions parallel those of Saul (1 Samuel 11), who hacks oxen into pieces, then sends the pieces throughout the area to call the Israelites to war against the Ammonites. The Levite sends out the unnamed secondary wife's body parts as a call to meet, to avenge the wrong of the Benjaminites. The irony and perversion of this scenario are that the one consecrated to holiness and to be in charge of ritual is the one who "becomes the agent of a grotesque antisacrifice that desecrates rather than consecrates. A woman's raped and battered body replaces the sacrificial animal."[50] Similarly, Pinkerton, one sworn to protect, to be an officer and a gentleman, is the catalyst for Butterfly's shame and death. The injustice of patriarchy and the horrific abomination of gang rape notwithstanding, that the Levite, one who must maintain certain rigors of cleanliness, sacrifices a defiled woman is yet another irony and negation of the Levite by the Deuteronomist. The Levite lies by omission in not telling the other tribes the full story of what occurred. In skimming over various details, it is even probable that the Levite actually killed the unnamed

---

[49]The Levite dissects her just like those in the Paris Museum had Sarah Bartmann dissected and placed certain body parts on display. See Patricia Hill Collins, *Black Feminist Thought: Power, Knowledge, and Politics*, 2d ed. (New York: Routledge, 2000), 136–37, 141–43.

[50]Yee, "Ideological Criticism," 165.

secondary wife himself. The Levite ultimately manipulates the details of his secondary wife's demise just as the Deuteronomist fully humiliates and censures the Levitical order and removes the Levite from the remainder of the story, a narrative ending in social chaos (Judges 20–21) that began in cultic chaos (Judges 17–18). Similarly, the composer Puccini so orchestrates the life and movement of Butterfly that one cannot help but see Pinkerton for the despicable lout that he is. Both the Levite and Pinkerton defame, destroy, and violate in premeditated fashion.

Violence and Scapegoating Today

Every newspaper, action film, Greek tragedy, and most opera and animated cartoons contain violence. Soap operas, professional sports, and biblical texts are full of violence. Violence does not emerge out of things or technology, but out of people's lives. All violence arises from disordered human relationships. A full engagement of life, which is antithetical to the violence that negates life, encourages unity and respect for all life.[51] One of the roots of the complex nature of violence lies in deep-seated, nonrational attitudinal and belief systems that sanction and allow violence. The fact that violence allows for the scapegoating of the Butterflys and unnamed first and secondary wives in the world is *misbegotten anguish* personified. These ingrained attitudes of callousness, brutishness, and indifference have the capacity to objectify and dehumanize others. Such personal and institutional beliefs often erupt into violence. By definition, the realities of racism, sexism, classism, ageism, and homophobia make scapegoating indigenous to the fabric of American governmental institutions. These practices have been carried out against particular racial and ethnic groups by the dominant culture to name them inferior and other to the extent that these oppressive ideologies have become a part of the socialization of American life. Such oppression forces those deemed other into powerlessness, which results in a misbegotten anguish where the victim internalizes this powerlessness as rage, self-destruction, and individual and communal pain. Such an impact on the oppressed community then may result in heightened crime, addiction, and domestic violence, due to frustration and self-hatred engendered by

---

[51] Michael N. Nagler, *America Without Violence: Why Violence Persists and How You Can Stop It* (Covelo, Calif.: Island Press, 1982), 5, 40.

the systemic oppression.[52] The scapegoats end up scapegoating themselves.

Systems, institutions, patriarchies, misogynies, or supremacies frame the evil of oppression, notably gender oppression. The control of societal power, and overt and covert violence, evolves with accompanying attitudes and values. These traits are inextricably linked with male dominance of women in the narratives analyzed here. Within systems, one must note the quest to create a sense of legitimacy and authority over women. In human life and literature, men usually exert physical power; that is, men make or take a woman, and women must surrender or submit. The exercise of her "feminine wiles," one strategy for countering male supremacy that involves feigning weakness, hiding feelings, and appearing helpless, is again a reaction that further entrenches male oppressive behavior. The equating of maleness and manhood with an exercise of strength, power, domination, and being tough fosters a misbegotten anguish; such violence often emasculates and makes victims of those men who have no access to power.[53]

Violence as hazardous play is destructive, antisocial, and degrading in its consequences; is habitually deliberate; and is complex. One can view violence as the breakdown of social order or as the maintenance of a pattern of dominance.[54] Some of how this hazardous play has evolved becomes more vicious as pertains to recent sociocultural developments. For example, major social change has occurred in the United States with the shift from an agrarian, to an industrial, to a postindustrial or technological society. From the 1850s to 1970s, factory building, energy harnessing, and urban development meant the downsizing of family farms and the growth of cities. Along with the development of new energy sources— from steam and coal to thermal and nuclear energy—came tremendous advances in the sciences, which had a major impact on public health, medicine, communication, sanitation, housing, nutrition, and transportation. With the emergence of personal computers, industry and modern life have moved from a base of

---

[52]Lynne B. Iglitzin, *Violent Conflict in American Society* (San Francisco: Chandler, 1972), 77–81.

[53]Ibid., 85–92.

[54]Nancy Armstrong and Leonard Tennenhouse, eds., *The Violence of Representation: Literature and History of Violence* (London: Routledge, 1989), 24; Michael Kowalewski, *Deadly Musings: Violence and Verbal Form in American Fiction* (Princeton: Princeton University Press, 1993), 7.

manufactured goods to one of information technology. With layoffs, downsizing, and mergers has come a three-tiered system of workers: knowledge workers, those who service knowledge workers, and a permanent underclass who do not have the training and skills to be part of the other two groups. An anomie, or rapt confusion produced by the accompanying dislocation occurs with such vast changes. Parallel to these changes are the ensuing changes in values. The industrial era valued an American cultural and civil religious ethos embodied in the Declaration of Independence and the Protestant work ethic. With a different sense of freedom, abundance, and accessible communication came a focus on the values of material acquisition, personal entitlement, and a thirst for instant gratification of sensual experiences. Without stipulating cause, statistics show that with a huge increase in dysfunctional and disrupted family life—particularly through debt, drugs, family violence, broken homes, inadequate parenting and schooling—violence is now a national public health epidemic, a viral outbreak of misbegotten anguish. Numerous sociological, biological, and psychological risks come into play in the manifestation of violent behavior. Violence occurs when these risk factors are triggered and when healthy communication fails, causing personal, institutional, and societal dislocation. Even with these determining factors, most people commit violent acts as their choice; few crimes are committed as a result of medical disorders that totally incapacitate individual control.[55]

Because of these choices, then, scapegoating is the process of releasing the negative forces of guilt and the psyche. Apparently, primitive and "respectable" societies and the sometimes elitist intellectuals need scapegoats. The scapegoat is the target of misbegotten anguish. Such a revolution, built on lies, personifies conquerors that pledge and often covenant victory over evil and death. The human desire for "righteous self-expansion and perpetuation" pushes us to develop social and personal lies, the absurdity that undergirds the human condition: In seeking our own good, we do evil.[56] The scapegoat apparatus, the tool for immortality, is the revolution.

---

[55]Raymond Flannery, *Violence in America: Coping with Drugs, Distressed Families, Inadequate Schooling, and Acts of Hate* (New York: Continuum, 1997), 10, 28–35, 98.

[56]Ernest Becker, *The Denial of Death* (New York: The Free Press, 1973), 95; Charles Bellinger, "Ernest Becker and Soren Kierkegaard on Political Violence," in *Church Divinity*, ed. John Morgan (Bristol, Ind.: Wyndham Hall Press, 1987), 25, 124, 135, 141.

PART II

Power, Control, and Loss

Bombs bursting: over plains and fields,
In mid air, at ground zero;
Bombs raping the land,
Despoiling creation.
Someone got trigger-happy
And decided to play grown-up
With explosive toys,
Relegating the millions of lives slaughtered
To the pile with children's discarded toys,
Justifying the costs of perceived liberty.

Neither justification, jeopardy,
Nor population control needs
Grant us the sanction
To practice global idolatry:
To decide who should die, when they should die, and where they should die;
And how they should die, and how many should die.

Sensationalized, dreaded response mechanisms:
We see violence on screens
All the time;
Violence lessens our humanity.
Even a single victim should make our hearts break!
But we don't even have a second thought
About the other thousands of victims
Who died needlessly today,
Because we sent the missiles and the personnel
To fire at the count of three, two, one, "fire."

3

Contracting
Mechanistic
Muscles

War and Colonialism

A glance at history—ancient and recent—gives witness to the ongoing reality of total warfare. The move to conquer and rape the land of its natural resources for the sake of greed and economic gain attests to colonialism. War has shifted from hand-to-hand combat to the anesthetized, sanitized, and remotely controlled fighting of Scud missiles and biological or germ warfare. In the process of killing people in wartime, we managed to poison the land with chemicals such as Agent Orange. We have taken the gift of "having dominion over the earth" to the gluttony of scarring, polluting, and destroying the land. As a global people, we have been horrific stewards of the land. Some of us have been greedy and lacking in vision. We have skillfully convinced ourselves, in ingenious ways, of objectifying those deemed other, so that genocide legitimated by war holds no shame, remorse, or guilt; so that, in the words of Pete Seeger, we build "ticky tacky houses" over burial grounds without removing the remains; so that we blot out the sun with our skyscrapers, and we stack too

65

many people in claustrophobic caves and call such gated towers a "city" (but not the City of God!), a city that gives witness to our deluded imagery of life on Earth. The conquer-or-be-conquered mentality has certainly come to be a substantive thread among the sociocultural and political fabrics and tentacles of our world. We bask in the success of the Gulf War, which ended after one month of brutal air attack and one hundred hours of ground combat with only 148 American soldiers killed. (But with more than 100,000 ill-trained Iraqi troops missing or killed in action.)

This chapter examines the attitudes, the belief systems, and the complexity of violence amid the systems and processes of war and colonialism. I review the devastation exacting 200 million deaths in the twentieth century as a violent species of population control, and the stories of *Saving Private Ryan,* and the Jezebel and Elijah saga. I explore war and colonialism amid systemic, institutional violence from a global perspective, and reflect on the collaborative mentality that creates a sense of patriotic, manifest destiny as a civil, religious, evangelistic call to fight to the death in a holy jihad.

Devastation Personified: 200 Million Body Bags

Cui Bono, meaning "for whom is this good?" or "Who would profit from this?" is a central question when exploring issues of war. Essentially we are asking at what level a given government deals in good faith from a perspective of justice and ethics with and for the people over which they have authority. All governments have had ancient or contemporary spin doctors to support particular state-constructed agendas, to laud successes and conceal defeats. Part of the language of the spin doctor is to express, ignore, or suppress the dictates of the dominant group or party, which also shapes information regarding oppression and political power or impotence. The language of politics also illumines the ethics, behaviors, and attitudes of the dominant culture regarding the poor and the oppressed, any deemed other.[1] And politics allows those with power to control populations of people by any means necessary.

War, atrocity, or massacre caused the murders of between 180 and 200 million people in the twentieth century, a much larger total than during any other century in human history. Approximately 165 wars or tyrannies in the twentieth century killed more than 6,000

---

[1]Frank S. Frick, "Cui Bono?–History in the Service of Political Nationalism: The Deuteronomistic History as Political Propaganda," *Semeia* 66 (1994), 79–83.

people each. Five of these events took more than 6 million lives each. Twenty-one events claimed between 600,000 and 6 million lives each. Sixty-one acts of government-sanctioned violence claimed between 60,000 and 600,000 each, and seventy-eight events killed between 6,000 and 60,000 each. Although these numbers are subject to interpretation and a wide margin of error and debate, many of the worst atrocities occurred in the dark, unseen, and remain unrecorded. The numbers killed in the twentieth century are also so high because there are so many more people available in the world to kill. Between 4 and 5 percent of all human deaths in the century were intentionally caused by political violence, from terrorist bombings and executed dissidents to battlefield fatalities to starvation among refugees and those at hard labor in concentration camps.[2]

One can divide twentieth-century carnage between the East and the West. In 1911, the Eastern hemoclysm, a Greek term for "blood flood," began with the ousting of the Manchu dynasty in China, leading to thirty-eight years of Civil War and a Japanese invasion. The slaughters of the interregnum shifted to a greater bloodbath in 1949, and then again in 1976 when the Communists united their power under Mao. When viewing the carnage as a continuum, this chapter of Chinese history was a sixty-five–year year hideous atrocity that took 75 million lives. The Western hemoclysm began with the Balkan Wars (1912–13), which provoked the First World War. Four of the most powerful monarchies in Europe were toppled, creating a power vacuum ultimately filled by the Nazis in Germany and the Communists in Russia. Russia entered the conflict during World War II. Stalin's death in 1953 finally snuffed out the Western hemoclysm after 80 million Russian deaths. World War II actually connects the two halves of the hemoclysm. In addition, there were several massacres and wars in Indochina from 1945 to 1980. The first of the series (1945–54) was parallel with World War II, which triggered a chain reaction that led to other wars, which left 5 million Indochinese dead, a total Matthew White does not include in the numbers for the two hemoclysms.[3]

The thirty most prominent atrocities, however, do not include the many concentrated episodes of brutality that affected smaller numbers of people. If we examine the many twentieth-century mass killings—including military and civilian casualties—divided by the

---

[2]Information found on http://users.erols.com/mwhite28/war-1900.htm#introduction in July 2001.

[3]Information found on http://users.erols.com/mwhite28/atrox.htm in July 2001.

populace of the country that suffered the losses, particularly noting the most brutal religion, race, or ideology, an interesting pattern emerges—there is no pattern. The casualties cross classes, sizes of communities, races, and religions. All have exterminated others in the names of various belief systems, involving gods or lack of gods. The political spectrum involves right wing, left wing, and those in the middle; monarchies; dictatorships; and democracies. There is no one group, ideology, or system to blame for the heinous brutality of the twentieth century. "Every major category of human has done its share to boost the body count, so replacing, say, Moslem rulers with Christian rulers, or white rulers with black rulers, is not going to change it at all."[4]

Counting deaths from state projects that resulted in mass famine, deliberate killings, or cold-blooded murder of unarmed noncombatants, Adolf Hitler, Mao Ze-dong, and Joseph Stalin are our leading figures. Their rules resulted in the following numbers of murdered persons: Hitler—34 million; Stalin—20 million; and Mao—15 million, though Mao's failed attempted to restructure China—the Great Leap Forward—resulted in an additional 30 million dead. The following individuals, listed alphabetically, were each responsible for more than a million unnecessary, unjust, or unnatural deaths by instigating or escalating war, famine, or resettlement, or by allowing individuals under their control to commit murder:[5]

> Chiang Kai-shek (China: 1928–49)
> Enver Pasha (Turkey: 1913–18)
> Hirohito (Japan: 1926–89)
> Hirota Koki (Japan: 1936–37)
> Ho Chi Minh (North Vietnam: 1945–69)
> Kim Il Sung (North Korea: 1948–94)
> Lenin (USSR: 1917–24)
> Leopold II (Belgium: 1865–1909)
> Nicholas II (Russia: 1894–1917)
> Pol Pot (Cambodia: 1975–79)
> Saddam Hussein (Iraq: 1969–)
> Tojo Hideki (Japan: 1941–44)
> Wilhelm II (Germany: 1888–1918)
> Yahya Khan (Pakistan: 1969–71)

[4]Ibid.
[5]Information found on http://users.erols.com/mwhite28/tyrants.htm in July 2001.

How senseless such hemoclysms and bloodletting are, and how such atrocities are glorified become more apparent in wrestling with narratives that involve war and bloodletting: *Saving Private Ryan* and the Jezebel-Elijah saga.

Killing Fields, Holy Wars, and Conquests

World War II was a pivotal event of the 20th century and a defining moment for America and the world. It shifted the borders of the globe. It forever changed those who lived through it, and shaped generations to come. It has been called "the last great war."[6]

Saving Private Ryan, Steven Spielberg's 1998 war drama, realistically recreates a grisly account of a D day invasion and its immediate aftermath during World War II. The story opens with a short prologue in which a World War II veteran brings his family to the American cemetery at Normandy. The musical score underlying the drama is rife with dissonance, echoing the pain, stress, and quasi-triumph. The horns and drumbeats reverberate in counterpoint to the sound of a tattered "Old Glory" rippling in the air. The returning veteran is in tears. With a flashback fading to June 6, 1944, we meet Capt. John Miller and the American GIs approaching the Normandy Omaha Beach in a landing craft. They are met with devastating German artillery fire and are picked off like wooden ducks in a shooting gallery. This mass slaughter of American soldiers is riveting, compelling, and unforgettable. Many of them are blown in two. The relentless battle is "a crucible that defines the absoluteness of slaughter…[T]he warfare becomes so intense and all-consuming that the very air seems filled with battle. Shrapnel hangs there, every shard in razor-sharp focus, as if molecules of the film itself had been startled out of the emulsion."[7] The soldiers are all so young.

As the shooting renders some of them temporarily deaf, it seems almost a blessing that they are spared the sounds of violence, since they cannot avoid the sight of it. Amid death and carnage, Miller's men slowly move forward and are finally able to take a concrete pillbox. On the beach among so many broken bodies is one with the name "Ryan" stenciled on his backpack. Stateside, the Army

---

[6]Quote found on http://www.rzm.com/pvt.ryan/movie/movie.html in July 2001.
[7]Quote found on http://mrshowbiz.go.com/movies/reviews/SavingPrivateRyan_1998/review.html in July 2001.

Chief of Staff, Gen. George C. Marshall, learns that three Ryan brothers from the same family have all been killed in a single week. Marshall requests that the surviving brother, Pvt. James Ryan, be located and brought back to the United States. Marshall notes that after the Sullivan brothers had all been killed together on a ship, the general consensus was that no two family members should serve together in combat. Reading a letter that President Abraham Lincoln had written to another mother who had to bury five sons, Marshall is determined that James Ryan be returned to his family. Captain Miller and his eight-man squad of D day survivors are sent behind enemy lines on a public relations mission to do the impossible, to rescue the last son of a devastated Iowa family and bring Pvt. Ryan back alive.

Miller chooses a translator, Cpl. Upham, who is skilled in language but totally naive regarding combat, to join his squad with Sgt. Horvath and privates Mellish, Caparzo, medic Wade, cynical Reiben, and southerner Jackson, an ace sharpshooter who always prays and calls on the Lord while preparing to aim, a prototype of World War I's Sgt. York. Clearly for Jackson, as for Sgt. York, this war is a holy war of sorts. Having previously experienced action in Italy and North Africa, the close-knit squad starts out on its journey through areas still thick with Nazis. After they lose one man in a skirmish at a bombed village when the private tries to rescue a child, some of the men begin to question the logic of losing more lives to save the life of one soldier. Why is the life of Private Ryan worth more than their own?[8] When questioned about the math, why eight lives are being jeopardized to find one, Capt. Miller replies that duty supersedes logic and math. And that not only did God make him an instrument of warfare, but the chain of command goes up, never down.

Miller is particularly sensitive to the needs and stability of the men under his command. He rationalizes the mission, not the men. He has lost ninety-four men under his command, and is touched by each loss. At one point, Upham, the translator, insists during a skirmish that they should not kill the remaining German, because he is a prisoner of war. As the squad's morale deteriorates, Miller is able to help them regroup by finally telling them the answer to the riddle for which they have taken bets: What did Capt. Miller do before entering the service? He was a high school English teacher.

---

[8]Information found on http://www.movieweb.com/movie/privateryan/ in July 2001.

When they do find Ryan, Ryan refuses to leave his squad, which is standing guard at a bridge. Miller hopes that another soldier one day may be able to say that saving Private Ryan was the thing that made sense. During the battle at the bridge, Upham, the translator, freezes and cannot bring the ammo or support to his comrades in the tower as they are being savagely stabbed. He stands on the stairs, and the same German soldier he defended earlier, who killed the soldiers in the tower, looks at him with disdain and then passes him by. Minutes later, when Upham sees that Captain Miller is dead, he kills the one German who passed him on the stairs; the others are taken as prisoners of war. When planes arrive and give relief, Ryan is able to stand and see that Captain Miller is dead. Then we hear the voiceover of General Marshall, reading his letter to Mrs. Ryan:

> Nothing, not even the safe return of a beloved son can compensate you or the thousands of other American families, who have suffered great loss in this tragic war. But I might share with you some words which have sustained me through long nights of peril, loss, and heartache. And I quote: "I pray that our Heavenly Father may assuage the anguish of your bereavement, and leave you only the cherished memory of the loved and lost, and the solemn pride that must be yours to have laid so costly a sacrifice on the altar of freedom." Abraham Lincoln. Yours very respectfully, George C. Marshall, Chief of Staff.

When the film fades back to the present, Ryan is with his family as he has a rhetorical conversation at Captain Miller's grave. Ryan says that every day he thinks about what Miller said on the bridge. "I didn't know how I'd feel about coming back here. I hope that I was enough. I hope I earned what you did for me." Ryan then poignantly says to his wife, "Tell me I've led a good life. Tell me I'm a good man." She replies, "You are."

The film's historical consultant was Stephen E. Ambrose. Ambrose's 1994 bestseller *D-Day: June 6, 1944* depicts the true story of 101st Airborne's Fritz Niland, whose story parallels *Saving Private Ryan*. The plot of *Saving Private Ryan* is partially inspired by Niland's story, one of four brothers from New York state who were soldiers during the war. Two Niland brothers were killed on D day. Another was missing in action in Burma and presumed dead, though he actually survived. Fritz was located in Normandy by an Army chaplain, the Reverend Francis Sampson, and then taken out of the combat zone.[9]

For war purposes, conquest at Normandy was significant. The Americans had to be successful at Omaha Beach. With the concurrent British and Canadian landings at Gold, Juno, and Sword beaches and the American landing at Utah, the Allies were able to establish and hold a beachhead on the Normandy coast. Ambrose notes that there were many actual officers like the fictional Capt. Miller. In actuality, the Americans sustained about 2,400 casualties at Omaha on June 6. Spielberg unstintingly depicts the destruction on the battlefield, a radically different treatment from earlier World War II films that let soldiers die quick, romantic, noble deaths, never knowing what hit them. Ambrose argues that ninety-nine percent of the time, soldiers clearly know what hits them. The eighteen-year-old soldiers are terrified, and "they're not at peace with their maker or anything else like it." Spielberg's Omaha Beach is deafening and chaotic juxtaposed against the earlier battles of this genre, which Ambrose argues "are too clean, too neat, too surgical, too short, too good to be true."[10]

Saving Private Ryan provides an extraordinary illustration of the violence, fear, loneliness, and emotional instability American soldiers experience as they partake of killing and witnessing their fellow soldiers dying in dreadful fashion. This movie helps one begin to glimpse and then comprehend the pain and suffering American fighters battled and the distress, the post-traumatic stress syndrome, that sometimes even years of counseling can never console. Upham presents a humanist view of war. Having never fired a rifle in battle, he is terrified to death of the whole idea. Upham and a lot of other GIs may have asked until the end of their lives the same questions that Ryan raised fifty-five years after the war at Capt. Miller's Normandy gravesite: Have I been a good man? Was it worth it to risk eight lives to save my life? What about the families of the squad members that did not make it? Such nationalistic violence provoked many similar and different questions in ancient biblical texts, particularly in 1 Kings 16–22; 2 Kings 1–2, 9: the Elijah and Jezebel saga. Here the biblical texts utilized will be those relevant to the movements of Elijah, Ahab, and Jezebel.

---

[9]Information found on http://private-ryan.eb.com/page1.html in July 2001.
[10]Ibid.

1 Kings 16 chronicles that during Ahab's reign of twenty-two years he did evil in the sight of God, more than any king ever before; his sins parallel those of Jeroboam. (The Deuteronomist criticizes Jeroboam because he made sacrifices at places other than the temple, made graven images of Yahweh, and had the audacity to set up a priesthood outside of the house of Levi.)[11] Ahab, son of Omri, married Jezebel, the daughter of King Ethbaal, and proceeded to worship and serve Baal and erect an altar to that Canaanite deity. 1 Kings 17–2 Kings 10 is the story of the Northern kingdom, which features stories about Elijah and Elisha, Ahab's reign, and the destruction of the Omride dynasty. First Kings 17 introduces Elijah the Tishbite and tells of his encounter with the ravens and of his exchange with the unnamed Sidonian widow woman and her son, whom Elijah brings back to life after Elijah cries out to the Lord. As the drama continues in 1 Kings 18, God tells Elijah to go and see Ahab, as Samaria is troubled by a terrible famine. Ahab calls the prophet Obadiah. Obadiah is one who both reveres the Lord and remembers when Jezebel was killing God's prophets (18:4). Ahab offers Obadiah a strategy for securing the safety of their livestock, and then they part company. Obadiah and Elijah cross paths, and Elijah requests that Obadiah tell Ahab he, Elijah, has arrived. Knowing what he does about the connection between Ahab and Jezebel, Obadiah questions the job and safety of the prophetic office, and Elijah recounts how God has provided protection and care. Twice during this pericope, we are told that Jezebel killed God's prophets (18:4; 18:13–14), a foreshadowing of an act of retribution. Obadiah goes to announce Elijah's arrival to Ahab; Ahab comes to meet Elijah (18:16).

When the two meet, Elijah takes Ahab's inventory, accusing Ahab of breaking many commandments. Elijah tells Ahab to summon all Israel to the event and also challenges the prophets of Baal and Asherah to meet him at Mount Carmel, signifying Jezebel's complicity in that she feeds them. The audience, familiar with the Deuteronomist agenda, knows that sooner or later Jezebel will have to be accountable for practicing idolatry in the eyes of Israel. When all are gathered, Elijah preaches, "If God is God, then follow God; but if Baal is God, then follow Baal" (18:21, NRSV, altered). The contest begins on Mount Carmel with Elijah's challenge, perhaps

---

[11]J. Benton White and Walter T. Wilson, *From Adam to Armageddon: A Survey of the Bible*, 4th ed. (Belmont, Calif.: Wadsworth, 2001), 42.

his dare, that the Baal worshipers summon Baal to answer them by creating a fire under the sacrificial bull. Even after midday, "there was no voice, no answer, and no response" (18:29). Elijah makes an offering and an oblation, calls on the God of Abraham, Isaac, and Israel to make known the Godself as God in Israel, and the fire of God falls on the sacrifice and consumes the offering. Elijah then has every Baal prophet seized and slaughtered at the Wadi Kishon.

In 1 Kings 19, Ahab tells Jezebel what happened, and she vows revenge and ironically calls for her own death if she cannot subdue Elijah. Elijah flees and goes to the wilderness, where he experiences two epiphanies with visits from an angel of the Lord. Then Elijah encounters God at Mount Horeb in sheer silence, only a gentle whisper. God tells Elijah to anoint Hazael as King of Syria, anoint Jehu as king of Israel, and anoint Elisha as Elijah's replacement. This chapter ends with Elisha's call to be a prophet. As opposed to historical documentation, 1 Kings 20 is more theological reflections assessing the quality of Ahab's faith[12] as he deals with foreign policy matters, finds favor, and receives a harsh word: Ahab's death is foretold. In 1 Kings 21, Ahab has to deal with domestic affairs, notably the question of Naboth's vineyard. Upset and not appreciating that Naboth would not and could not give, trade, or sell his land because it is an ancestral inheritance, Ahab goes home like a spoiled brat and sulks. Jezebel inquires as to why he is so depressed and conspires against Naboth to get the land for her husband. Her plan is successful; Naboth is dead, and Ahab journeys to take possession of the land located in Jezreel. God tells Elijah to go and confront Ahab, to pronounce retributive justice: Since you have killed, Ahab, just as the dogs licked Naboth's blood, dogs will lick up your blood also. This is really bad news.

Not only is Ahab indicted, but the prophetic word is that all men of Israel will be cut off from Ahab, and his house will have the same outcome as the house of Jeroboam, because Ahab provoked God to anger and has caused Israel to sin. Elijah also announces that Jezebel will be eaten by dogs within Jezreel, that anyone of Ahab's house dying in the city will be eaten by dogs, and that anyone of Ahab's house dying in the country will be eaten by birds. Ahab immediately assumes an attitude of penitence, repentance, and humility, and God promises to not bring punishment during Ahab's

---

[12]Choon-Leong Seow, "The First and Second Books of Kings," in *The New Interpreter's Bible Commentary: A Commentary in Twelve Volumes,* vol. 3 (Nashville: Abingdon Press, 1999), 146.

lifetime, but that disaster will come upon Ahab's house during Ahab's son's lifetime (1 Kings 21:27–29). Following three years of peace (1 Kings 22), war breaks out and Ahab is advised by his prophets to go to Ramoth-gilead for the skirmish as the Lord will make Ahab triumphant. Only the prophet Micaiah proclaims that Ahab will be enticed to battle to meet his death. Not aware of the folk adage "a hard head makes a soft behind," Ahab orders Micaiah imprisoned, and goes to war in disguise, but is mortally wounded in battle. Ahab remains propped up in his chariot until he dies in the evening. 1 Kings ends and 2 Kings begins with rebellion on the part of unfaithful Israelites or foreign uprisings. After having encounters with Ahaziah's soldiers, who are consumed by divine fire, Elijah and Elisha meet again as Elijah winds down his ministry to assent to the prophetic ministry of Elisha. In 2 Kings 2, Elijah and Elisha travel about, cross the Jordan River, Elijah gives Elisha a double portion of his gifts at Elisha's request, and Elijah is taken up to Yahweh in a chariot of fire. The ministry of Elisha then unfolds around "issues of life and death, [with] Elisha in each case acting to bring, sustain, or restore life and avert death."[13] When Jezebel reappears, the text really focuses on King Jehu and the demise of the house of Omri.

Jehu receives word from the Lord that he, Jehu, is to become "king over the people of the LORD, over Israel. You shall strike down the house of your master Ahab, so that I may avenge on Jezebel the blood of my servants the prophets, and the blood of all the servants of the LORD" (2 Kings 9:6–7). After obediently seeing to the deaths of King Joram of Israel and King Ahaziah of Judah, King Jehu goes to Jezreel to find and assassinate Jezebel (2 Kings 9:30–37). The eunuchs throw an adorned Jezebel to her death at the command of Jehu. Her blood spatters everywhere; the horses trample her. When they go to retrieve her body for burial, they find only her skull and her hands, which fulfills the earlier prophecy. "In the territory of Jezreel the dogs shall eat the flesh of Jezebel; the corpse of Jezebel shall be like dung on the field in the territory of Jezreel, so that no one can say, 'This is Jezebel'" (2 Kings 9:36–37). Following the words spoken of God through the prophet Elijah, everyone who remained in the house of Ahab, including his seventy sons, the chief men, any priests, or close friends, is slaughtered and fed to the dogs and birds: a bloody, gruesome business (2 Kings 10:1–11); individual innocence was not a part of the equation.

---

[13]Ibid., 185.

With the redaction of the Deuteronomist and the tradition of reader response, Jezebel and Elijah have become polar opposites. Readers love Elijah and hate Jezebel; he is the essence of good, she the archetype of evil. Jezebel is couched in horrific hostility, beginning with her name, a perversion of the Hebrew term that means "dung," which also implicates her religious preference for Baal worship. Though their names announce the faith commitment of both characters, the Deuteronomists condemn Jezebel, but applaud Elijah.[14]

> Entrapped by hostile editors and male lords, Jezebel appears as evil object, neither speaking nor acting. Free of editorial restraints, Elijah appears as good subject, exalting himself in word and deed. She is female and foreign; he, male and native. She comes from the coastlands; he, from the highlands. She thrives in a sea climate; he, in a desert climate. She belongs to husband and father; he, neither to wife nor father. She embodies royalty; he, prophecy. Both bear theophoric names that unite them in opposition: Jezebel the Baal worshiper and Elijah the YHWH worshipper. The details of an economic text yield an abundance of polarities.[15]

Jezebel is condemned or undermined at every turn. The Deuteronomists set her up so that her own people oppose and undermine her. She is a chess piece in a political marriage and ends up living in Elijah's homeland. In turn, Elijah goes to her home turf. She is met with hostility, and he is greeted with hospitality. She is condemned for idolatry, for supporting and having power over the Baal prophets. The prophet Obadiah fingers Jezebel for Elijah by connecting her with the Hebrew verb "to kill" *(harag)*. Phyllis Trible notes that Elijah sees Jezebel's religious commitment. She is a consummate theologian and missionary, as she advocates her faith and provides abundantly for the upkeep and resources of the Baal prophets. Then she goes to the aid of her husband, Ahab, and has Naboth charged, convicted, and stoned to death; the men do not question her. Nevertheless, Jezebel and Elijah remain in polar opposition, though they execute similar behavior. Elijah derides Ahaziah without fear. Jezebel derides Jehu without fear, but Elijah wins. Jezebel loses. Elijah is taken up to Yahweh in a fiery chariot,

---

[14]Phyllis Trible, "Exegesis for Storytellers and Other Strangers," *Journal of Biblical Literature* 114 (1995): 3, 4.
   [15]Ibid., 4, 5.

and nothing is left of Jezebel but a skull and her hands. Ultimately, both characters are zealous for their respective gods, and they both scheme and commit murder as mirror images of each other.[16] What then, do *Saving Private Ryan* and the Elijah/Jezebel sagas have in common? Violence, misbegotten anguish, war, and colonialism.

Making It Plain: Colonialism and War Unfurled

Albert Memmi, in his *The Colonizer and the Colonized,* defines a colonized as one who, externally, has been stripped of much. The colonized are robbed of power and cultural artifacts that provide one with a sense of purpose: the stories, histories of origin, oral traditions, documents, and any legacy they might want to pass on to their offspring. Those colonized or oppressed can acquiesce and assimilate, which results in self-denial, or they can embark on self-discovery. Colonialism inverts the desires as it destabilizes the established hierarchy of what is important. The colonized often run into difficulty when trying to affirm the essential realities of precolonial traditions and those of the colonizer.[17] The domain of domination for the colonizer is the colony.

A colony is a land mass or territory that may or may not be inhabited that an outside power acquires by conquest or government or settlement by a people not indigenous to that territory. Colonialism is imposed foreign rule. A colonial relationship begins when one government or group of people claims sovereignty and enforces political control over another people or land mass. The relationship ceases when the colonized become fully self-governing or they fully assimilate into the political structure of the colonial power. The nature of colonial relationships has varied over time. The schematics for colonialism range from settlement by nationals of the colonizing country, to some colonies that have loose government, to others that have strict supervision. Some colonies have been settled sparsely, others heavily. Regardless of the strategy, colonialism is a philosophy, political strategy, and process of violation and imposition.

Understanding stewardship and dominion to mean presupposing authority and domination in the names of conquering, manifest destiny, and adventure, European nations espousing Western Christendom began subjugating other parts of the world. These

---

[16]Ibid., 6–7, 9, 12–14, 17.

[17]George Allan, "Conservatives, Liberals, and the Colonized: Ontological Reflections," *Process Studies* 23 (Winter 1994): 256, 257, 268, 269. See Albert Memmi, *The Colonizer and the Colonized,* trans. Howard Greenfield (*Portrait du colonisé précédé du portrait du colonisateur* [Corrêa: Editions Buchet/Chastel, 1957; Boston: Beacon Press, 1967]), 120.

events, which began more than five centuries ago, are "the earliest known example of globalization…An Appeal for Peace is now made necessary at the dawn of the 21st century because of the present day consequences of a global culture of war and colonialism dating back to the fifteenth century…The culture of war has set into motion and institutionalized destructive policies through the laws and processes of domination, militarism, subjugation, and exploitation."[18] The kind of globalization exhibited here is colonialism.

"Colonialism is a culture of war, violence, domination, exploitation and genocide."[19] As a system, colonialism imposes state or imperial laws, rules, and controls by colonial pioneers or settlers, in the lands and territories of independent peoples who have lived in these areas long before the colonial settlers arrived. Colonialism functions to secure and protect the settlers' own interests at the expense of, and without concern for, the original peoples' and nations' survival. Colonialism seeks to destroy and eliminate the preexisting peoples and their culture from the land to allow the settlers to attain dominance. In the process, colonialism devastates and ruins the sociocultural traditions and the natural environment. The devastation is a product of the arrogant, insatiable desires and needs of a market economy, the industrialization of the various environments, and the people who are solely interested in amassing wealth and resources by viewing all living realities as property. Colonialism is the art, science, and business of influential domination of peoples, nature, of all life. Because colonialism produces absolute annihilation of entire groups of people, it embodies a culture of genocide. Genocide, the epitome of war exacted by one group against another, hinges on bigotry and racism, which gives permission to the colonizer to dehumanize people deemed other and to destroy their ways of life. To control and rob the people and the earth, colonizers establish a system of domination through creating genocidal laws and policies that are intended to eliminate the original peoples and cultures and to thwart new births within their groups. Colonizers seek to brainwash and condition the children and the impressionable so that the colonized become active with, and assimilate into, the dominant colonial milieu. The other option is to self-destruct. Genocide takes the form of massacres and prohibitions against the physical and cultural survival of original peoples so that they are inhibited from

---

[18]"The Basic Foundations of Colonialism, International Law, and U.S. Indian Law," found at http://www.pasifika.net/pacific-action/hap/nalgifts.html in July 2001.
[19]Ibid.

passing on their culture and the life traditions of their own land to new generations. Genocide also functions to assure that colonialism, violence, racism, and coercion occur through state policies of forced assimilation of the particular indigenous peoples into the population at large and into the urban areas of the oppressive, dominating civil culture and social order.[20] Colonialism is not a modern phenomenon, but an ancient one.

Colonialism began during antiquity, particularly under the rule of the Egyptians, Babylonians, and Persians. Most scholars argue that the Phoenicians were the earliest overseas colonizers, with colonies along the Mediterranean Sea from about 1100 B.C.E. Phoenicians wanted to expand and control trade. Many Greek city-states were expanding along the coasts of the Black Sea, the North Aegean, and southern Italy by the eighth century B.C.E. The Greeks needed more commerce and more arable land to sustain a growing population. The two most famous Greek city-states, Sparta and Athens, were colonial powers in the sixth and fifth centuries B.C.E. During the medieval era, after the collapse of Rome in the fifth century, there was little overseas colonization. The Vikings, however, did a great deal of colonialization during the ninth and tenth centuries. They controlled much of the British Isles and originated settlements in Greenland and Iceland.

Modern European colonialism began in the fifteenth century in two overlapping eras: From 1415 to about 1800, Spain and Portugal led the colonial expansion in the East Indies and the Americas; from 1800 to World War II, Great Britain led European expansion into Africa, Asia, and the Pacific. In phase one the Portuguese, with great political stability, an advantageous geographic position, and maritime experience, were the first Europeans to sail around the southern tip of Africa to South and East Asia, mainly to dominate the spice trade. The Dutch and the English seriously challenged Portugal's Eastern trade monopoly by the late sixteenth century. The Dutch launched their empire at the Cape of Good Hope, finally drove out the Portuguese, and controlled Java and Ceylon (now Sri Lanka) by 1800. In 1757, the English East India Co., establishing itself in India, began formal colonialization of that mainland.

European nations wanted to colonize the Americas to obtain new land for agriculture, precious metals, freedom from religious

---

[20]Ibid.

persecution, and an opportunity to convert the Indians to Christianity. Once colonies were established, they only traded with their particular parent nations in Europe. Spain's vast empire spread across the bulk of Central and South America. The Portuguese mainly colonized Brazil. The Spanish and Portuguese tended to create mixed settlements that incorporated the indigenous populations of their territories, while the French and British settlers in North America usually formed colonies where they eliminated or displaced the original or previous inhabitants.

By the early 1800s, the European empires had largely deteriorated. Most Portuguese, Spanish, and French colonies in the Americas gained independence during and after the Napoleonic wars. The Dutch also lost their few holdings in the New World and happily practiced illegal trading with the colonies that belonged to foreign powers. Although Britain lost its original North American colonies, who gained independence in 1776, it continued to be a major colonial power, controlling India, Canada, the Cape of Good Hope, and Ceylon. Britain's late eighteenth-century colonial empire provides a historical bridge between the first and second waves of European expansion.

The second era of colonialization began from about 1815 to 1880 with a focus on well-established European interests. The second phase of this era, from 1880 to 1914, was a time of more determined colonialization. The colonizing of Africa—except for Ethiopia, which resisted Italy's conquest attempts—and parts of Asia and the Pacific was completed, with a global network of colonies. Britain, with the most substantive holdings, was joined by France, Germany, Belgium, Portugal, the United States, and Japan with significant holdings. The arguments regarding the driving forces for the colonialization efforts are varied, from the demands of capitalism and need for raw materials and places to divert surplus capital, to diplomatic and strategic motivations, to a continuation of earlier efforts.

The twentieth century saw the end of modern colonialism, due to the crumpling of the European balance of power and successive global wars. Colonies developed national awareness, and the lack of any justification for empire after 1945 resulted in widespread decolonization. Within about thirty years, centuries-old colonial empires were almost totally torn apart. Many former colonies now see colonialism as an imposed, systematic exploitation by stronger powers who fostered economic codependency and backwardness, racism, and psychological dysfunctionality.

The potential for colonization is intrinsic to a world made up of political bodies at fundamentally different stages of technological and economic development where the powerful remain tempted to control the weak. Power disparities make colonization possible, but not inevitable or necessary. The powerful do not always want to expand, and the weak sometimes have the capacity to resist. While nineteenth-century colonizers thought they had a moral obligation to control and civilize backward folks, colonialism exacted significant costs despite some of the benefits, to the colonizers and the colonized. Economically, colonialism was a mixed experience.

The catalyst for much of the historical colonialism and genocide rests in the papal authority at the Vatican. In eighteen documents called "papal bulls," a succession of popes authorized "rights of discovery, conquest, extermination, genocide, and subjugation to the Christian European colonizers of that time."[21] For example, Rome told the king of Portugal to "capture, vanquish, and subdue" infidel peoples, placing them in perpetual slavery, and to rob them of all of their worldly goods and possessions. In 1493, shortly after the first voyage to the Americas of Christopher Columbus, a Jewish convert, Pope Alexander VI, released the Inter Cetera bull of May 4, where he called for the overthrowing and subjugation of all barbaric nations for the purposes of building and propagating the Christian Empire.

The Inter Cetera bull, and many prior papal bulls, became the basis of global colonization for many empires of Christendom, including Spain, Portugal, France, England, and Holland. (N.B. Russia had left Rome back in 1100 C.E. Russia's only non-European colony was Alaska.) These colonial empires thought they had a divine right to acquire and manipulate the infidel nations and had a right to abscond with lands and goods. Other nations, such as Japan, China, Turkey, and the United States later joined these states or empires of the West, of Christendom, also known as the Family of Nations in Europe. This society of colonizers ultimately led to the failed League of Nations, and then to the United Nations. Today's world power structures, including the United States, Canada, Australia, and New Zealand, in league with dominant transnational corporations, base their methods of uniting the world's resources and subduing the world's peoples on the model of Christendom's paradigm for empire building and colonization. The existence and

---

[21]"Basic Foundations of Colonialism."

activities of the World Trade Organization (WTO), the Multilateral Agreement on Investments (MAI), the International Monetary Fund (IMF), the Global Agreement on Trades and Tariffs (GATT), the Asian Pacific Economic Council (APEC), the North American Free Trade Act (NAFTA), the Trilateral Commission, the Human Genome Diversity Project, and the Biodiversity Convention indicate current international trends which signal a new amplification of colonialism.[22]

The corporate patenting of living things as property within the global trade agreements of transnational corporations and nation-states effectively avoids the consent of all peoples. The massive corporate mergers have afforded selective monopolization through transnational corporations. Such action allows these corporations to be exempt from environmental and labor laws and protective collective agreements such as the Law of the Sea. Such power and authority allow for the rape and heinous destruction of the earth.[23] Lands and people have been wronged, particularly in the name of religion.

The apartheid system of slavery in the United States merged with Christianity to create an apologetics and a sustained relationship. Christianity aided and abetted colonial violence and oppression, allegedly as part of God's will. That slaveholders rationalized slavery with biblical texts reiterates the reality that Christianity, from its origins, had to make accommodations with diverse discourses to ensure its survival. With scriptural sanction and the assumption that slavery was central to God's plan to convert so-called heathen, inferior persons, these arguments supported the oppressive colonial analysis of economy, race, class, and religion.[24] The same manifest destiny that created the United States has been one impetus for the conquest of other peoples, of other lands. Puerto Rico is one case in point.

U.S. troops first invaded Puerto Rico and the Philippines in 1898, at the end of the Spanish-American War. This foray began the occupation and colonialization of Puerto Rico by the United States. Puerto Ricans have mounted various acts of resistance, dealing with cruel colonial circumstances and draconian tactics to control various political activists. The U.S. military continues to use Puerto Rico as

---

[22]Ibid.

[23]Ibid.

[24]Kimberly Rae Connor, "Everybody Talking about Heaven Ain't Going There: The Biblical Call for Justice and the Postcolonial Response of the Spirituals," *Semeia* 75 (1996): 114–16.

the main U.S. military base in Latin America, including more than fourteen sub-bases throughout the island, and uses two tiny populated islands connected to Puerto Rico as bombing ranges. This type of colonialism taps into the military but also affects Puerto Rican citizenship status. Although Puerto Ricans have had a nominal kind of U.S. citizenship since just before World War I, which allowed the U.S. government to recruit Puerto Rican men, Puerto Ricans who do not live within the United States cannot vote during governmental elections, even for president. Puerto Ricans have also engaged in U.S. draft resistance and evasion, notably since the numbers recruited are disproportional to their numbers within the population.

Along with the usual conflicts, colonial violence has also been perpetrated by forcing the sterilization of large numbers of Puerto Rican women as part of experiments that benefit multinational pharmaceutical companies. Additional colonial violence occurs through economic exploitation. U.S. corporations operate in Puerto Rico tax-free as poverty levels are escalating in the country, whose natural resources have been stripped. While Puerto Rico is a Spanish-language country, the English-language court system presides over the "security" work of various departments of military police, bureaus of investigation, and domestic forces. Resisters to this colonial violent situation are war resisters. "Colonialism itself has always been a form of war, and Puerto Rico remains—at the beginning of the century the UN had hoped to declare an era without colonies—one of the world's last direct colonial enclaves."[25]

While some may argue for the benefits of colonialism, there is a term in Kiswahili that indicates the damage caused by five hundred years of exploitative colonialism in Africa, which included slavery and imperialism: *Maafa,* "disaster or terrible occurrence."[26] One of the primary motives for the tremendous exploitation by Germany, France, Britain, Belgium, and Italy was to acquire Africa's tremendous mineral wealth, including coal, gold, diamonds, and bauxite. The colonial governments cared little for the Africans and forced the indigenous peoples to work under harsh conditions. Despite the horrendous situations created by persons like Belgium's King Leopold II, who had villagers flogged or their hands or heads cut off during the 1830s, there were persons such as missionary David Livingstone who did treat Africans with great respect.

[25]http://www.gn.apc.org/warresisters/news/pfp99pr.htm
[26]http://www.mrdowling.com/610ar.htm

Livingstone was horrified at the way the Portuguese and the Boers treated African people. African colonialism ended in most of Africa after World War II. The reasons influencing this feat of liberation included four key factors: (1) the Soviet Union and the United States, the two military super powers, both wanted to shape Africa by supporting nationalist movements; (2) Gandhi left South Africa to lead a successful movement to terminate British colonial rule in India, which provided inspiration to many African leaders; (3) With the vast destruction of Europe during World War II, those European governments could not then send troops to Africa to contain and suppress nationalist movements; (4) A class of elite Africans, who were well educated in Western universities, saw how those colonial powers were exploiting their home nations.[27]

The last vestige of home-based colonial rule was apartheid in South Africa. Although British colonial rule ceased when Britain gave South Africa its independence in 1910, Blacks were not given any power. In 1948, apartheid or apartness, was begun under the rule of the National Party. Apartheid called for separate categories of the races and forbade interracial living, work, or owning land in similar areas: "Bantu (black Africans), coloured [*sic*] (people of mixed race), white (the descendants of the Boers and English), and Asian (Indian and Pakistani immigrants)." Non-whites had to carry passes. All Black South Africans were forbidden to participate in the governing of South Africa.[28]

Surely the tears of Black South Africans meet in the seas and oceans of the world, mixed with the trail of tears of Native American peoples. The oppression of Native peoples in the United States developed as imperialist actions of conquest and colonialism under the guise of Christianity. Because of the vast missionization and colonialization of Indian peoples, they can comfortably speak of God as "he" in English, where they would never do so in their own language. Indian peoples refer to a spiritual force that infuses the entire world, manifested in numerous ways that cannot be adequately translated as God. American Indian cultures do not privilege human beings as do Euro-American cultures. This need to dominate may logically flow from the philosophical and scientific thought of Aristotle, the Renaissance, and then Descartes. Native peoples have a tremendous respect for all of created order, which affords a

---

[27]Ibid.
[28]Ibid.

philosophy of harmony and balance of daily life, one of reciprocity, which is the foundation for balance, and spatiality, which privileges place over time. European and Euro-American theological and philosophical history usually privileges time. The significance of space/place for Indian culture makes it clear why Indian existence and spirituality finds such an attachment to land and particular territories. This connection is significant for Indian spiritual and cultural ethos—existence, symbols, ceremonial structures, kinship ties, and a tribe's symbolic boundaries for its universe, central to communal life. The major differences between Euro-American and American Indian cultural values are indicative of why the ongoing relationship between the two continues to involve conquest and colonialization, which produces eco-devastation of Indian peoples' territories. Thus, colonization exacts too great a price, for it has produced oppression that we describe as environmental racism, which affects all of creation: problems of systemic ecological and social injustice, which demands a communal, theological, and ethical response.[29] The Euro-American archetypal heroes and stories of conquest have encouraged denial, which has yet to account "for their history of systemic violence in the world and their easy proclivity for rationalizing any act of military or economic colonization and conquest as somehow good...Stories of conquest are complemented by stories of utilitarian rationalization."[30]

Colonialization has arisen from the Western thrust of individualism over communal life that shapes all theoretical and intellectual thought and posturing. Colonialization has produced rampant ecological injustice: the rape of the land, as in blasting and coal mining, resulting in vast devastation, flooding, and soil depletion. With a systemic, philosophical, intellectual, militaristic, political, and economic colonialization, Native peoples have been forced into vast poverty and dysfunctionality. This reality plays itself out in high infant mortality, alcoholism, incarcerations, tuberculosis, and diabetes. Righting relationships with American Indians regarding sovereignty and the return of lands opens the door to the reshaping of Western values, which could affect our environmental injustices, for such cultures work to live in balance with all created order, cognizant of environmental limits.[31]

---

[29]George Tinker, "An American Indian Theological Response to Ecojustice," *Ecotheology* 3 (1997): 88, 90–93, 96, 99, 100.

[30]Ibid., 101.

[31]Ibid., 102–7.

Many colonizers are able to colonize successfully because they have mastered the art of conquest and do not mind engaging in war to accomplish their purposes. War is a dynamic, aggressive engagement of hostile fighting that includes bigotry, genocide, crime, injustice, abuse, and scapegoating. Those who sanction war also usually practice self-justification so that they can make themselves look good, be right, and take on the mantle of alleged justice. War as scapegoating allows the establishment of peace and unites enemies against others, sometimes former friends, a genuine revelry of hypocrisy.[32] Modern war is usually a state of openly declared, armed hostile conflict between states or nations, a state of antagonism and hostility. Yet war predates organized nation-states. War pertains to matters of history and society, particularly the problems that emerge. The French Revolution was a catalyst for the practice of training large groups of men to participate in potentially self-destructive acts. This particular event portrayed the significance of popular armed engagement. After the Industrial and Agricultural Revolutions, increased numbers of eligible males and material resources could be targeted for use in warfare. During the nineteenth century, a positivistic notion of war developed that included a philosophy about society, human nature, notions of the state, and various ideas concerning management. These concepts gave military scientists affirmative goals during a time of peace, when the major military events in Europe were Prussia's victories over Austria and France. Militarism, a nineteenth-century negative label for structures or systems, places inordinate value on glorifying war, military virtues, and soldiers. As more and more states replaced feudal systems, and as democratic and national armies replaced bands of military artisans, the perversions of war became more apparent. Some philosophical positivists saw war as a grand event of state, but this view was shaken after the two world wars of the twentieth century.[33] Even so, in the twenty-first century some still advocate war because of their stringent religious beliefs and understanding of their particular sacred texts.

Many legitimate their stance on war and violence with quotes from the Hebrew Bible. While the Bible tells us who we are, what we ought and ought not do, we must be careful not to oversimplify and eisegete information about war that does not exist in the text.

---

[32]Ted Peters, "Violence in War and Peace." Editorial, *Dialog* 36 (Fall, 1997): 242–43.

[33]Theodore Ropp, "War and Militarism," in *Dictionary of the History of Ideas: Studies of Selected Pivotal Ideas,* ed. Philip P. Wiener, vol. 4 (New York: Charles Scribner's Sons, 1973), 500–508.

One type of war ideology in the Bible is the ban, when God demands war that includes the total destruction of women, men, and children, sometimes domestic animals, destroying entire cities. As these bans express Israelite culture, one can argue that they were concerned about an ethics of war, particularly about the question of justice regarding the ban. The first use of the ban in the Hebrew Bible occurs in Genesis 14 with Lot's rescue by Abram's military tactics.[34] One example where the text does not use the word for ban *(harem),* but implies a connection with divine justice is 2 Kings 9–10, where Jehu comes to purge the Omride dynasty, as cited earlier. Fulfilling Elijah's prophecy (1 Kings 21:20–24), Jehu comes to take down Ahab's house. Ahab is viewed as an "unethical incorrigible idolater," encouraged by his "foreign, zealous, Baal-worshipping wife," Jezebel, who victimized Elijah and other Yahweh worshipers. Ahab dies in battle (1 Kings 22:37).[35] Jehu kills Jezebel and all the house of Ahab. This directed fighting resembled a ban. The Deuteronomist views Jehu from a positive perspective. Only the author of 2 Kings presents the purging of the Omride house that "evokes the ideology of the ban as God's justice."[36] Yahweh uses genocide to colonize the Northern Kingdom of Ahab.

Despite the many civil wars or wars within nations and ethnic cleansings, with their profound suffering, that have occurred as recently as the 1990s, there are many persons committed to peacemaking and to the prevention of war. The number of declared wars between independent nations has been reduced. An ethic of peacemaking has been the subject of much discussion, and several scholars have reached a consensus on ten peacemaking practices and principles that can help sustain peace, regardless of our capacity to affect war and to come to quick solutions. These practices have been incorporated within countries throughout the world:

1. The nonviolent direct action practiced by Gandhi and Martin Luther King, Jr., helped to quell the violence and stifle civil war in East Germany prior to the fall of the Berlin Wall.
2. An invitation for reciprocation and reducing the threat to the opposing side through independent initiatives afforded face-saving options to Serbian military forces and political asylum

---

[34]Susan Niditch, *War in the Hebrew Bible: A Study in the Ethics of Violence* (New York: Oxford University Press, 1993), 4, 5, 8, 10, 11.

[35]Ibid., 72.

[36]Ibid., 73.

to Yugoslav soldiers, with assistance from Germany, Russia, and the Fellowship of Reconciliation.

3. By using cooperative conflict resolution strategies that uphold a people's culture and history, solutions seem to be more attainable.

4. Critical to peacemaking is the acknowledgement of, or onus for, the injustice and the conflict, and work toward repentance and forgiveness; for example, the United States is partially responsible for Serbian military expertise and violent behavior.

5. In advancing democracy, human rights, and religious liberty, it becomes important to recognize what exacts loyalty, what is being threatened, and which elements foster peace, which ones nurture violence.

6. Because economic scarcity is a catalyst for war, we need to foster just and continuous economic growth, as the Marshall Plan did in supporting European economic recovery.

7. Peacemaking requires the identification of the emerging global cooperative forces, for example, in the Hague, Russia, in concert with NATO's being less trigger-happy.

8. The process of strengthening the cooperative efforts with the United Nations and international peacemaking actions for human rights requires a balance between rigid rule and flexible compromise, particularly in situations between NATO and Serbian diplomacy.

9. Peacemaking requires a reduction of the production, trade, and use of offensive weapons.

10. Peacemaking and sustained freedom necessitate efforts by grassroots peacemaking and voluntary groups.[37] These concepts are not merely theoretical abstractions, but instances of applied peacemaking that become even more relevant when we assess the long- and short-term effects of war.

Although the Berlin Wall is down and Communism is no longer viewed as the Evil Empire, not a day goes by that someplace in the world is not the site for raging internecine wars in a post–Cold War cosmos. There are men and women who resist war. Others honor their citizenship and believe that sending their sons and daughters

---

[37]Glen Stassen, "Nonviolence in Time of War," *Sojourners* (July-August 1999): 18–21. See also Glen Stassen, ed., *Just Peacemaking: Ten Practices for Abolishing War* (Cleveland: Pilgrim Press, 1998).

off to war or engaging in war themselves is a noble calling. These raging wars are not simulated games, but major, violent events that involve sophisticated technology that not only makes war more deadly, but more efficient. Scud missiles become computer games with such accuracy that total war strategies make both civilians and combatants legitimate war targets. In the last forty years, most of the wars have been fought on the soils of Africa and Asia under the directions of former colonizers, especially the United States, Britain, the former Soviet Union/Russia, South Africa, Belgium, and India. During such wars, violence is directed against the civilian population in many ways.[38]

Girls and women living near military bases, or those in refugee camps, often become prey for soldiers in the area. They frequently are victims of abduction, forced prostitution, or rape. The connections between war and the control of women's bodies and their sexuality and reproduction through sanctioned sexual harassment, rape, and militarized prostitution is evident in history. Female political prisoners become the victims of multiple, militarized, genocidal rape. Women are raped and molested as an act of war because "the humiliation for women of giving birth to the enemy's children symbolizes the destruction of the community."[39] Such catastrophic violation of women's sexuality has occurred not just in Yugoslavia but in Germany by Soviet soldiers (1945), in Bangladesh by Pakistani soldiers (1971), and in Kuwait by Iraqi soldiers (1990–91). Documentation shows that even UN peacekeepers have committed sexual abuse and rape against women and girls in Cambodia, Mozambique, Somalia, and other regions. These perpetrators are often supported by the larger military system. After all, young, virile males must have some way to release the stress acquired through military duty, mustn't they? Not only is such behavior tolerated, but militaries around the world often promote prostitution near military compounds to "comfort" their troops. This prostitution has sociocultural, psychological, and economic implications for all those needed to maintain all related services: male partners, club and brothel owners, local governmental and health officials, ministries of foreign defense, all male soldiers, and local male civilian customers.

---

[38]Lois Ann Lorentzen and Jennifer Turpin, eds., *The Women & War Reader* (New York: New York University Press, 1998), xi, xii; Jennifer Turpin, "Many Faces: Women Confronting War," in *The Women & War Reader,* 3–5.

[39]Turpin, "Many Faces," 5.

Wartime also sees an increase in domestic violence, of rape and battering. War affects every system, from military agencies and hospitals to office buildings and educational facilities. War has a tremendous impact on the local environment, despoiling and contaminating earth and water systems. Nations involved in war also siphon off monies for any social and educational spending to bolster military coffers. Contextually, war can recur because of the link between militarism and patriarchy.[40] Within this dialectical relationship,

> [M]ilitarism relies on patriarchal patterns, and patriarchy relies on militarization...Militaries rely on male privilege and female subordination in order to function...[S]tructural conditions are complemented by cultural ones: militaries need men and women to behave in stereotypes ways...[I]n order for societies to be patriarchal or male dominated, military values must predominate—that masculine values must be privileged over feminine values, and masculine values must become equated with military ones. Those values will be evident in various cultural forms, including gendered, militarized rhetoric, in popular culture, and in religious symbols.[41]

War and Colonialism: Upfront, Close, and Personal

War is a product of colonialism and colonizing attitudes: economics and conquest. War is an in-your-face phenomenon that requires a collaborative mentality even when only one person calls the shots. War is personal as it affects the soldier and the soldier's friends and family. War is about anthropological notions of creation that allow for gross devastation and destruction of the Earth and the humanity that inhabits it. Thus, on one level, permission to exact that kind of destruction assumes that someone or something gives one permission to destroy and violate. War is the epitome of misbegotten anguish: the ugliness, the broken bodies, the destruction, the dishonesty often perpetrated to get a nation to consent to war, and the objectification of another that allows one human being to kill another in the first place. *Saving Private Ryan* and the Elijah/Jezebel saga make this reality quite plain.

---

[40]Ibid., 3–11.
[41]Ibid., 15–16.

In *Saving Private Ryan,* there is a tremendous sense of manifest destiny, that we must fight the war to save the world. As Private Jackson, a superb marksman, always prays when he aims and then fires, without equivocation this is a holy war to him. As General Marshall refers to the letter of Abraham Lincoln there is a sense of historicity and patriotism that transcends time. The gesture of fighting takes on a nobility, an elegance. There is never an apology for the war itself, though there is an apology for the deaths of Mrs. Ryan's other three sons. The push for taking Omaha beach at Normandy clearly has evangelistic overtones. In the middle of being cut down like lambs to the slaughter, the soldiers continue to press forward to take the beach. This kind of zeal is born of a belief system, whether that be in a god, a philosophy, a discipline, or a principle of justice or survival. Similarly, the violence in the Elijah/Jezebel saga is brutal.

After the evangelistic call to worship the right god, Elijah not only triumphs in calling on and then witnessing to the power of his God but then slaughters all the Baal prophets. Elisha calls on God and creates two pogroms where a hundred men lose their lives because they have come inquiring on behalf of their king. After the divine hit is given on the remainder of the Omride dynasty, Jehu zealously kills all of Ahab's household. He goes so far as to order the steward of the palace, the governor of the city, the elders, and guardians of the royal princes, who were responsible for their upbringing, to kill the seventy sons, decapitate them, and bring their heads to him at Jezreel. Then all these men and any remaining persons in the house of Ahab at Jezreel are murdered. This was holy war. This was up close and personal. Both narratives explicitly or implicitly authorize mass genocide for the purposes of a higher good. What are our options? Can we with the same kind of zealousness demand peace?

A postcolonial reading notes the complexity of all relationships, particularly at the point of contact between the oppressed, the colonized, and those who want peace and those who desire war, beyond binary opposition to an experience of critical engagement and mutual transformation. These complex relationships involve an exchange of ideas, reciprocal appropriation and confrontation. Such categorization emerges out of the context and writings of Africans, Indians, and Latin Americans, with the plethora of theory arriving later.[42] We have much to learn, and we must look beyond

---

[42]R. S. Sugirtharajah, "A Brief Memorandum on Postcolonialism and Biblical Studies," *Journal for the Study of the New Testament* 73 (1999): 3, 4.

our enlightenment model of logical analysis to do so, particularly given that as detestable as war is, no person or government can impose or force peace.

Walter Wink posits that when we impose or force peace, the troubled groups retrench along ethnic lines and are then unable to imagine any kind of future life where they could possibly live in peace with other racial/ethnic groups. Others retrench along the patriotic, nationalistic lines, or lines of economics and imperialism. In searching for solutions, Wink reminds us that the Bible is a book of hope and of tragedy, of prescription and description. There are times when the prophetic voice is silent, only to remind us that God is a God of history. When America as the "great white hope of the world" goes through our market of various modes of attack, each time being a little more aggressive, there may be times when some people will not repent. These are the times, certainly, when America, that is the United States, needs to repent for our dependency on power and force. Nonviolence is an incredible tool, and we are still not sure of how to invite others to embrace it.[43] Until we do, and until the vast majority of persons in the world are willing to practice nonviolence, without perpetually making former enemies friends and former friends enemies, we are in trouble. Until the need to conquer other people and other lands subsides, we will have those willing to evangelize inviting others to join the civil religious liturgy of war and colonialism, until at some point someone makes a mistake and presses a button that destroys us all.

---

[43]Fletcher Farrar, "A Time to Weep, Interview with Walter Wink," *Sojourners* (July-August 1999): 21.

Mr., he's called
Regardless of his actions;
Slut, tramp, hussy she's called:
If she has an illicit affair;
If she sells her body to feed her babies.
If she likes to sleep with bunches of folk,
She becomes trash, shunned, other.

She be other, also
If she is female:
Victorian sensibilities of ladyhood,
Contemporary realities of career women
Are but opportunities for folk
To ridicule and not take women seriously,
Women who work hard everyday.

Women: poor, in between, and not so poor
Women made to feel inferior,
Women undermined by other women;
Women lied to and treated childlike
By men who ought to know better;
The oppression ripples on
Like an avalanche, destroying
Everything and everybody
In its path.

How is it that we continue
To read Eve's story all wrong?
Continue to think that an awesome God
Could in anyway create one gender inferior to another—
So much so that many have permission
To systematically destroy
That which is female, is woman, is girl-child
On the basis that she lacks a penile appendage,
That she has XY genetic coding,
That we have lied and made her become catty
And spoiled and incompetent:
A porcelain vase waiting to be smashed.

Such a lie,
A barbarous, nasty lie
We perpetrate on over half the species.

4

Cheating, Defaming, and Abusing Eve

Sexism, Seduction, Gender, and Domestic Violence

Many women purchase *concealer,* a type of below-the-eye makeup, and wear sunglasses indoors not to look younger, but to disguise blackened eyes. Some women become passive aggressive in their actions because this type of behavior is the way they survive in abusive relationships, roller coasters of chaos and emotion. Every city in the country has battered women's shelters because women need sanctuary from abusive husbands. At the same time, there are instances, though much fewer, where women have physically abused men, and the men stayed in the relationship for the same reason that many women do—for the sake of the children. Until recently, women could not make major purchases without their husband's signature. Today some women still choose to be called and be known as "Mrs. Joe Brown," relinquishing their given and maiden names for the sake of, perhaps, a sense of being owned; perhaps out of a sense of pride that they captured a sought-after man. In many cultures, women were/are the property of either their father or their husbands or their sons or other male relatives. Such a status of objectification allows for an abuse of power and for manipulation.

This chapter analyzes the role of traditional and cultural mores at work in the living out of sexism within the context of sociotheological attitudes and the misuse of power. First, I define the nature of sexism and introduce the biblical and cinematographic case studies. I discuss the attitudes of patriarchy, conquest, and emotional hijacking that lead to sexism and flesh out various components of politics and power at work in gender oppression and abuse. I explore the particular realities, ironies, and paradoxes regarding gender and domestic violence. I analyze the silent oppression and violent seduction (1) in "The Women," (2) as a brother's revenge within the story of Dinah and Shechem (Gen. 34), and (3) as the brothers' rebellion in "Seven Brides," naming the dynamics of sexism and the onus on women and men for the proliferation of such gender violence.

Gender Oppression/Sexism Defined

From the fall of the Roman Empire through the 1960s sexual revolution, to the present day, women have been viewed as sex objects, and masculine privilege over women's bodies and their sexuality has never ceased. The myths of male superiority, great sexual prowess, and vanity that justify male pleasure at any cost embodies sexism and gender oppression in forms of misogyny and male supremacy. A classic insecure misogynist was Aristotle Onassis. Onassis went from a jealous, crude tobacco salesperson to a polished, diplomatic shipping magnate and spouse of Jacqueline Kennedy Onassis. The young Onassis brutally beat his women and continued as he aged to pursue many women at one time, for he saw himself as a lover and playboy. He pursued heightened political, economic, and erotic pleasure simultaneously. Other men engage in practices of dehumanization through psychic warping, a mental and emotional dysfunctional behavior. Other male supremacist practices include an inability to relate to people who are different, and of transferring guilt and responsibility to his victim. Those who practice sexual oppression are paralleled in popular media. During the 1960s and 1970s, movies went from covert misogyny or sympathetic indifference to brutality and violent abuse. Contemporary film and pornography not only treat women as objects, including lewd and lascivious poses, but depict actual enactments of rape and physical, mental, and emotional abuse.[1] One of the crucibles of sexual violence in America was the slave plantation.

Amid depravity and stereotypes of the virile, chivalrous, Southern gentleman and his delicate, pure, Victorian wife, slavery institutionalized acts of brutality, abuse, and humiliation perpetrated on the slave family, as the woman became the broodmare, the man a stud bull. The plantation master saw slaves as bestial, lustful, and inferior. Nevertheless, he could ravage his slave women, humiliate his wife, and help procreate bastard children that he could then sell. Thomas Jefferson's life testifies to these conundrums. Jefferson had numerous affairs and bore numerous children by Sally Hemings, which recent DNA testing bears out. The Jefferson-Hemings affair served as the primary text for William Wells Brown's novel, *Clotel, or The President's Daughters,* first published in London in 1853, revised edition published in the United States in 1864. Unfortunately, Jefferson was not particularly fond of his slave children.[2] Children imply a family, and family was and continues to be the primary institution where women experience oppression.

The historic development of the division of moral labor within the institutions of family, economy, and state have occurred along gender lines. The stereotypical categories have usually been rights, justice, and having agency for males; the categories of caring, responsiveness, and communal concerns, notably personal relationships, have been the purview of females. Steeped in occupational rather than gender stereotypes, these belief systems are related to culturally based educational and socialization processes. These realities call for moving beyond the justice/care dichotomy to an ethic that involves both justice and care for the purposes of reckoning with the potential for harm and violence occurring within personal interrelationships and human community. Different kinds of moral commitment shape our thinking and actions, including a focus on ethical commitments that shape our conduct, or human virtues, or the guidance of a friend held in trusted esteem.[3] In sum, "nothing intrinsic to gender demands a division of moral norms which assigns particularized, personalized commitments to women

---

[1]Bernard Braxton, *Sexual, Racial and Political Faces of Corruption* (Washington, D.C.: Verta Press, 1977), 7–8, 13–16, 19–24.

[2]Ibid., 38–39.

[3]Marilyn Friedman, "The Demoralization of Gender," in *Justice and Care,* ed. Virginia Held (Boulder, Colo.: Westview Press, 1995), 61–77.

and universalized, rule-based commitments to men. We need nothing less than to 'de-moralize' the genders, advance beyond the dissociation of justice from care, and enlarge the symbolic access of each gender to all available conceptual and social resources for the sustenance and enrichment of our collective moral life."[4] Our individual and communal lives are rife with violence as a means of social control.

Violence often plays a major role as a tool of social control in societies where gender stratification is germane. Such violence affords a means of domination, subordination, and control.[5] Who is controlled? Who is the battered spouse? The battered spouse or partner may be you. For sure, she is the attorney, the doctor, the next-door neighbor; she may be a member of your staff, your daughter or daughter-in-law, your CEO, or your minister's spouse. Battered wives/partners occur across class and culture and across racial/ethnic backgrounds. Violence is increasingly a norm in many families, and no religious group can state that the families within their group are nonviolent. Violence tends to escalate in homes that subscribe to hierarchical relationships within more traditional, legalistic understandings of marriage. Some that subscribe to familial male dominance based on their sacred texts, often in misunderstanding the concept of submission, engage in violent behavior. Violence occurs less in homes that operate on a more egalitarian model where couples share power.[6] The need to control the domestic scene often results in sexual violence.

Sexual violence linked with sadism and masochism can involve cruelty and pain. *Sadism,* the term for emotional gratification that results from causing another pain or suffering, derived from French author Marquis de Sade (1746–1814), may or may not involve sex. De Sade's novels depicted his own sick sense of women as sex objects and violence. German psychiatrist Richard von Krafft-Ebing coined the term *masochism,* from Leopold von Sacher-Masoch, who wrote novels that portrayed sexual pleasure between lovers by the infliction of humiliation or pain, to name that sexual pathology. Such practices were part of the Hitler and Third Reich regime. Hitler, attracted to

---

[4]Ibid., 73.

[5]Jalna Hanmer and Mary Maynard, "Introduction: Violence and Gender Stratification," in Jalna Hanmer, *Women, Violence and Social Control* (Atlantic Highlands, N.J.: Humanities Press International, 1987), 11.

[6]Jim and Phyllis Alsdurf, "Wife Abuse and the Christian Home," *Daughters of Sarah* 13 (July/August 1987): 7–10.

Jewish actresses, practiced sadism with lower-class women and masochism with upper-class women. The Nuremberg trials attested to the heinous so-called scientific medical experiments that involved sadism, sexual perversion, and bestiality under the hands of Dr. Josef Mengele, a barbaric practitioner of sexism and racism. Charles Manson, who saw himself as a disciple of Hitler, led his "family" in murders and orgies, where Manson physically arranged people's bodies and forced them to have mixed and same sex oral and vaginal/penile intercourse both to remove all inhibitions and to attempt a simultaneous orgasm, which never happened. For Manson, women had two functions: to satisfy men sexually and to give birth. Manson's proclivities and habits echo the Machiavellian tendencies of the Borgia family, those sensibilities of Pope Alexander VI (whom the Vatican commemorated with a stamp in his honor in 1999) and his children (particularly Lucrezia and Cesar), where incest, murder, and exploitation were the justified means to sexual and political ends,[7] clearly a perverted sense of "All in the Family."

Violence against women and children occurs on individual, institutional, structural, cultural, and interrelated levels. Individual violence occurs on a global scale with particular cultural twists regarding practices concerning dowry, *sati* (widow burning), widowhood rites, and genital mutilation. These are in addition to rape, sexual harassment, sexual coercion and assault, domestic violence, or female sexual slavery. Institutional violence, often cloaked in silence and invisibility, works to rationalize, support, and depersonalize individual acts of violence. Many legal and religious institutions foster practices that give assent to family violence, often giving credence to family honor, economic subordination of women, and the control and discipline of women—denying women their basic human and civil rights. Collective cultural and structural belief systems that condone gender violence involve the uses of violence to: maintain control and power; champion White male superiority ideology; support a property- and profit-based economy; support militaristic values of dominance; and support win-lose solutions. The interrelatedness of violence emerges when violence is normative, pervasive, impersonal, and invisible.[8]

Because many "invisible" women experience sexual violence in their lives, to talk about a continuum of violence can include the

---

[7]Braxton, *Sexual, Racial and Political Faces,* 44–51, 59–70.
[8]Dorothy Van Soest, *The Global Crisis of Violence: Common Problems, Universal Causes, Shared Solutions* (Washington, D.C.: NASW Press, 1997), 116–24.

variety of types of force, coercion, and abuse used by men to control women and can begin to unpack the complexities regarding the impact that sexual violence has on women. How a particular woman defines, reacts to, and then copes with sexual violence over her lifetime is also a complex issue. Referring to a continuum of violence allows women to name the links between aberrant and typical behavior and see and explore their own particular experiences. Some women experience repeated episodes of violence that may not include physical violence but instead emotional outbursts, emotional withdrawal, questioning women's activities, and efforts to control women's social relationships and contacts,[9] including threats against their children.

The tremendous amount of violence within our society reeks of sadistic choice, tyranny, and rebellion, particularly with the contagion of physical and sexual abuse against children by family and strangers. Girls and women of color are stalked like prey. Statistics and the portrayal of sexual violence through literature, popular culture, and mass media reveal the preponderance of sexual abuse, often depicting it as desirable, normal, and natural. The denial about the depths of this problem also creates an environment where stereotypes and myths portray the majority of rapists as Black and the majority of victims as White females. Such myths and lies not only make victims invisible but often place the blame on the victim as well, especially with so-called private, domestic abuse. When such abuse escalates to murder, the woman's death is often trivialized. Even the reporting of a man's killing his brother versus the account of a woman whose husband murders her and then takes his own life shows a dismissal of the woman's life.[10] The headlines for the news stories show "how differently the writers treat murders of women by their partners or former partners: 'Man charged with murder in brother's death' and 'Husband, wife die in dispute.'"[11]

In society, the courts, and the church, victims of sexual violence, particularly of rape, are often blamed for the crime. Myths about Eve and her being the cause for the alleged Fall (which was actually an expulsion) linger and continue to underlie much of the oppression

---

[9]Liz Kelly, "The Continuum of Sexual Violence," in Jalna Hanmer, *Women, Violence and Social Control* (Atlantic Highlands, N.J.: Humanities Press International, 1987), 47, 48, 49, 51, 54.

[10]Linda A. Bell, *Rethinking Ethics in the Midst of Violence: A Feminist Approach to Freedom* (Lanham, Md.: Rowman & Littlefield, 1993), 21–26.

[11]Headlines from *Atlanta Journal and Constitution*, 6 December 1992, cited in Bell, *Rethinking Ethics*, 25.

of women. Some men believe that they own their wives and give assent to the traditional "obedience clause," wherein a wife or female partner is forever at the beck and call of her mate, including sex on demand. The practices of male chauvinism, where women are the property of men, and the perpetuation of the myth of virginity subscribed to by many faith traditions have solidified the stigma of rape for the victim. The traditional inferiority of women and the virginity myth that posited that virgins had particular mythical attributes that made them more desirable and worthy than women who had already had sexual intercourse have had a tremendous impact on rape cases. Until the mid-1970s, the rules of evidence allowed a defense attorney to introduce information pertaining to the victim's sexual history, while laws were in place prohibiting the introduction of the sexual history of the rapist's past. When rapists are from middle- and upper-class backgrounds, when they have high standing in the community, and when the rape victim is older and not considered ideally beautiful, the victim is often not believed. With the new laws, rape victims receive better care; they are questioned by female detectives; and hospitals now have rape kits to acquire and protect the evidence. However, cavalier, misogynist, institutional attitudes of corruption and power allow rape, sexual exploitation, and violence to continue to occur,[12] for the guys are really just sowing their oats, aren't they?

The male of the human and non-human species usually displays more aggression than the female. Human children also show such aggressive behavior delineated by gender as early as age three. Boys tend to be more physically aggressive and engage in rougher contact than girls.[13] This same aggressiveness sanctions a batterer's behavior. The variables that shape a battered woman's response are her options and sanctions. Options concern the occupational, social, and economic resources she can access. The more options, the more likely she is to leave. Those who remain in abusive situations are limited; that is, they are usually unemployed or poor, have low-paying jobs, have a high school education or less, and receive negative attention from the persons and agencies they seek out for help. Internal and external sanctions are the mechanisms within the sociocultural realm that function to control their behavior. The societal external sanctions involve the clergy, police, legal, and

---

[12]Braxton, *Sexual, Racial and Political Faces,* 123–32, 146–48.

[13]Kenneth E. Moyer, *The Psychobiology of Aggression* (New York: Harper & Row, 1976), 153–54.

medical care systems. Until recently, Western law sanctioned the battering of women by their husbands or male partners. The law against wife beating was not addressed until about 1970, though it was made illegal by 1870. Even today, batterers are often able to break the law without experiencing sanction. No wonder victims are often reluctant to press charges. Not only do women often not press charges because they are afraid of retaliation from their batterer; they are often told to stay in these abusive marriages by their clergy. Physicians often underestimate a woman's abuse and may not identify cases of spousal abuse or may be more likely to dispense medication than to help the woman leave. Certainly staying in the relationship will undoubtedly result in more violence. The normally supportive venue of family often falls apart when a female has been subject to male violence. Internally, women's sanctions usually concern epistemology, ethics, and the use of power. Since women tend to be relationally based in their ethical analysis, a woman's commitment to preserving the relationship will come into play, even though she is the object of abuse. With a tendency toward an epistemology of connectedness, women will likely relate to the discomfort and pain of the other one, her male partner. Accustomed to thinking about the other and with her maternal thinking, the battered woman is usually unable to move the attention from the other, her abusive partner, to herself. Some women do not defend themselves out of an attempt to heal an old hurt they sense in their batterer. In terms of power, women often have fear when it comes to using power for their own self-interest: the fear of being selfish, of being abandoned by the people they care about, and of being destructive. Women often misinterpret acting on behalf of their own interest as being arrogant and selfish. Ultimately, women tend to be at a greater physical and psychological handicap in abusive situations, and are forced to make a choice as to whether they work to save their economic safety and well-being, or their physical safety and well-being.[14] Sexual/gender oppression violates, manipulates, and minimizes the vitality of persons whom a perpetrator concludes are somehow his property. The levels of vulnerability, silence, and skewed identity of gender predators and their victims emerge in film and biblical narratives.

---

[14]Carolyn F. Swift, *Women and Violence: Breaking the Connection*, Work in Progress Series (Wellesley, Mass.: Wellesley College, 1987), 3–15.

Cinematographic and Biblical Case Studies

Seven Brides for Seven Brothers, an incredibly sexist, misogynist 1954 musical film has phenomenal choreography, but romanticizes gender oppression. Based on the work of Stephen Vincent Benét, who adapted the story of "The Rape of the Sabine Women," this frontier film tells about the lives of six fur-trapping brothers who go into town to find spouses after their eldest brother, Adam, returns with a wife from town. The other Pontipee brothers end up kidnapping the women, who spend the winter at the ranch because the brothers cause an avalanche by firing their rifles as they clear a mountain pass. Such patriarchal, sexist rape fantasies were considered great entertainment and in good taste when this movie emerged on the silver screen.[15]

Music and dancing are the veils that mask and thus romanticize the blatant gender oppression. From the very beginning, the songs daringly state misogynist themes, but in the beautiful lyricism of Adam's voice and his charisma and wilderness aura, the depth of the actual violence goes by the wayside. He belts out his personal desire to participate in gender exploitation in a sweet, energetic format. In town for supplies, he asks the store manager for a wife from under the counter, along with his purchases of lard and chewing tobacco. He wants a wife, a widow woman not afraid to work. As he leaves the store, he places his desire in song, rhyming his desire for a "bride" with her "beautiful hide."[16]

"Bless Your Beautiful Hide" indicates the tenor of the entire movie—blatant sexism, ensconced in a picturesque, frontier mountainous setting of Oregon territory, circa 1850, where the man is the Lord and Master and the woman is to do his bidding. The relationship begins with a lie of omission, as Adam fails to tell Milly that he has married her so that she can be chief cook and bottle washer tending to his six siblings. Milly agrees to marry Adam because the ethos of the town is that a girl does not have the right to stay single, and Adam is the first man she has encountered who does not make her have an "awful sinking feeling" in her stomach when she says yes. The preacher is hesitant; others think it is indecent; but Milly is unaware of what she will meet when they get to the homestead. Milly, in her naivete, is actually delighted to be marrying

---

[15]James Monaco, et. al., *The Movie Guide* (New York: Perigree Books, 1992), 832.
[16]Gene dePaul and Johnny Mercer wrote all the songs for *Seven Brides for Seven Brothers*. Adam Pontipee, the oldest brother, sings "Bless Your Beautiful Hide" as the opening number.

Adam, despite the brief courtship of five minutes, because she does not think she is much of a bride in her outfit. When they stop by a pond, Milly's innocence and fantasy about marriage emerges in the song she sings about what a "wonderful, wonderful day" it is: "Seems I've gone and grown up to a bright, merry, fairy, fairy land."[17]

When they arrive at the homestead, Milly is met by the other six brothers and a house that is like a pigsty. Adam introduces her and shows her the kitchen as the boys continue to fight and act barbaric. Not to be outdone, she pushes up her sleeves and goes to work. But when she calls the brothers to the meal and they continue to act like pigs, she overturns the table and tells them to eat like hogs. Milly runs upstairs to the bedroom and reads the scripture, which gives us the first hint that the light may be dawning on her: "Neither cast ye your pearls before swine, lest they trample them under their feet, and turn again and rend you" (Matt. 7:6, KJV). Realizing that Adam wants a washerwoman, cook, and hired girl, Milly tells him that she will work alongside him, but she will not sleep with him. In that moment one sees that Milly can stand up for herself. When Adam beds down for the night in the tree outside their window, Milly acquiesces, since it does not seem right for a bridegroom to spend his wedding night outside in a tree. Adam counters, saying it was her idea, not his. Milly replies that she was pretty mad at him and that she has a lot of dreams about love and marriage. Milly then sings that "When you're in love, really in love, you simply let your heart decide it…when you're in love as I'm in love with you." Knowing how it will be with his brothers if he spends the night in a tree, she agrees for Adam to come back inside. In humorous relief, he falls on the bed, and the bed collapses. Disgustingly, the theme song, "Bless your beautiful hide" emerges in the background as the camera pans to the hallway, where the brothers all knowingly smile. The audience learns later that Milly and Adam had sex, because we find out that Milly is pregnant: a rape fantasy played out. Adam has made his conquest and has tamed Milly.

Milly sets out to tame the brothers and make gentlemen out of them. She coaches the boys so that they can learn how to court women. They go to town for a barn raising, do a spectacular dance number, and end up in a fight. When they return, all the brothers, except Adam, are filled with melancholy. They too want women.

---

[17]Ibid., Milly's first solo, "Beautiful, Wonderful Day."

When Adam sings to them about Milly's book on the Sabine women of Roman days, the brothers head to town to kidnap the girls, and cause the avalanche so their folks cannot follow. Upon the brothers' successful return, Milly and Adam have a spat and Adam goes to the trapping cabin. Milly keeps the girls with her to protect them. When the snow thaws, the townspeople come for the girls. When they hear a baby, each of the girls claims the baby is hers. The fathers stand behind the girls, with shotguns in hand, and the preacher marries them to the Pontipee brothers. Throughout the film, the music of "Going Courtin'" and "When You're in Love," paint a romantic scenario to lessen the crimes of kidnapping, endangerment, and perhaps rape.

The film *The Women* involves 135 women and no men onscreen, but men are ever present in the thoughts, words, and deeds of the women. The opening trailer for the film announces: "Out of the boudoir, onto the screen, Clare Booth's story of 135 women and no men. Dowagers and debutantes let their hair down and claws down." Debuting as a play with 666 performances on Broadway and 84 performances off Broadway, the film makes an interesting commentary on the need for feminist action, the realities for women regarding societal pressures, and female bonding, particularly in the upper middle- and upper-class settings. The narrative opens with a joyous, wealthy, and loving Mary Haines, a socialite with an adorable daughter and a husband, who we find out has been having an affair with the seductive Crystal Allen, who sells perfume in a local department store. Of all of Mary's girlfriends, the most backbiting and cattiest, Sylvia, makes sure everyone knows of Mary's husband's infidelity, including Mary herself, through a gossipy manicurist. Mary's mother, Mrs. Watson, tells Mary to do nothing; this is just a phase Steven is going through. At a boutique, Mary and Crystal meet and have heated words. Mary decides to get a divorce and, with other friends, goes to Reno for a six-week divorce. Several women who are seeking divorce land at Lucy's ranch, including Mary's nemesis, Sylvia. Mary also gets a call that her former husband has married Crystal, in the eleventh hour before her Reno divorce is finalized. After Mary returns to New York, she learns that her ex-husband is unhappy. Crystal is spending up a storm and having an affair with the husband of the Countess, another friend Mary met at Lucy's ranch. Mary decides to fight to win her husband back and uses some of the predatory principles Crystal has used. When the story ends, someone comes and tells Mary that Steven is waiting for her. When asked, "Don't you have any pride?" Mary responds with, "A woman in love can't afford to have pride." "Filled with witty repartee and vicious gossip, *The Women* portrays a world where women seem to do nothing but obsess over men."[18] In sum, *Seven Brides for Seven Brothers* celebrates a rape fantasy and the violence of lies and kidnapping. *The Women* honors the dysfunctionality of women trapped in a patriarchal system who violate each other through scapegoating. The biblical case study is the "Rape of Dinah," where lust overrides love, and the response of the girl's family results in murder.

Dinah, the daughter of Leah and Jacob, goes to visit the women in the area. Shechem, a prince and son of Hamor, is obsessed with Dinah and rapes or physically violates her. Subsequently we learn he allegedly loves her, speaks tenderly to her, and asks his father to arrange for Dinah to be his wife. Jacob hears of Dinah's defilement and does nothing because his sons are still in the field. Hamor comes to speak to Jacob about the same time that Jacob's sons arrive. When they find out what happened, they are outraged. Hamor tries to smooth things over by saying Shechem longs for Dinah, and asks that Jacob give her hand in marriage to Shechem; basically, let us swap daughters all around. Shechem reiterates and literally says, "name your price." Jacob's sons answer, "Impossible, you have disgraced us." The only way they are willing for the marriage to occur is for every male in Hamor's family to be circumcised. Hamor and Shechem are delighted at the bargain they have struck. They relate the story to their family about their newfound friends and the condition of circumcision, a small price to pay for the swapping of daughters and the sharing of livestock that will occur. But Simeon and Levi, two of Jacob's sons, are not satisfied. They take their swords and find the men, who having complied with the circumcision agreement, are still in pain. Levi and Simeon proceed to murder Hamor, Shechem, and all the males, and take Dinah from Shechem's house. Jacob's other sons plunder the city, because their sister has been raped, defiled. Jacob tells Levi and Simeon that they have disgraced him and brought him nothing but trouble, especially with Canaanites and Perizzites, who also live in close proximity. Jacob fears the destruction of himself and his household. The two brothers reply, "Should our sister be treated like a whore?" (Gen. 34). The

---

[18]Monaco et. al., *The Movie Guide,* 1077.

rape, circumcisions (for some, mutilations), and murders certainly do not make for bedtime stories, and press the envelope on violence to death. Where the music romanticizes violence in *Seven Brides*, the narrator shifts the agenda to minimize the rape of Dinah in Genesis 34. What underlies the violence in the films and the biblical narrative are the patriarchal, misogynistic, manipulative ethos from which these narratives derive.

Attitudinal Complicity: Patriarchy, Conquest, and Self-righteous Violation

The yin and yang of the masculine lived experience arises in the marvelous accomplishments in the arts and sciences over against the dastardly deeds of individual and corporate exploitation, pollution, war, religious persecution, and sexual and domestic violence. On this continuum rests a panoply of sociocultural norms, conventions, and legacies that define what it means to be masculine, a history of contradictory behaviors.[19] All men are not patriarchal boors. Many, including my own beloved father, have vast capacities for compassion, sensitivity to human need, a keen sense of judgment, incredible inner strength, warmth, sociopolitical chutzpah, intellectual prowess, and artistic gifts. On the other side of such genuine humanity rests the selfishness and need to dominate and manipulate. These acts of domination and manipulation are central for the analysis here. Violence is largely the purview of men; notably some states in the United States as yet have no female prisons. Those statistics that state female crime is up by any large percentage are skewed; that is, if there were five female-committed crimes in one time frame and the number doubles the next time statistics are checked, the increase is 50 percent, but still involves only ten acts of violence, while the male population may have committed three hundred criminal acts in that same category. Statistics on male violence, the continuum of behavior, and the prevalence of male violence reflect the vast complexity of masculine violence. To begin to understand this phenomena, one needs a systemic approach, delving into the biological (sexual and physical), sociocultural, economic, individual, and mass personality profiles. Thus, one response to the recidivism rates and career criminals is that the moves toward reform tend to focus on only one area of action. Interestingly, male-run corporations that engage in consumer victimization and

---

[19]Lee H. Bowker, "On the Difficulty of Eradicating Masculine Violence," in *Masculinities and Violence,* ed. Lee H. Bowker (Thousand Oaks, Calif.: SAGE Publications, 1998), xi.

ecological destruction parallel behavior that keeps men incarcerated;[20] and some men in both spheres do violate women.

Globally, male violence against women is a complex process of control and domination, designed to accord men power and authority. Such violence occurs at the hands of strangers, casual acquaintances, and intimate partners. The continuum of such violence holds subtle and blatant oppression, lethal and nonlethal battering, sexual and nonsexual victimization, and serial murders. The more economically dependent a woman is on a man, the greater probability that he will perpetrate violence against her. Such violence often occurs as the result of instances where she challenges him about money matters, where he perceives she is not doing her wifely duties, or where he becomes jealous. Such bouts of violence not only exact pain and demean the woman's humanity but also act as fodder for her then becoming a perpetrator herself. Many women in jails and prisons were themselves victims of gender oppression, including incest, rape, and sexual abuse. Usually incarcerated for drug and property offenses, female inmates may have been victimized as children, but almost always they have been victims of adult domestic violence. Once imprisoned, these women often experience sexual abuse and extreme policing and control by other inmates and poorly trained and often aggressive correctional officers. The various cultural systems of abuse and patriarchy expose women to violence worldwide.[21] Within the varied systems of domination and coercion, violence is one tool in the "arsenal of patriarchal control mechanisms."[22]

One fourth of the college men interviewed by Neil Malamuth in 1981 noted that they were open to using force to get sex.[23] Over one half of them said they would try to rape someone if they would not be caught. In both cases, these young men signaled an attitude of entitlement, which meant they could coerce sex when they desired, especially in dating situations. Are these sociopaths and psychopaths? For the most part, probably not. Sexual perpetrators are everyday,

---

[20]Ibid., xi, xiv, xiv, 1.

[21]Neil Websdale and Meda Chesney-Lind, "Doing Violence to Women: Research Synthesis on the Victimization of Women," in *Masculinities and Violence*, ed. Lee H. Bowker, (Thousand Oaks, Calif.: SAGE Publications, 1998), 55–57, 72–80.

[22]Ibid., 79.

[23]Cf. the evaluation in Neil M. Malamuth, Daniel Linz, Christopher L. Heavey, Gordon Barnes, and Michele Acker, "Using the Confluence Model of Sexual Aggression to Predict Men's Conflict with Women: A 10-Year Follow-Up Study," *Journal of Personality and Social Psychology* 69/2 (1995).

ordinary men. These men are often dubbed a good provider, a staunch supporter or pillar of the community. When raped by these alleged archetypes of health and good citizenship, many women never tell or press charges because the man's status in the community literally assures her that no one will believe him capable of such behavior. When and if the perpetrator is confronted, he will often be confused as to why all the fuss is being made. His confusion will probably arise out of the reality that even in the twenty-first century, explicit or implicit sexual violence is often excused, legally and medically speaking. For example, husbands could not be prosecuted for raping their wives until 1975. Freud's early practice focused primarily on upper-middle-class women from Vienna. After revealing the nature of the sexual assaults, Freud initially took them seriously, diagnosing hysteria based on childhood incestuous assault. Caught in denial, Freud retracted his theory. Surely that many Viennese fathers could not be molesting their children. The depth of Freud's denial permeates his notion of the Oedipus complex, assuming that his patients were really on fantasy trips. Freud's theorizing helped to keep incest hidden. When denial and secrecy fail to cover up sexual assault, sexual assault is usually justified explicitly through rationalizations and pornography. Even medical journals have argued that sexual activity between women and men require male dominance.[24] In other instances, society blames the victim of sexual assault. Sexual violence continues to be tolerated, for "it is socialized behavior and a means by which male supremacy is enforced and perpetuated…[which explains] the rapist's attitude of entitlement, lack of remorse, and failure to respond to pleas of conscience…The men who beat their wives or children at least felt some regret after the assault, viewing their own behavior as a loss of control. The incestuous fathers, however, rarely showed remorse."[25]

To shape one's ethic of care by only focusing on individual relationships obscures one's level of responsibility, is limited, and too apolitical. To have a system steeped in altruism without a substantive sense of justice allows people to not claim their own onus in the process, and usually omits concerns for themselves and others outside their immediate family. Such a philosophical base

---

[24]Judith Herman, M.D., *Colloquium: Sexual Violence,* Work in Progress Series (Wellesley, Mass.: Stone Center for Developmental Services and Studies, Wellesley College, 1985), 2–5.

[25]Linda Gordon, "The 'Normality' of Incest: Preliminary Findings of an Historical Study" (unpublished ms., University of Massachusetts Department of History, 1981), cited in Herman, "Colloquium," 4–5.

allows one to live in denial, unconscious of the needs of others who suffer abuse, who are oppressed and starving within a reality of xenophobia, racism, ethnocentrism, classism, and heterosexism. The subtlety of some violence affords ambiguity, concedes that there is no specific perpetrator to blame, and applauds a sense of indifference. An ethic of care must reckon with the vast complexities of systemic oppression. An ethic of care must be cognizant of prevailing power systems, become political, and not be trapped into a virtue ethic that places women in a system dominated by a patriarchal agenda. An ethic of care must not valorize love at the expense of freedom, and can embrace the healing powers of laughter and play, in concert with an ethic of freedom; in no instances being paralyzed by futility or relativism.[26] One's sense of freedom has an impact on her or his total well-being, particularly one's mental and emotional health, as related to being the target of abuse.

Psychologically, a man abuses his female partner by labeling her with cultural phrases that ascribe particular norms, that is, depictions of reality, desired states or values, and ethics of behavior. Such behavior involves elements of cultural systems coupled with some physical violence, together creating effective violence mechanisms. Batterers may use economic and social systems to dominate their victims, often pulling the victim's friends into the manipulative scenario. In reality, anyone can play the masculine role. Masculine violence targeted against others, mixed with sexual aggression, has escalated and exceeds the levels present during ancient hunter-gatherer societies, where their system of social control had a greater sense of unity and strength than contemporary systems in the United States. Yet we probably have less extremely high levels of masculine violence today than was the case during the era of embodied manifest destiny with westward, frontier expansion.[27]

Men also often control women through individual and collective ways, particularly within the institutional familial setting of heterosexual monogamy. Within many families, husbands are able to procure "unwaged sexual, emotional and physical servicing from women in exchange for protecting them from other men."[28] Viewing instances of spousal and sexual abuse within the power relationships

---

[26]Bell, *Rethinking Ethics,* 36–48.

[27]Bowker, "On the Difficulty," 4, 6, 7, 12–13.

[28]Jill Radford, "Policing Male Violence–Policing Women," in Jalna Hanmer, *Women, Violence and Social Control* (Atlantic Highlands, N.J.: Humanities Press International, 1987), 43.

of such a family reflects the baseline of patriarchal power within monogamous heterosexuality and male supremacy. Such activity crosses lines of class and race. All women in such family systems largely depend upon male goodwill.[29] Women learn their expected stereotypical behavior from their family systems and from the media.

Media portrayal of gender images gushes with stereotypical messages: Girls exude affection and giggles, are gentle, are obsessed with physical appearance, and practice good behavior. Boys typically are aggressive, strong, athletic, independent, adventurous, and are in charge of their surroundings. These standards of behavior are not a biological given, for gender roles emerge from society, not biology, despite the physical differences. Human beings create a society, that society creates an objective standard about the dynamics of society and the related human behavior, and then society creates people. We extend the gender differences beyond the particulars of biology to ascribe a particular behavior that we then expect everyone to internalize, making boys thus naturally rough, tough, and aggressive, though often emotionally repressed. Toys and toy commercials promote this kind of behavior. For girls, the industry promotes beauty, daintiness, nurture, and hospitality. The work of Sarah Sobieraj shows how toys and toy advertising support the social construction of patriarchy by overwhelmingly focusing on domination as a significant male gender idea with and without connections to violence. All oppressive male behavior ultimately harms women in their quests for career advancement and personal esteem. Teaching such behavior also makes men prisoners to a mindset of domination, wherein they are forced into a set pattern of behavior as well.[30]

> Girls are not biologically obsessed with their looks, predisposed to cleaning house, or enthusiasts of the color pink. When boys emerge from the womb they do not instinctually seek validation through superordination or intimidation. These ideas are externally imposed and consumed by children at face value...Television is capable of creating a desire for something and providing directions

---

[29]Ibid., 30–45.
[30]Sarah Sobieraj, "Taking Control: Toy Commercials and the Social Construction of Patriarchy," in *Masculinities and Violence*, ed. Lee H. Bowker (Thousand Oaks, Calif.: SAGE Publications, 1998), 15–21.

on how to behave. The culmination of this constant bombardment is social control.[31]

That art mirrors reality is evident in the number of episodes on prime-time television from 1976–1990 that focused on rape. The programs shifted from always depicting the rape as a surprise attack by a deranged, violent stranger to showing acquaintance and date rape. Previously silent victims became more vocal with more prominent roles that allowed them to air their needs, experiences, and feelings. One overarching factor that did not change was the focus on the masculinity of the male protagonist or detective. Assailants became more normal-looking individuals, but with a propensity for dangerous, racist, sexist, unhealthy, violent thoughts and ideas. Fortunately, on the small screen and in reality, advances have been made in the protocols for relating to rape victims within social and legal practices. Today, a woman is not automatically viewed as the cause of her own rape. Further, there are refined police procedures, hospital protocol for examinations and for collecting and preserving evidence, crisis hotlines, and therapy for victims following the attack. Unfortunately, within fictional television and in larger society, most tend to blame individual deviance for sexual assaults, and few if any focus on or pay attention to the organic elements such as socialization, universal violence, and the objectification of women in all forms of media (particularly videos), in the rampant use of pornography, or in patriarchal social systems. The diverse range of victims and the intersections of class, race, and rape are rarely fully explored in prime-time television episodes.[32]

Gender oppression includes the violence perpetrated not only against women and children but also against lesbian/gay/bisexual and transgendered persons. In his study about violence against gay men and lesbians, David Comstock sees a change with World War II and what follows. Gay men and lesbian women, after the war, wanted to remain in the cities where they had had wartime assignments, making larger metropolitan areas centers for lesbian and gay life. When these groups were less visible, there was some intolerance, but that escalated to more open hostility when gay men and lesbian women became more visible. Comstock's analysis demonstrates the systemic and socially constructed nature of

---

[31]Ibid., 27.

[32]Lisa M. Cuklanz, *Rape on Prime Time: Television, Masculinity, and Sexual Violence* (Philadelphia: University of Pennsylvania Press, 2000), 154–58.

homophobia and anti-gay violence. The perpetrators are usually groups of young men, and a stranger to the victim. The homage given to masculinity and patriarchy in our culture makes it open season against lesbians, gays, transgendered, and bisexual persons. The violence explodes across race and class. The particular racial differences occur because White perpetrators attack more lesbians and gay men of color than victims of color in general. Teenagers perpetrate violence against gay men as part of a sport, partially as imposition of community norms and social activity. Some participate because they have a sense of enforced idleness and they lack power because they are teenaged and young adult men living amid patriarchal capitalism. The blatant violence results not only from patriarchy and gender-role socialization—what it means to be male or female, what is feminine, masculine, and other—but the social location of homosexual persons. Particularly for adolescent perpetrators, they have little or no power in their family systems. They are beginning to physically resemble adults, but are often marginalized and forbidden or restricted in their sexual activity. Because they do not yet have a wife to own, boss around, or control, society grants them permission to show off their physical prowess by beating up those deemed other, particularly homosexual persons. In this arena, they have power and some autonomy, external to their home environment and to the workplace to which they ascribe.[33] For the young, old, rich, and poor, the assent that patriarchy gives to abuse makes for some harsh realities, absurd ironies, and sad paradoxes.

Realities, Ironies, Paradoxes: Domestic Violence Takes the Stage

The statistics regarding sexual and domestic violence are staggeringly painful and sobering, particularly as one notes the inappropriate use of authority and the misguided teachings of faith communities, notably in the Christian church. Such misguidance reveals the tremendous abuse of power found within intimate relationships deemed appropriate under the rubric of patriarchy and religious hierarchy. Such is not the message of Christ. The restoration to wholeness of battered women is antithetical to the desires of men in power who believe that they are well within their rights to control, manipulate, or abuse their partners, wives, or girlfriends. Battered

[33]Susan E. Davies, "Gaybashing: Roots in a 'Decent' Identity," *Christianity and Crisis* 51 (November 18, 1991): 365–67; Gary David Comstock, *Violence Against Lesbians and Gay Men* (New York: Columbia University Press, 1991), x, 111.

women accustomed to mistreatment fear change, as they know the pain, but not the unknown life without this abusive male. Many churches and other faith communities would rather live in denial than acknowledge the need for divorce. Our society still nurtures patriarchy and has difficulty dealing with telling the truth about abusive men.[34]

Sometimes there is an elitism and arrogance within the United States, because we believe we are the best, the most powerful and awesome, the most educated, and the most humane nation in the world. Yet we bear the shame of many countries we shun. Although 165 countries already have ratified the United Nations Convention on the Elimination of All Forms of Discrimination Against Women, we, the "home of the free and the brave," have failed in our duty. We have managed to join the ranks of Iran, Afghanistan, and North Korea in not adding our voices to those that say No! to discrimination against women. Senator Jesse Helms rules the roost of the Senate Foreign Relations Committee, and he adamantly refuses to let this measure gain approval. What a sad state of affairs when more than 50 percent of the population in the United States cannot by law be guaranteed protection for their basic human rights in the political, sociocultural, economic, legal, and civil realms of life.[35] The all-too-familiar plight of abused women in the United States and the world finds many parallels in the story of the Sabine women.

"The Rape of the Sabine Women" is a story of how these women were kidnapped from their families at a religious festival to help populate Rome, and how the Romans won over their minds and hearts by violence accompanied by sugary words and childbearing. According to the Roman historian Livy, who lived about the time of Jesus Christ, Romulus and Remus were twins born to a Vestal Virgin, Aemilla, a.k.a. Rhea Silvia, and to the Roman god Mars, a fertility god and later a god of war. Like Moses, the babies were threatened with death, so their mother placed them in a basket and put them on the Tiber River. The twins grew up and killed their uncle for having put his mother in prison and for mistreating their grandfather. After restoring their grandfather to the throne, the boys quarreled, and as with Cain and Abel, Romulus killed Remus. With the Roman state now stronger, they needed to populate the area. In one account,

<hr>

[34]Reta Halteman Finger, "The Dangerous Task of Healing." Editorial, *Daughters of Sarah* 13 (July/August 1987): 3.

[35]"The Shame of the Senate." Editorial, *San Francisco Chronicle,* 14 July 2000.

Romulus invited people from other countries to come and live in Rome. He then kidnapped young, unmarried women from the Sabine tribe. The girls' fathers were scandalized and outraged, so the Sabines attacked Rome. The kidnapped women, now content and pleased, helped to stop the fighting and negotiated peace between their fathers and their husbands. In another account, Romulus, with the backing of the senate, sent emissaries to other tribes hoping to build alliances and to effect marriages. The neighbors scoffed at them, and Rome was upset. Romulus began to think about using force. He invited neighboring tribes to a religious festival, and many people came, including the entire Sabine population. The Romans provided great hospitality as the Sabines marveled that Rome had grown so fast. While everyone focused on the festival, Romulus' men kidnapped all the girls. The festival ended, and the grief-stricken parents went on their way, noting that the Romans had violated the laws of hospitality. Romulus told the girls that they would not have been kidnapped had their fathers cooperated and not been so inflexible. But now, as Roman wives, they would have all the civil rights and material rewards of Roman citizenship and they would have children. Who could ask for anything more? Romulus suggested they let go of their anger and give their hearts to the men who already possessed their bodies; besides, a good relationship usually begins with an offense. Their husbands would make up for their losing their parents and their country by being extra kind to the women. The men swore their undying love and passion. The women were won over. Abused women are often won over by sweet words and hard knocks.

Admitted to a hospital's emergency room, a severely battered wife is diagnosed with a spontaneous abortion. The doctor fails to document on her chart the split lip, black eye, and the bruises on her ribs, stomach, and face. Although the doctor tells her she could have bled to death, he literally sees nothing. Why? The doctor fails to see the woman's injuries because he knows the abusive husband. This abused woman's first battering assault occurs on the first day in her new home with her husband. After thanking his friend who gave them a ride from the airport, her husband beats her for flirting. So, afraid, intimidated, and with her shyness exacerbated, she hesitates to welcome her husband's friends he brings home. Damned from both sides, she becomes obsessive about trying to please him, maintaining a meticulous house, having her every hair in place, running to get him a beer when he walks in. Yet one hair in the bathroom sink lands her a punch to her chest. She finally gets away from him when her abusing husband is transferred to Germany. When he is on leave and their baby cries, he threatens to shut the child up permanently. When he leaves and she finally files for divorce, her pastor tries to discourage her. She goes to another church and later completes her college and seminary degrees. Having denied and buried her pain, fear, and anger for so many years, she finally breaks down.[36] She is met with compassion and is able to begin the healing process, after twenty-five years. She now ministers to others and vows to never "allow God's love to be so misused as to ever trap another woman into a marriage of death."[37] Other victims of spousal abuse have not received such grace and have ended up committing murder to avoid continuous persecution.

Raised in a Midwest town where religious conservatism and male chauvinism were the touted norm, Shirley Etsinger felt unloved and worthless. So when an upperclassman began to woo her in high school, she felt accepted, and she eventually agreed to marry David Rock, though she had misgivings. She was at a disadvantage because she had no other options or role models; besides, he never pressured her to have premarital sex. In five years of marriage, his preferred sexual activity was to get drunk, beat her, and then masturbate over her body while accusing her of being frigid. Unaware of the option of annulment, she was too embarrassed to go to counseling, and when she did go to an attorney, he said her experience was not uncommon and to just go to a marriage counselor or a minister, which they never did. Unable to escape, she poisoned her husband in May 1972; was indicted on a first-degree murder charge; and on the bad advice of an inexperienced male lawyer, she plea-bargained for second-degree murder. No one questioned the abuse despite the psychiatrist's testimony of incompatibility. All her appeals were turned down. As of 1987, she had a new female attorney. Etsinger grew, sought training, did volunteer work in the prison, and embraced her faith after moving from a dead, legalistic, oppressive church.[38]

---

[36]Doris Gateley (Alias), "For Better, For Worse: The Story of a Battered Wife," *Daughters of Sarah* 13 (July/August 1987): 4–6.

[37]Ibid., 6.

[38]Judith Steward and Shirley Etsinger, "Behind Bars: One Victim Speaks Out," *Daughters of Sarah* 13 (July/August 1987):12–13. See also, Angela Browne, *When Battered Women Kill* (New York: Free Press, 1989); information found on http://members.xoom.com/jdgiustina/bws.html in July 2001.

Whereas Etsinger ultimately defended herself, other women have been fiercely beaten by strangers who have ambushed them. Following the brutal beating, strangling, and sexual assault by her assailant while she was on a casual countryside walk, Susan Brison knew fear for her safety and a hesitancy to speak about the act and shame. The attack left her with multiple head injuries, her eyes swollen shut, and a fractured trachea. People were horrified when told she was the victim of an attempted murder, but seemed nonchalant or uninterested when she noted that this crime began with her being sexually assaulted. People take sexual violence as a given, yet also cling to denial about its reality and commonness. Sexual violence has become such a daily reality that many think testosterone authorizes male violence against women. Many rapes and sexual assaults go unreported because many in society still blame the victim. We cannot imagine what pleasure the rapist derives nor can we imagine the trauma, humiliation, and pain of the victim. In Brison's case, much of the post-assault experience felt unreal because so many of her family and friends simply could not deal with the rape. Even those best intentioned often fail to offer the support so needed at such a time. Brison notes that we have a difficult time empathizing with the victim. In crime films and novels, we are seduced into empathizing with or being intrigued by the detective who solves the crime or by the assailant. Ironically, once they are detained, criminals have rights, and victims have none. Some of Brison's family and friends thought that if they just did not talk about the event, it would all go away. Some were so burdened that they did not know how to communicate their own pain to the victim. Some relatives took benign stabs at theodicy by saying that Brison would be stronger for having gone through the assault and would be able to help others. Ultimately, everyone has to make sense out of meaningless, futile violence amid all the taboos surrounding rape and talk openly about the violence, trauma, and sex. Our ignorance about how to respond to such catastrophic violence often results in denial and silence. These kinds of behaviors only make it that much more difficult for the rape victim to heal. Those who have not been so traumatized will definitely not be able to understand why survivors tend to blame themselves and often are unable to blame the perpetrator. In the process of recovery, Brison learned to transcend being stuck between fear of her assailant and her appropriate anger at him, along with self-blame juxtaposed against her own powerlessness through political and physical empowerment.

Learning to fight back helped Brison get her life back, but it was a changed life.[39] Often, women are taught not to fight back, which feeds into the fear that rape produces and serves as a control factor to keep women in their place.

> Sexual violence is a problem of catastrophic proportions—a face obscured by its mundanity, by its relentless occurrence, by the fact that so many of us have been victims of it…[One can, however,] survive it, and even to flourish after it…This is not to say that the attack and its aftermath were, on balance, a good thing or…"a real blessing from above." I would rather not have gone down that road. It's been hard for me, as a philosopher, to learn the lesson that knowledge isn't always desirable, that the truth doesn't always set you free. Sometimes it fills you with incapacitating terror and then uncontrollable rage.[40]

A random act of violence is terribly despicable. But when pastoral/clergy sexual abuse occurs, there is an overwhelming shattering of trust. This violence is like incest because of the levels of intimacy and vulnerability. When a person comes to a pastor or counselor, the balance of power tips toward that professional because he or she represents authority. Often when such a travesty occurs, the victim is afraid to come forward for fear of reprisal and misunderstanding on the part of the congregation. Often some members think the pastor should not be asked to resign, that the victims and congregation should just forgive and forget. In many instances, when someone does come forward, there are those who have been aware of the pastor's misconduct, but have never taken steps to see the behavior challenged. Pastoral sexual perpetrators may seem to display remorse in public, but they often vent their anger against their victims in private. For the victim of clergy sexual misconduct, the experience often involves entrapment, confusion, obsession, fear, and betrayal. The pastor's actions have betrayed the call God has on her or him and has betrayed the duty and responsibility he or she has to protect the fragile location of the person being counseled. These sexual indiscretions have oppressed, have violated. The exposure of the accusations also traumatizes the congregation. Some want to blame the victim and support the pastor.

---

[39]Susan J. Brison, "Surviving Sexual Violence," *Second Opinion* 20 (October 1994): 11–18.
[40]Ibid., 21.

The congregation may sustain irreparable damage. At no point, however, should a premature reconciliation be attempted between the pastoral perpetrator and the congregation, for it undermines and thus prohibits the justice-seeking process and the later restoration of all persons to authenticity and integrity. The call is to make justice emerge out of unjust actions.[41]

Silent Oppression and Violent Seduction, Revenge, and Rebellion

Silent oppression and violent seduction in the film *The Women* leads to undermining, nasty, cheap behavior. The patriarchal quagmire that forms the context for this film smothers the vitality of all the female characters. Although no male ever appears on the screen, men's background presence stymies any sense of female freedom and self-actualization. The need to always be in relation with a male, even with an unfaithful, abusive, or manipulative male, shapes every conversation and every action. Like many women today, those in this film confuse being protected with being controlled. Somewhere in the myth of the American nuclear family that has particularly arisen in the last forty years, women of means have been put on the pedestal. Accepting the Victorian mode of conduct violates the energy of a relationship. When such energy is dampened or erased, people begin to do and say unconscionable things. For example, in the film, Mary's mother tells her daughter to accept her husband's philandering ways, because such violence is cyclical and generational: Her dad played around on her mom. Mary's mother excuses the adultery, saying that a man only has one escape when he hits middle age. When women get restless, they redo their homes or offices. When a man becomes restless, he must see a different self in a woman's eyes, eyes other than his wife's. Mary's mother contends that Steven does not really love the girl with whom he's cheating, for if he did, Mary would have sensed that fact. Mary counters that she is not chattel, that she and Steven are equals. There is so much denial, pretense, and avoidance that Mary finally goes on a trip to Bermuda with her mother, but quickly returns when one of her gossiping friends contacts her on vacation. Gossip and fashion seem to be the priority for the women who live in this fragile, but wealthy world.

---

[41]Christine Hamilton-Pennell, "Pastoral Sexual Abuse: One Congregation's Ordeal," *Daughters of Sarah* 13 (July/August 1987): 20–24. See Beth Van Dyke, *What About Her? A True Story of Clergy, Abuse, Survival* (Mukilteo, Wash.: WinePress Publishing, 1997).

Though the male presence is silent, it is oppressive. The silence seduces their wives into playing games. All the women are preoccupied with fashion, decorating, gossip, and vacations. Never does the discussion touch on books, intellectual pursuits, the women's dreams, spiritual concerns, or social justice issues. In their greed for gossip, they objectify their other women friends, and thus end up objectifying themselves, to the point that some condone adulterous practice. The "other woman" also gets short shrift, according to Crystal. After a fashion show, Crystal asks Mary what she is kicking about; she has the position, money, and so forth. "You [wealthy] women bore me," Crystal says. Crystal would break up their home, but Steven likes the sentimentality of the "traditional" home. Mary tells Crystal to forget about Steven. The salesgirls, having overheard the vicious conversation, think that Mary should have kept her month shut. All the gossiping about Mary and Crystal comes to a head in a local scandal sheet. These women are so psychologically and mentally oppressed, despite all the external trappings of success, that they work hard to destroy each other. They feed on sensationalism and crises. This kind of mind-set crosses class lines as well.

The maid runs to tell the cook about what she has overheard in a conversation between Mary and Steven (the camera trains on the maid and never shows Mary and Steven). After listening, the cook replies that no man likes the fact that only his wife loves him. The maid continues to recount the story as we hear the implications of the "Simon says" childhood game in the mouth of "Steven says." In one sense then, the film shows women being puppets of their husbands. On the other hand, it shows how women are always reacting against what their husbands and society regard as their proper role in life. In her kitchen-table wisdom, the cook notes that the first man who can figure out how a man can love his wife and another woman is going to win the prize (Nobel) that they give out in Sweden. What is at stake here?

Ultimately, *The Women* exposes a privileged lifestyle and bogus understanding of marriage. Many women seemed trapped and helpless to deal with the relationships they find themselves in, so they demean and are condescending to other women. That Steven's female secretary is harsh and mechanistic in her treatment of Mary when she comes to get the divorce papers signed perhaps indicates not a sense of being mean, but a sense of seeing the ridiculous games people play in marriage. One finally sees some critical thinking emerging when daughter Mary asks her mother, Mary, why people get divorced. Mary's answers are incomplete. The viewer is only left with this illumination for a few minutes, because when several women are on the train to Reno for their six-week divorces, the Countess remarks that she did not pick her husbands for character. Upon the women's arrival, the manager of the Double T Ranch also brings in a bit of reality. Lucy notes that she does not feel sorry for the divorcing women, because they feel too sorry for themselves. They feel so sorry that they either fight over men, compete for men, or see marriage as a notch on a belt. After getting her divorce and returning to New York, Mary learns that Steven is not happy. She sets out to play the same game on Crystal that Crystal and Mary's so-called friends played on Mary. Thus, being a manipulative con artist is "the way to get and keep a man"!

Such a mind-set glorifies gender oppression and patriarchy. Both men and women are complicit in the propagation of emotional and psychological gender violence. This violence penetrates every fiber of every person and teaches that women cannot be trusted, are immature, and will sabotage one another, so men do not have to worry about being faithful or being controlling. In this culture, the women expect men to be adulterous and never question the amount of control the men exercise, even in their absence.

The violence of "Dinah's Rape" is emotional, physical, and spiritual. Silent oppression is rife in Dinah's story in several ways. Jacob never expresses his outrage against his daughter's rape or against the defilement of Israel. Further, when Hamor requests not only the hand of Dinah but of all of their daughters, the daughters, their fathers' property, have no say in the matter. Their voices are not heard. Dinah's voice is not heard. That Shechem has the gall to rape Dinah and then demand that his father, Hamor, ask Jacob for her hand in marriage is bizarre and ruthless. Even Shechem's language of love regarding Dinah in no way mitigates what he has done, though his language does tend to make the reader more empathetic to him. I find such sensibilities unconscionable and problematic, even though this behavior follows Israel's legal tradition, where the father makes the arrangements for the marriage, and in which Shechem's rape of Dinah requires him to marry her, as stipulated in Deuteronomy 22:28–29.[43] Even if Dinah and Shechem

---

[43]Terence Fretheim, "Genesis," in *The New Interpreter's Bible: A Commentary in Twelve Volumes,* vol. 1 (Nashville: Abingdon Press, 1994), 577–78. Deuteronomy 22:28–29 says that if a man rapes an unbethrothed virgin, he has to pay the father, marry the woman, and "he shall not be permitted to divorce her as long as he lives." See also Exodus 22:16–17.

actually fall in love, that the rape is left hanging in the air is the height of dysfunctionality. Hamor and sons do not balk at the requirement of circumcision for the marriage deal, because as they exchange daughters, they merely exchange property, but the livestock and animals that come with the girls will also be theirs. The girls are objects of trade, by virtue of their gender. The silence is juxtaposed with, and is part of, the violence.

The violent seduction of Dinah is never resolved, as the author of the text presses us to watch the stories of the brothers. Brothers Levi and Simeon are outraged with Shechem, and using "trickery as vengeance," they offer circumcision as a compromise, as the only way Shechem can marry Dinah. What emerges is both a lack of respect for Jacob and his sons, and a lack of respect for working with kinship relations when Levi and Simeon take over. One of the ironies of the story is that Shechem as most favored is supposedly an honorable man, one who will respond with integrity. Dinah's brothers focus more on their own injured honor than on their sister. Further, that the brothers actually call their sister a harlot or whore because she was raped violates Dinah all over again. Their skewed vision embodies the trickster motif. When women are central to the action, the relationships end up being about the men. Thus, the rape and enforced silence push the seduction of the reader into downplaying the impact of the rape on Dinah and looking for some greater good.[44] The brothers exact their revenge, perhaps as repayment for the assault on their own character, since the rape of Dinah has become about them, not about Dinah. That the brothers murder every male, plunder the city, and kidnap the women and children seems to be overkill. That Jacob is self-absorbed to the point of thinking about the troubles that will result for him because of his sons rather than dealing with their crimes also seems a pathetic and most understated response. The absence of God's voice seems to indicate displeasure, but leaves a vast, awful emptiness amid a satiated nadir of violent death. The death in *Seven Brides* is the death of innocence and naivete; the brothers' violence is dismissed, and *Seven Brides for Seven Brothers* mirrors "Rape of the Sabine Women," with its rape fantasy, kidnapping, and childbirth leading to a happy ending for all. In addition to the obvious problems with all these case studies, in reality (1) they are based on stereotypes, and (2) there are scenarios today that disturbingly parallel the accounts cited here.

---

[44]Fretheim, "Genesis," 576–81; Susan Niditch, "Genesis," in *Women's Bible Commentary,* ed. Carol A. Newsome and Sharon Ringe (Louisville: Westminster/John Knox Press, 1992), 23–24.

Such stories are popular and ring true because of the stereotypes embedded in culture that justify gender oppression. First, since women are equated with nature, they become objects, are property, and thus, must be subdued. Two, viewing women in this way as eternal mothers provides an opportunity to devalue women, so that women must fail to live up to impossible standards and so that women should not be included in religious iconography. Three, through men's claiming that women are insane, hysterical, and irrational as they rely on their intuition, women can be silenced and invalidated. Four, categorizing women as subhuman, inferior, or weak allows society to disregard the lives of women and to trivialize their worth. Five, viewing women as sin-bearers, a concept noted as early as the second century by Tertullian and seconded by John Chrysostom in the late fourth century, is an option to blame women for the negativity and evil in the world. Six, thinking of women as sin-bearers moves one to the logical conclusion that women are the gateway to death, which justifies the negation of women's wisdom, heritage, and culture.[45] Unfortunately the indoctrination has worked so well that many women and men, across age, class, and race lines fully accept and even pontificate about the inferiority, neediness, and weakness of women: the power of misbegotten anguish as hostile, pathological activity, for some even celebrate misogyny and patriarchy. In a recent Bible study class, an ordained woman opened the session proclaiming that she loved her dad and had a great husband; thus, she fully embraced the patriarchal system and the sole concept of God as Father. No one asked her if her earthly father had ever sacrificed one of his daughters as Jepthah did, if her husband had an unnamed secondary wife as the Levite had, or if her husband considered her to be his property.

When lived out, such careless statements justify gender oppression and the related violence. Such carelessness sets up churches to be irresponsible in the wake of clergy abuse. The congregants will be tempted to disbelieve the victim, to want to protect the church's reputation, and to blame the victim: misbegotten anguish rooted in deceit, pain, and cruelty. The congregants will often empathize and sympathize with the abuser, excuse the abuser's behavior, and protect the abuser from the consequences of her or his behavior. One of the most painful scenarios occurs when the

---

[45]Pamela Cooper-White, *The Cry of Tamar: Violence Against Women and the Church's Response* (Minneapolis: Augsburg/Fortress, 1995), 46–55.

congregation wants to invest in cheap grace, where they sweep everything under the rug, quickly forgive the abuser, and move on.[46]

Neither society nor faith communities can afford to just move on from sexual oppression and violence of any kind. We can no longer feign ignorance and become paralyzed by misbegotten anguish. Laws have been made, and most institutions have codes of conduct against sexual harassment. However, some remnants of sexual oppression are so entrenched within our society that much work is left to be done. As long as women themselves condone and teach gender oppression and as long as sexual orientation provides a license to judge, ridicule, and kill, the levels of gender and sexual oppression will increase; the misbegotten anguish will abscess; the tragic deaths, the battered spouses, and the abused children will continue.

---

[46]Marie M. Fortune and James Poling, "Calling to Accountability: The Church's Response to Abusers," in *Violence Against Women and Children: A Christian Theological Sourcebook,* ed. Carol J. Adams and Marie M. Fortune (New York: Continuum, 1995), 451–52.

Mainstream, middle class, marginalized:
Terms about dollars and sense and lifestyle.
Cents don't go too far,
Yet the educated sensibilities,
A cultured existence
Spun to create an image,
though perhaps not of God,
Elevate the absurdities of invisible borders
Firmly embedded in the fabric of systems
And governments, and groups of people
Where power brokers make final decisions.

Mainstream, middle class, marginalized:
3Ms of interrogation
Of Life's classified imagination
That somehow delineated individuals
And societal groups become
Markers of distinction:
Producing millions of wannabes.
Upper class, underserved, underrepresented
Tell a story some of us would rather not hear;
Many of us loathe all those stationed at the borders.

5

Conjugating
Elitism

Classism and Caste-ism

Many in the United States of America argue that we seek a
classless society as an American ideal. Many countries in Europe
perpetuate a blatant class system. Marxism and communism are
political constructions dependent on a notion of warfare between
class systems. The Beatitudes in Matthew 5 remind us of class with
the evocations of blessedness to the poor, the meek, and those who
hunger after spiritual foods and righteousness. Jesus' response to the
quest for life in the kingdom by the rich young man implicates the
distinctions between rich and poor. What one wears, the school one
attends, where one lives, what one considers recreational, and who
one associates with derive from our social location in a particular
class of a given society.

This chapter analyzes the impact of individual and systemic
attitudes and actions on the experience of classism in the United
States. After exploring and defining various aspects and meanings
of class, I then review the contextual narratives of the parable of
the unjust steward (Luke 16) and the film *Cry, the Beloved Country*. I
ponder the various actions that undergird classism, such as social

stratification, and search for a vocabulary from the two narratives, in which we can begin to name the indicators of classism as we hope for a more inclusive, less fractured society, steeped foundationally in normative ethics.

Class Unveiled: Silk Stockings, Nylons, or Crew Socks

The term *class* as a social category appears during the Industrial Revolution era. Prior to the 1770s, the common use of the term pertained to a group or division in colleges and schools. The terms *the poor* or *poor laborers* emerged in the eighteenth century, indicating the relationship between wage earning and poverty. In the early nineteenth century, the phrase *working class* or *classes* emerges to indicate economic process, beyond the earlier implied hierarchy of possessions and social rank. The differentiation in ranks, that is, higher, middle, upper, lower-middle, and so forth appears between the 1790s and the 1890s. The late appearance of the terms designates the change in attitude toward them and the character of the divisions. Throughout history, the notion of depicting societies as whole groups of people has been prevalent, particularly when justifying or explaining inequities among how certain groups of people were treated. Sacred texts such as the Bible, the Koran, and the Vedic texts have used such language of social stratification. Augustine and other medieval theologians used these religious mythic texts to justify slavery and other peonage systems.[1]

Many thinkers conceptualize society as a dichotomy: the top, the rich and powerful, and the bottom, the poor and powerless, those who wear silk stockings and those who wear nylon hose or polyester crew socks. The use of such categories has not been consistent, though the foci of the dichotomies tend to break down regarding wealth, power, or relationships. For many ancient thinkers such as Plato and Aristotle, the division concerned free persons and those enslaved, according to biological predisposition. For some theologians in the fourth century, the dichotomy pertained to property: owners and nonowners, regardless of whether one favored the elite or the oppressed. These dichotomies may have been long-standing because of our tendency to highlight extremes and polarities, and because they help some individuals to promote their particular causes or interests.[2] Other thinkers have developed a tripartite model.

---

[1]Lewis A. Coser, "Class," in *Dictionary of the History of Ideas: Studies of Selected Pivotal Ideas,* vol. 1 (New York: Charles Scribner's Sons, 1968, 1973), 441–42.
[2]Ibid., 443.

Aristotle posited the class categories as the very rich, the very poor, and those in between. In the medieval church, the tripartite categories included "those who pray, those who defend the country, and those who toil...clergy, nobility, commoners."[3] In the eighteenth century, Adam Smith revised the terminology of old priests, knights, and commoners to that of "proprietors of land, proprietors of stock, and laborers...those who lived by the rent of land, those who lived by profits, and those whose income was the wage of labor."[4] For Aristotle, the middle class ought to be the basic class, the mean between the extremes of rich and poor. For Karl Marx, the two opposing classes, the bourgeoisie and the proletariat, are the basic classes, and the middle class is less stable or enduring; the dichotomy dominates, and the trichotomy is a temporary deviation. With the nineteenth century, more and more complex models for class stratification emerge. The more diverse the criteria, the more any one class marker will have a lower rank, affording the ability for such a ranking system to have both consolatory and compensatory functions, where one rank can offset another. Max Weber noted that to focus solely on economics as an indicator of class is insufficient. He distinguishes between several markers and gives priority to status, class, and power. Status pertains to prestige or honor, to lifestyle. Class concerns economic status, particularly people who either have similar life possibilities or who share a similar experience in the marketplace. Weber understood power to mean the capability of a person or a group to impose its will on others, even if there is opposition from the others, based on political or economic resources. Other thinkers have added additional class markers, including education, occupational prestige, ethnic group position, kinship, etc.[5] Other scholars analyze social stratification based on particular functions.

Medieval and scholastic church thinkers such as Thomas Aquinas explored the concept of function based on a sense of calling or duty, which also allowed for inequality. Luther concurred that people are called to participate within a particular social structure and ought to live within their own class. Yet the differentiation does not inherently create distinct values or ranks. How to see the different functions of humanity in conjunction with the various offerings or contributions

---

[3]Ibid.
[4]Ibid., 444.
[5]Ibid., 445.

of social classes remains important to sociology. Following Adam Smith, the functioning categories concern proprietors of land, proprietors of stock, the new dynamic strata of the new industrial order, and laborers. Karl Marx's theory of stratification rejects the notion of many classical economists who assume basic common interests to all classes.

Marx sees a basic conflict of interests among the classes. Different classes have always been divided by different interests, as they stand in opposition; there has always been a class struggle. Marx saw class conflict as central to the relations between industrial capitalists, landowners, and wage earners. While many earlier economists saw the tripartite divisions as natural to humanity, Marx viewed the matter contextually and saw such relations as a reality for a given historical period. While class struggle has always existed, the players in the battle continue to change. Marx also talked about class as related to the import of class awareness or class consciousness, when the socioeconomic factors are supported by sociopsychological matters. In later writings, including the incomplete *Das Kapital,* Marx also developed multidimensional schemes, where society can experience differentiation on multiple levels. Essentially for Marx, class differentiations arise from antagonistic confrontations, where the class struggle is about the fight for power between the exploited and exploiters, the rulers and ruled, the oppressed and oppressors.[6] One of the issues germane to our understanding of class is how one understands the source and nature of equality and inequality in analytical systems.

Most thinkers have rejected the notion of a divine or supernatural justification for human inequality. Some French social reformers, such as Claude-Adren Helvétius and Etienne Bonnot de Condillac, followers of Locke, argued that all human beings are similar at birth; others, such as Jean-Jacques Rousseau argued that two distinct kinds of inequality exist at birth, the natural and moral differentiation. Rousseau argued that the distinctions pertain to the reality of private property. Thus, only the political inequalities are socially and morally significant. Another key concept, particularly for an American audience, is the notion of the availability of equal opportunity amid a society of unequals. Saint Simon stood in opposition to Locke's disciples and argued that society is congruent with the natural reality for humanity, which is inequality. Thus, people fall into the categories

---

[6]Ibid., 446.

of (1) leaders and guides, those with rational scientific capabilities; (2) manual laborers, those with key motor capabilities; and (3) the artists and religionists, those with sensory capabilities. While thoughts of inherent differences within humanity is long-standing, Saint Simon also pressed for the import of organizing society in a manner that allowed all persons of a society the best possible opportunity to fully develop their capacities. Ultimately, at the beginning of the twenty-first century, the industrial societies in the world all have sharp class distinctions, where people are in particular class categories, many through achievement and merit.[7]

Building methodologically and theoretically on the work of Pierre Bourdieu regarding the logic of practice, Joan M. Martin uses Bourdieu's[8] four conceptual tools as she defines class. Martin contextually uses Bourdieu's notions of fields (figuration or network involving objective relations), practice (an activity generated via dispositions, perceptions, and schemes), habitus (typical or habitual condition), and class, which is also a habitus.

> Class is a mode of social grouping defined by a specific set of social relations…into simply a category of economic materialism defining everything in relation to the means of economic production,…but [is] a universal explanatory principle for all relations….not real groups of people, but it is the conditioning that differentiates the existence of peoples within social spaces…Class is also a category for Bourdieu which enables not only distinction in embodiment, manners, and taste; class, as a conceptual tool, also permits the investigation of hierarchical modes and uses of "symbolic power" or "symbolic violence" in the social world shared by classes—for example slaveholders, their wives, overseers, and the enslaved.[9]

Some scholars describe social class based on occupation, with the following categories: professional, managerial and technical, skilled non-manual, skilled manual, partly skilled, unskilled, and armed forces. Professional workers include doctors, lawyers, scientists, CEOs, CFOs, managers of large corporations. Managerial and technical workers include farmers, teachers, shopkeepers, and

---

[7]Ibid., 447–49.

[8]Joan M. Martin, *More Than Chains and Toil* (Louisville: Westminster John Knox Press, 2000), 55.

[9]Ibid., 66–67.

white-collar workers. Skilled manual laborers include carpenters, master builders, shop assistants, nurses, electricians, and plumbers. Semi-skilled manual workers include pipe fitters, rapid transit drivers. The unskilled manual workers include bartenders, porters, housekeepers, and general laborers.[10] The various occupations afford a particular lifestyle and a particular kind of access, but again are not the only determinants of class, though some groups of people automatically deem other persons inferior based on their vocations. Since time immemorial, the elites in the dominant culture have tried to convince other people that things within the status quo cannot change, especially when it comes to the distribution of monies. They claim that everything in the world and the world itself is set and fixed.[11]

Author David Brooks argues that many of America's elite are not the WASP elite, but the résumé gods. When the *New York Times* lists nuptials, for example, the data emphasized about a person includes college degrees, graduate degrees, career path, and parents' profession—the indicators or markers of current upscale Americans. All kinds of talented and ambitious Americans have gained access to these markers in recent years, particularly persons who are not White, male, or Protestant. American higher education has provided two legacies from the late 1950s and 1960s that have contributed to this shift: one, the focus on merit systems, on brains and not bloodline; second, the political and sexual rebellion that challenged the usual ideas of success where a social code based on respectability, income, and possessions helped to move individuals toward lives based on spiritual and intellectual ideals, with a sense of creativity and personal emancipation. Brooks calls these new energetic entrepreneurs "bourgeois bohemians"—Bobos.[12] This prosperous educated group has disdain toward thoughts of being hostages to consumerism and have become connoisseurs instead. In deference to conspicuous consumption, this class views acquisitions as reflections of their own personalities, moving for the practical or the educational, the edifying. This group has an ethics that includes responsible self-control and utility. Bobos tend not to be overtly

---

[10]David Rose, Institute for Social and Economic Research, University of Essex. Information found on http://www.hewett.norfolk.sch.uk/curric/soc/class/reg.htm in July 2001.

[11]Editorial, *Tikkun* 12 (March-April, 1997): 7.

[12]Gary Rosen, "Summa Cum Latte: Review of *Bobos in Paradise: The New Upper Class and How They Got There* by David Brooks," in *Commentary* (May, 2000).

religious, but are concerned about spirituality. For those members of traditional faith communities, their interest is out of a need to be engaged with a moral community, not out of any sense of deep commitment or belief, which, of course, is not necessarily satisfying. Bobos tend to be tolerant in civic and personal matters, work for decency and fairness, and gently try to change and forgive things that are not working, but with no grandstanding. In all matters—social, political, and spiritual—Bobos tend to search for a peaceful midpoint. One of the fascinating realities is the democratic achievement of an elite ruling class based mainly on academic achievement, not on DNA, military prowess, or wealth. Rosen challenges the aptness of the label, given the august tradition of Bohemians. While this group of elites is undemanding, maybe even lax, its elitism may be problematic because it has allowed them to insulate themselves from the fallout of their own notions of what emerged from the 1960s focus on self-expression and personal liberation. In the wake of Bobos' success, the impoverished underclass has suffered greatly.[13]

Since capitalist societies do not have the "traditional juridically enforced class distinctions and [they promote] a belief in the legal freedom of persons...when everyone is formally free, how can there be class domination? Why do class distinctions persist between the wealthy, who own the means of production, and the mass of people, who work for them? The theory of exploitation answers this question."[14] The mystery is unpacked if one recognizes the exploitation that emerges with the transfer of the results of one social group's labor for the benefit of another group. The process of exploitation creates a hierarchy of power between different social groups. The social definition of the meaning of work, or what work is, and who works for which person or organization, and the social process that controls how the work results are dispensed and how people are paid for work determine the relations regarding power and authority.[15] This is particularly the case within capitalism. Capitalism is an economic system characterized by private or corporate ownership of capital goods, by investments that are

---

[13]Ibid.

[14]Iris Marion Young, *Justice and the Politics of Difference* (Princeton, N.J.: Princeton University Press, 1990), 48.

[15]Ibid., 48–50.

determined by private decision rather than by state control, and by prices, production, and the distribution of goods that are determined mainly by competition in a free market.[16] Sometimes in analyzing such systems, we confuse capitalism with mercantilism. Mercantilism is the theory or practice of mercantile pursuits or commercialism. Such an economic system developed during the decay of feudalism to unify and increase the power and especially the monetary wealth of a nation by a strict governmental regulation of the entire national economy. This regulation usually occurs through policies designed to secure an accumulation of bullion, a favorable balance of trade, the development of agriculture and manufacturing, and the establishment of foreign trade monopolies.[17] To explore notions of capitalism as relates to class, we turn to a review of the parable of the Unjust Steward (Luke 16) and the film *Cry, the Beloved Country.*

Class by Design: Ancient and Modern Parables

Central to Luke's gospel are these four parables: a shepherd with a lost sheep paired with the parable about the housewife with a lost coin, followed by the parable about a father with obstinate sons paired with the story of a man with a disappointing worker. In each parable, something that is wrong is made right. In the case of the unsatisfactory worker, he receives approval from his master. This worker, known as the unjust steward, has been slandered, falsely accused. If his work is found to be below par, he will probably end up in the mines, since that is the place where a steward like him (often viewed as a slave) would be sent for punishment. So the steward realizes what is at stake, which is why he does not want to lose his status. He says he cannot dig and does not want to have to beg. He cannot afford to be fired and made to leave the household. The steward cuts deals with those who owe his master, allows them to revise their IOUs, and the same master that earlier critiqued him when he was falsely accused, now praises him for his ingenuity, even though the master is taking a cut in profits. For persons of faith, all are like the unjust steward, all will need some "awesome and surprising approval, unbiased by our merit, which we call grace."[18]

---

[16] *Webster's New Collegiate Dictionary* (Springfield, Mass.: G. & C. Merriam Co., 1981).
[17] Ibid.
[18] Christopher Bryan, "The Slandered Steward." Editorial, *Sewanee Theological Review* 42 (1999): 126.

One must ask the question, What is the steward up to in Luke 16? If we assume the skillful authorship of Luke, we can then search for an answer that is not dependent on who recognizes the steward's cleverness nor the details of the transactions. Handling and negotiating resources that do not belong to him, the steward will face dire straits if he is dismissed, so he uses the remaining time to connect with those who are in his boss's debt. Then he will have those same people to fall back on when he loses his job. If taken in conjunction with the parable of the rich man that follows, a message that one can derive is that one should use his or her worldly goods to acquire friends. Thus, when the goods are gone, the individual will be welcomed into the eternal kingdom. Our time on earth is short, and we cannot take wealth or anything else with us when we die.[19]

Clearly the rich man has tremendous wealth, and the steward is being dishonest, given the amounts of the debt and that someone tells the rich man that the steward is "squandering his property." A major challenge is how one interprets the steward's action of reducing everyone's debt. There are several options. One, by reducing the individuals' debts, the steward cheated the master. Two, by excluding the interest that was included in the debt, as prohibited by Deuteronomy 23:19–20, the steward was acting out of moral agency. Three, the steward lessened the debt due by subtracting the amount of his own commission, which was figured into the debt. The text is ambiguous on these matters. The first two options decrease the master's income, and the first option is illegal. The third choice depicts the steward as generous by giving up his share. The second choice paints the steward in a good light, but the amount of interest is excessive, so scholars vary about how to reflect and assess the nature of ancient economics. R. Alan Culpepper suggests we follow the first option, particularly given the limited data we have. Although the precise delineation of who the "lord" or "master" is in Luke 16:8, the steward's boss or Jesus, is unclear. Whichever person is the master, he creates an environment of goodness and honesty, binding the debtors by honor to respond in kind to the steward's gracious benevolence. The final verse to this pericope, Luke 16:13, adds closure and asserts that no one slave can serve two masters–a slave will hate or despise one master and will love or be devoted to the other–and finally, no one can serve both God and wealth. One must

---

[19]Michael Ball, "The Parables of the Unjust Steward and the Rich Man and Lazarus," *Expository Times* 106 (August 1995): 329–30.

not idolize money or become enslaved to it, for God requires total loyalty.[20]

In considering this parable as a demonstration of class issues, the Lord/master is upper class and the steward is working class. The steward has a certain status in working for this Lord/master, for there are particular phenomena that transcend money and access. He has become accustomed to a particular lifestyle and to holding an office that is held in some esteem. His position has given him certain privileges based on his relationship with the Lord/master. If he is fired or forced to leave the master's employ, he will not only be embarrassed, he may go to prison. Being terminated or going to prison would change his profile and probably make it impossible for him to have the same kind of access he had previously. So he makes the master's debtors offers they cannot refuse. Thus, if he is fired, he may be able to get employment with one of the individuals he bargained with. Yet they may decide that he would operate their business just as he did for his present master. Would they have to assume that in all probability, the steward would someday shortchange them? Shifting from an employee-employer relationship to that of father and sons, we observe some ramifications of class and class oppression in a different time and a different place.

Darrell J. Roodt directed *Cry, the Beloved Country*, a film based on Alan Paton's classic novel that portrays how two fathers come to grips with deep personal loss (the death of their sons) and the emotional scars of South African apartheid. This 1995 adaptation tells the story of the Kumalo and Jarvis families, the first major film produced in South Africa after the end of mandatory apartheid rule with the election of Nelson Mandela as president.[21] Set in Natal, South Africa, 1946, the opening scenes belie the devastation and evil that lurk at the periphery, though they are central and foundational, deep within the entrails of the soil itself. A little girl runs along a picturesque, pastoral countryside with a beautiful valley, rushing waters, and a road that climbs seven miles. She brings a letter from Johannesburg to Father Stephen Kumalo, respectfully called *umfundisi,* the local Black priest. He fears opening the letter and knows he must go in search for his sister. In a voice-over, Kumalo ponders:

[20]R. Alan Culpepper, "Luke," in *The New Interpreter's Bible: A Commentary in Twelve Volumes,* vol. 9 (Nashville: Abingdon Press, 1995), 308–9.

[21]Information found on http://allmovie.com/cg/x.dll?p=avg&sql=A135800 in July 2001.

This is a journey I have always feared—where my people have gone, never to return. The young men have gone to the mines, so the young women go to find them. For who can enjoy the lovely land and the sun that pours down on the earth, when Whites will not live equally with Blacks? A land where the White man has everything and the Black nothing.

The Rev. Stephen Kumalo pastors in a poverty-stricken farming community. For the first time, he will go to Johannesburg to search for his son Absalom. Absalom left the rural area a while ago and is missing. At the train station, we see James Jarvis, a South African White, who we later learn is a wealthy landowner. He picks up his daughter-in-law and grandson from the train station. The elder Jarvis speaks about his son as a dreamer who opened a house for Black boys. Kumalo is leery of the big city, and being naive and too trusting, he experiences some of the seamier side of this den of iniquity as he is robbed and beaten quite soon after he arrives. He does get to Sophiatown, looking for his sister Gertrude, who came looking for her husband and did not find him. To his deep regret, she is now a prostitute in order to be able to buy food for her son. Father Msimangu acts as the umfundisi's guide in Johannesburg. They meet the umfundisi's brother John, a politician, and learn that Absalom is now a petty thief who has a pregnant girlfriend. John has forsaken his faith in God and is advocating a violent revolution to overthrow South Africa's White apartheid leadership. The umfundisi finds his sister in a brothel and takes her away, and her Madam is furious that she is leaving. He does not know what to make of things, so he talks to a fellow priest and asks regarding his brother, "How can he have truth on his side and not God?" The question of where is God amid the struggle recurs implicitly and explicitly several times in the story. The umfundisi's compatriot asks, when you see so much poverty, pain, and suffering, how is one to respond? "Perhaps God is on [John's] side, and he does not want to know it any more."

The scene shifts from the squalor of the shanty town, an indicator of poverty and lower classes, to the lush African countryside. The police arrive to tell Jarvis that his son Arthur, a well-liked activist on behalf of the rights of the city's Black majority population, was shot dead and that they suspect a native gang. The earlier scenes of poverty indicate the two intersecting oppressions of race and class, for the language used to talk about the suspects undergirds this reality.

Father Msimangu and the umfundisi continue to search for Absalom and learn that he and his cousin have been in trouble, probably theft or smuggling. Absalom has been in a reform school, and the warden says he has hopes for Absalom. Msimangu and Father Kumalo find Absalom's pregnant girl friend, but even she does not know where he is. Msimangu is frustrated, loses his temper, and later apologizes to the umfundisi, asking for forgiveness, for he doubted whether the girl was actually Absalom's girlfriend. The scene goes completely black. Next, we see that the Jarvis family arrives by plane in Johannesburg to identify the body. At that point, the elder Jarvis is distraught and yells, "My son was their champion, you know!" In referring to Black South Africans, he calls them "bloody kaffirs," "bloody bastards," and he wants the police to catch whoever killed his son. During the funeral service, the film presents some intriguing camera angles. The audience first sees the funeral service, then the massive search for the killers as the police abuse several of those whom Msimangu and Kumalo questioned earlier. The camera returns to the receiving line after the funeral service, all set and choreographed to the deep voice of the umfundisi, who states:

> There is fear in the land, and fear in the hearts of all who live there. And fear puts an end to understanding and the need to understand. So how shall we fashion such a land when there is fear in the heart? The white man will put more locks on his door and get a fine, fierce dog. But the beauty of the trees and of the stars—these things we shall forgo. Cry, the beloved country, for the unborn child that is the inheritor of our fear. Let him not love the earth too deeply. Let him not be too moved when the birds of his land are singing. Nor give too much of his heart to a mountain or a valley. For fear will rob him of all if he gives too much. Yes, cry, cry, the beloved country.

The umfundisi and Msimangu check back with Absalom's girlfriend and ask what the police wanted, and she says she doesn't know. Jarvis then goes to his son's office to sort his papers. He is stunned by a journal entry that he reads, but it is in his reading that he begins to try to understand who his son really was. He reads, "Native crime is not the issue, but White crime. What sort of memorial do we want? What sort of memorial do we deserve? We call ourselves a Christian people. When prosperity comes to judge us, it will consign us to the sewers of history; as tyrants, oppressors, criminals." As Jarvis tries to grasp what he has read, the police come to say that they have found the three boys responsible.

Absalom confesses. He says that he was frightened and only had the gun for protection, but when the White man came, he shot him. He did not mean to kill him; they were committing a robbery. When the brothers John and Stephen Kumalo speak, it becomes clear that John wants Absalom to take all the blame. He argues that no one can really prove that the other two boys, his son and another boy, were there. Absalom is the scapegoat. Aware of these events, Jarvis visits the boys' club Arthur helped to start, again trying to understand his son. One of the teachers offers that "Arthur Jarvis was the only man, Black or White, who saw me for what I really am." Later that evening, still distraught and suffering insomnia, Jarvis asks his wife, "Why do we bring children into this world?" Dealing with his own angst, the umfundisi speaks with Absalom's girlfriend, asking if she wants to marry Absalom, for he does not want to take her into his family if she is not willing. She consents. A lawyer who believes in freedom for Blacks takes Absalom's case pro bono, and the trial begins. Absalom pleads guilty and the other two, including his cousin, plead not guilty. The drama occurs inside and outside the trial court.

The umfundisi goes in search of a parishioner's daughter. He ends up at the house where the Jarvis family members are guests for the duration of the trial. He is overcome and falls as he recognizes the elder Jarvis. Jarvis does not recognize him. The umfundisi tells of his mission and Jarvis replies that the servants and owners are not there, but he can wait. In a most poignant and vulnerable moment Jarvis tells the umfundisi that there is something between the two of them, but he does not know what that is. The umfundisi responds that "it is the heaviest thing of all my years." When Jarvis gently pleads with him not to be afraid, that he will not be angry, the umfundisi is still hesitant. The umfundisi replies, "The thing that's heaviest for all my years is the heaviest for all of your years. It is my son who killed your son." Stunned, Jarvis turns away momentarily and then replies, "I understand what I didn't understand. There is no anger in me." The umfundisi answers Jarvis' query about how he knew who Jarvis was, that it was from court. The conversation reveals that Jarvis had ridden his horse past the church where the umfundisi pastors. The umfundisi also remembered the son, Arthur, as "one who had a brightness in him." During this exchange, time and context are suspended; all past and all future transcended. They bid each other farewell, and the scene shifts back to the court.

The judge acknowledges that apartheid may have contributed to the case, but says that a judge's duty is not to apportion blame in a defective society and that he is not authorized to show mercy. Because of insufficient evidence, the other two boys are released. Absalom is sentenced to die by hanging. Shortly thereafter, Absalom and Katherine marry in prison. Msimangu later tells the umfundisi that he is giving up the world for a cloistered life to deal with his fear. He fears that "when the White man turns to loving, we will have turned to hate." The umfundisi replies that if his son does not receive mercy, he will go to the mountains as he has only done on two other occasions: when Absalom was sick unto death as a baby and when the umfundisi was tempted to commit adultery. Msimangu asks for prayers as he attempts this new thing and gives the umfundisi a contribution to help defray his expenses. As the umfundisi is about to leave, one of the matrons comes and tells him that his sister left during the night, but did not take her child. After the umfundisi leaves with Katherine, his daughter-in-law, and his nephew, Gertrude's child, the head of the local religious order tells Msimangu that the umfundisi is "the only truly Godly man I've ever met." Msimangu responds with a question, "Why does God not show him any mercy?"

As the umfundisi leads a service back at his church, Absalom dictates a letter to a Black priest from Pretoria. He seeks to comfort his mother and father, telling them he is not being treated badly, but that there will be no mercy for him. Then the rains that the congregation had prayed for come. The umfundisi goes to the church, putting out pans to catch the water because the entire tin roof is leaking. There are not enough pans to catch all the water. Jarvis stops by and asks if he can take shelter. In a bit of comic relief, the umfundisi remarks, "the roof leaks, the roof leaks in many places." Jarvis responds, "I know." As the deluge continues, the camera shows the gaze of two fathers, two very tired fathers, and a very wet church. Jarvis inquires about mercy for Absalom, and the umfundisi tells him that the execution is at dawn in fifteen days. They look at each other as the rain stops, and Jarvis leaves, saying that he will remember Absalom. Fifteen days later, with the beautiful, majestic terrain before him, the umfundisi leaves to walk to the mountain to pray. The two fathers meet again on the mountainside: Jarvis on a horse, the umfundisi walking with his staff.

Jarvis greets the umfundisi and notes that he thought the priest would be going up on the mountain on day fifteen. Jarvis has a letter for the congregation, which states he will build them a new church. After the umfundisi says the church will check with the bishop, Jarvis asks if the congregation would put a little stone with his son's name on it, "the one who had the brightness in him." As one father rides down the mountain, the other ascends to pray. Katherine goes into labor, and they are about to execute Absalom, as the umfundisi's voiceover follows:

> Who knows for what we live and struggle and die? Who knows what keeps us living and struggling while all things break about us? Who knows why the warm flesh of a child is such comfort when one's own child is lost and cannot be recovered? Wise men write many books in words too hard to understand, but this, the purpose of our lives, the end beyond all human struggle, is beyond all human wisdom. Oh God, my God, do not thou forsake me. Yea, though I walk through the valley of the shadow of death, I fear no evil, if thou art with me.

Absalom dies. The camera pans in a circular motion around a lonely, tired father on a mountaintop praying. With a blackout once more before the credits, we see a quote from the author of the novel, Alan Paton: "For it is the dawn that has come, as it has come for a thousand centuries, never failing. But when that dawn will come, of our emancipation from the fear of bondage and the bondage of fear, why that is a secret." Secrets and ambiguity are bedfellows in these two stories of loss. Secrets and ambiguity together can create a pathology that makes it easier to create arenas of stratification and class oppression.

Not in Our Neighborhood: Stratification, Classism, and Challenges

People experience stratification in several systems: religion, government, property, wealth, and labor. Within religion, the institution works toward providing unity through teaching and modeling common needs and values. In medieval society, the priest had high status because the society could afford to support a large, organized priesthood who ministered to a general populace of mostly illiterate people. The priesthood has less status in more advanced societies because "sacred tradition and supernaturalism lose significance as secular scientific knowledge becomes more important."[22] Government helps to establish a society around authority and law, with internal and external functions. Internally, government-enforced norms arbitrate conflicts and plan and direct society. Externally, government is in charge of diplomacy and war. Nevertheless, some factors hamper the power of government, such as officials, mores, and "the power of position vs. power of knowledge."[23] One's position determines social status: the higher the income, the more functionally important, and the smaller number of persons available to fill the position. Power and prestige are often determined by the possession or ownership of capital goods and productive goods. Technical knowledge functions to help one acquire a goal without participating in determining the goal. The process of recruitment to technical vocations (education) and the level of specialization affect the amount of status given to technicians.[24] The amount of status, clout, and privilege, or the lack thereof, can be noted through an assessment of class markers.

Class markers or indicators involve a variety of categories within sociohistorical, cultural, and economic life. Class status allows certain assumptions, privileges certain concepts, and disallows others. The amount of traveling one does and how one travels (staying with friends or in hotels, flying or driving, going a great distance to a variety of places or to local destinations) indicates class status. One's sense and understanding of geography and history; the amount of exposure to cultural activities in the home and community through music, art, books, theatre, museums, one's school experiences; and how one is able to make connections between facts learned can also be related to one's class. If one has not learned integrative thinking, where one can engage interdisciplinary discourse, this typically indicates lower class. How one uses communications technologies, employs grammar and protocols, and utilizes tone and gesture that outsiders would miss, indicates one's class. The language used by the managerial and professional classes is different. Since communication is embedded in social relationships, the ways in

---

[22]Wilbert Moore "Some Principles of Stratification," found on http://www.spc.uchicago.edu/ssr1/PRELIMS/Strat/stmisc1.html#DAVIS in July 2001.
[23]Ibid.
[24]Ibid.

which one signifies meaning pertains prominently to one's class. Some social class markers emerge when families and communities are position-oriented, where authority lies within the position a person holds in the community or family, not within the individual. Each class also has a particular way in which social class etiquette functions. In some lower-class settings, for example, the authority figure is always right. Class also shapes mobility, how many times people move, and whether or not they live in the same or similar neighborhoods throughout their lives. How people think, whether they have a disjointed worldview that comes from being on the bottom end of a division of labor society or they are able to engage in integrated thinking and understanding of connections that exist are all markers of class.[25]

Class markers shape an individual's attitudes, ways of thinking, and behavior. For example, college students from upper-middle-class families have their values, beliefs, and habits. They tend to drive luxury cars, value high-tech equipment, and wear expensive or designer clothes. Spring break means trips to Florida, the Bahamas, and Mexico. Such students will feel they are part of the majority and become quite comfortable. As their numbers reach a critical mass, their way of being and doing becomes mainstream. Those not a part of this social class start to disappear or become repressed. Working-class students hope to become upwardly mobile and are often trapped between two worlds. They are on the edge of this environment, looking in, but they are never invited to join "this brave new world." Imitation does not change their position; it only hides it. Purposefully, working-class students are discouraged from questioning the status quo value system, and so they do not pose a threat to the current social order. Students will continually have to deal with levels of socialization, questions of isolation and assimilation, and their level of class consciousness. Another demarcation of class concerns amount and locus of educational opportunities. Is there a tradition of higher education or is the student the first to go to college? How is the education funded, for example, trust fund or scholarships? As noted earlier, the upper-middle class includes university trained professionals and managers with comfortable incomes, job authority, stability, and independence. Working-class people are semiskilled, blue-collar workers and some

---

[25]Michael W. Gos, http://www.lee.edu/~mgos/but.html.

low level white-collar workers, who generally have less financial security and are rarely blessed to experience higher education. Class consciousness is the awareness or knowledge of being part of an entity that shares similar interests and burdens, and thus requires collaborative work if anyone is to succeed.[26] Issues of class tap every place in society on individual and communal levels, in areas of work, play, and faith.

For some faith communities, class creates just as great a schism as race. For example, the type of attire a minister wears exudes particular messages of class. If a minister dresses conservatively, the congregation may see clothing as a symbol of the sacrifices that a minister and family make as part of their ministry. If a clergyperson dresses ostentatiously, he or she may be seen as lacking couth. An individual's name, type of automobile, level of health and dental care, questions of smoking versus nonsmoking and the brand of cigarettes, and the forms of address for a given protocol all have to do with class indicators.[27]

Amid a prospering economy, a sense of well-being, and the freedom to be able to afford to make purchases beyond the necessities, live those who exist in urban ghettos. Each ghetto is a quarry of dilapidated housing, few retail stores, high crime rates, a proliferation of drugs, rampant gang activity, and a shortage of jobs. Such difficult living conditions test one's resilience, ingenuity, faith, and entire sensibility. While incredibly poor and very talented artists and writers have lived together in the ghetto, the impoverished are an isolated collective of the disadvantaged spawned by racist and classist exclusionary practices. Part of the impoverishment occurs because those who could leave have left. Second, the manufacturing jobs that used to provide income also have left. The absence of economic means and models of hope has led to the development of the underclass. The American dream has included moving to better neighborhoods. When the emerging middle class leaves the ghetto, then the ghetto community is even more disadvantaged. With the decline of manufacturing jobs, there has been a growing service industry market, but many of these have not been accessible for

---

26Kristin Tyler, "The Silent Minority: A Study of Working Class Students at Boston College, an Upper-Middle Class Campus" (master's thesis, Boston College, n.d.). Available online at http://www2.bc.edu/~tylerk/thesis.htm as of August 2001.

27Alma Faith Crawford, "Practical Tips to Effectively Confront Classism Through Your Ministry" (paper presented at UUA Ministry Days 2000, Nashville, June 2000). Available online at http://www.uua.org/ga/ga00/ministrydays/classism.html as of July 2001.

those in the ghetto. Many ghetto dwellers have not been in a position to compete for top jobs in technology, communications, or finance. Many ghetto residents have had poor or little education and far less work experience. William Julius Wilson posits in his 1996 book *When Work Disappears* that for the first time since 1900 the majority of the adults in most inner-city ghetto neighborhoods do not work during a given week. This startling announcement could be made even making allowance for those involved with child-care responsibilities and those who cannot work because of disability or age. Joblessness brings about the following experiences: low self-esteem; no income; stigmatization; and the loss of expectations that frame daily life, give activity meaning, and teach discipline. Joblessness makes it difficult to cope with daily life issues and fosters boredom and self-destructive behavior, helping one to internalize oppression. Joblessness also creates an environment where one may hurt another, may join a gang, or may be enticed to do drugs and alcohol. While there are some resources in the ghetto, including family and faith communities, the challenges for healthy survival are incredibly overwhelming.[28] Having noted some of the markers for class and some of the outcomes of class oppression, what do our narratives teach us?

Following some of the models of stratification and class cited earlier, Luke 16 situates a dichotomy where the master can loan and the others need to borrow. One can also see a trichotomy regarding the power structure, with the master being in the upper class, the steward in the middle, and the borrowers in the lower class. Another paradigm would see God as upper, the master as middle, the steward as lower, and the borrowers as underclass, a model paralleling the experience in the ghetto. The issue of who has the power and authority for decision making is most pronounced here. The text does not tell us how the master came to be so wealthy. Did he inherit his fortune? Work for his fortune honestly? Or, like some of the nineteenth- and twentieth-century robber barons in the United States, did he make his fortune at the expense of his workers (e.g., those who worked in steel mills and coal mines or those who laid tracks for the railroad)? That the master had a substantive amount of money makes it more possible for him to be one who has a sense of entitlement when it comes to power and authority. If one wants to

---

[28]Owen Fiss, "What Should Be Done for Those Who Have Been Left Behind?" *Boston Review* (Summer 2000). Also available online at http://bostonreview.mit.edu/BR25.3/fiss.html as of July 2001.

complicate the interpretation, one could see the master's statement of praise for the unjust steward as irony.

While he thanked the steward for being dishonest, he could have actually been ridiculing him with an implied, how dare you lower the debt! and an unspoken, you will pay for this. That he was in a class "superior" to the steward gave him certain privilege. Conversely, even though the master gets less money than he would have, had the steward kept the debts the same, he actually has more than he had before, because previously the debtors had not paid anything on their loans. They were in arrears. When bringing in matters of class, then, the situation is not just about debt, but about appropriate behavior across boundaries, the kinds of stigmas that develop when one individual or group is in debt to someone else who has a superior status based on social class. That the steward lessens the debt reverses the oppression that was in place from the large amount of interest. Does the steward have any real options?

The steward is in the middle: He does not own the resources, and does not owe the master anything but an honest day's work. But the text labels him dishonest. We are not told how to justify this accusation. The text says he was wronged, but later he wronged his master. Could this have been a case of projection? Did the master give the steward the benefit of the doubt, or did he trust his source of information more? Had the master been fair with the steward on previous occasions? The steward could have adopted an attitude that said, "Since someone lied about me and slandered my reputation, lord and master, I will 'slander' your coffers by making sure you do not receive the total amounts due." Such are some of the questions one needs to explore, particularly when reading such a story from a twenty-first–century purview. One needs to observe that any relations based on power are opportunities for abuse or praise. This parable also turns the question of retributive and distributive justice upside down and challenges us to think most carefully about how we negotiate relationships that ought to be built on trust. Trust is also one factor in the classism that emerges in *Cry, the Beloved Country*.

In this stirring drama, classism sits intimately with racism. The oppression of apartheid has been documented, as the celebrated saga of Nelson Mandela makes clear. The language of race and color differentiation and the separate seating for Whites and coloreds in the courtroom scene echoes the apartheid ethos of the Jim Crow American South prior to the 1960s civil rights movement. When the elder Jarvis reads his son's diary, which says the crime is White crime and that Whites will be known as tyrants, he has articulated the case of classism and caste-ism. The bus boycott and John Kumalo's rally against apartheid reflects the awful weight of classism. That the fertile countryside is a bas-relief for the sterility of justice that comes with oppression cannot be lost on the viewer. Yet the incredible transformation that occurs between the two fathers, both elder statesmen in their own right, is a stroke of the incredible. Both fathers have known deep anguish over the plights of their sons. Arthur Jarvis worked for change and justice and the dismantling of apartheid, and his father did not understand him or his actions. Absalom Kumalo became a petty thief, perhaps as a way to contain the rage he felt from the strictures of apartheid and the ugliness he saw in the shanty town, Sophiatown, and his father did not understand him nor his actions. But the story does not stop here. Several ironies must be addressed.

That the son of the umfundisi is named Absalom cannot be lost on the audience. Biblically, Prince Absalom, the third son of King David (2 Sam. 3:3), orders the murder of his half brother Amnon because Amnon raped his sister Tamar (2 Sam. 13:1–29). Absalom Kumalo goes to Johannesburg in search of his aunt, who has become a prostitute. Perhaps influenced by his cousin, by loneliness, by the pain of apartheid, Absalom Kumalo gets into trouble and ends up in reform school, yet with a caring warden who sees some possibility in him. In the Bible, Absalom conspires against his father, David, because he thinks David is losing control and stirring up too much discontent in the nation, which means if David is not careful, he will lose the kingdom and Absalom will not have an opportunity to be king. Absalom gains a following in Israel, is able to have himself named king in Hebron, and chases his own father out of Jerusalem (2 Sam. 15–16). Absalom Kumalo, conversely, is ashamed of what has transpired and stops writing to his parents. Prince Absalom attacks David in an area of Ephraim, but is himself defeated. Despite David's wishes, Absalom is killed by Joab. Absalom rides his mule under thick brush and his head is caught in the oak, leaving him hanging in mid-air when the mule goes on. Joab thrusts three arrows into Absalom's heart. Caught in a robbery attempt, Absalom Kumalo panics and shoots the White man, Arthur Jarvis, one of the few men in Johannesburg who fought for the rights of Blacks. In that twist of irony, of fate, then, Absalom Kumalo kills his "brother," Arthur. The respect that the elder Jarvis and Kumalo have for each other links them and makes their sons brothers. Here a just man and an unjust man die. Just as Prince Absalom dies hanging in a tree, Absalom Kumalo is hung by the neck until he dies. The pathology of apartheid-fashioned classism kills Arthur Jarvis and Absalom Kumalo. The privilege and arrogance that often comes with a life of royalty, which exacerbates classism, kills Prince Absalom. Ironically, despite the entrenched apartheid, everyone—Black, White, and colored—respect the umfundisi. He has the bearing and radiates the grace that ultimately washes away the boundaries of race and class. Is it the man or the office or perhaps both? What, finally, do the voices of the unjust steward, the Absaloms, the Jarvises and the Kumalos teach us about classism? In a most fascinating way, words said to David and his response (2 Sam. 18) when learning about the death of his son, in dialogue with the words of James Jarvis and Stephen Kumalo, provide a powerful lens in reverse for seeing through the glass of class oppression darkly.

After Joab kills Absalom, he sends runners to David, and twice they utter the sentiments that the Lord had delivered David from the power of those who rose up against him (18:28b; 18:31b). When realizing the full brunt of the message, David, deeply moved, utters "O my son Absalom, my son, my son Absalom! Would I had died instead of you, O Absalom, my son, my son" (18:33b). The Lord delivers David, but the priest questions why God does not offer mercy to the umfundisi. The Lord delivers and protects David from the oppressive power rising up against him, but rather than being lifted up above that which will oppress, for the umfundisi and Jarvis, "The thing that's heaviest for all my years is the heaviest for all of your years. It is my son who killed your son." Prince Absalom is murdered by Joab to protect David. Absalom Kumalo murders Arthur Jarvis out of fear. The nation-state of South Africa murders Absalom Kumalo out of a sense of revenge and retributive justice. The umfundisi brings up the recurring topic of fear in the land. Consequently, classism is the misbegotten anguish of perpetuated and embodied fear: fear of difference, fear of the other, fear of lack, fear of powerlessness, fear of losing control. This level of fear becomes exponential in oppressive political situations steeped in the socioeconomic politics of survival. This level of fear becomes exponential in situations where you have the authority to negotiate with someone else's money, as the unjust steward did. Classism perpetuates the misbegotten anguish of grief connected to economics, trapped in pain and punishment. Classism embodies misbegotten anguish as hostility within individual and systemic politics that are often misinterpreted as racism. Fear intensified turns to desire, which metamorphoses as greed, and compounded becomes pain, which exacts a rage that requires a reaction—a need to covet, to hoard, to be superior, to be unique. Such a pathology allows for a level of denial that supports an acquisitive mimesis, that ultimately robs everyone's spirit, creates more lonely people, and intensifies the distance between the haves and have nots.

PART III

Powers
and
Pathologies

Trees with green leaves and red leaves
And yellow leaves and purple leaves
Live in the same gardens,
Each bringing a different kind of beauty;
Each helping sustain the oxygen levels
We humans need to live:
Growing out of red soil and black soil,
Beige sand and brown clay.
We don't complain,
We rejoice in the inherent beauty.

But the color of our skins
With the accompanying cultures
Have been and remain an issue:
One of division and pain and strife
And impotence, and hate, and whoremongering.
And buying and selling human cargo,
Idolatrous practices at the altar of insatiability,
Gluttonous practices riddled with an abject sense of the self:
Forgetting, God gives life, and none other.

As we extend an invitation to embrace the pageantry of color
God created within humanity,
May we see clearly
The many diamonds, rubies, topaz, and pearls,
The gems of humanity created by God
As holy, magnificent, unsaleable
Uncommodifiable, unobjectifiable good.

6

Corrupting
the
Rainbow

Racism Personified

In Alice Walker's book *In Search of Our Mother's Gardens: Womanist Prose,* Walker provides a four-part definition to the term she coined, *Womanist.*[1] One part of the definition entails a little girl questioning her mother. The little girl asks: "Why are Black people so many different colors, from milk white and pale ivory to darkest ebony and blue black?" Her mother responds: "We are different colors, like the rainbow." In talking with my student Juana Francis one afternoon when we were creating a dialogical sermon for an International Women's Day Liturgy, under the auspices of the Center for Women and Religion, Graduate Theological Union, Berkeley, we saw the irony and idiotic sensibility of racism. How is it that human beings get disturbed over the different color of someone else's skin, given that everything in nature has different colors? Even water, soil, and sand have varying colors! Trees and flowers and

---

[1]Alice Walker, *In Search of Our Mother's Gardens: Womanist Prose* (San Diego: Harcourt Brace Jovanovich, 1983).

rivers and oceans are different colors. Why in the world shouldn't human beings have different colored skins? Race is at the seat of a lot of pain, hatred, and demonization. Racism is the cauldron of stereotypes and lies and the need to project insecurities on various people brought in chains or under false pretenses to this country for the sake of the omnipotent mercantilism. (The dollar was not invented until after the American Revolution!) The colonists needed cheap labor, people who could defy the unrelenting heat, dampness, and mosquitoes to plant cotton, sugar, and rice. Those enamored with manifest destiny had to cheat folks indigenous to this land so that the pilgrims and their descendants could conquer some land. Other folk were brought from the Far East and were forced to build railroads. With the bombing of Pearl Harbor, second- and third-generation folk on the West Coast, but not from Hawaii, nor the Midwest nor the East Coast, were put in internment camps because they had the wrong skin tint. (Those of German heritage were not interned since they were not all that different.) In all these instances and in countless other documented American historical moments, a people who could be, were made *other* because they looked different.

Racism often arises out of ignorant taboos and notions of the exotic, the unattainable, and often the desirable, the forbidden fruit. This chapter interrogates history and selected narratives to determine how human actions and attitudes nurture the sin, the arrogance, and pathos of racism. After reviewing various dynamics of racism, I provide an overview of the narratives for Spike Lee's film *Jungle Fever* and the biblical story of Samson and Delilah (Judg. 13–16). I then reflect on the *dramatis personae* of both stories and the characters' actions and attitudes with regard to the stories' complicity or complacency around racism. I conclude by both exploring the contextual nature of racism and offering suggestions as to what changes must occur if we are ever to stem the tide of such a pernicious, repugnant reality.

Racism Revisited from History

Racism, an ugly global phenomenon, invades systemic socioeconomic, political, and monetary structures rife with oppression, discrimination, prejudice, and exploitation. Racism is ubiquitous and pervasive. This pathological bigotry is present when: (1) people, because of their race, have limited freedom of choice in work, movement, or residence; (2) participation in the political process is limited because of race; (3) people are barred from full participation in acquiring economic power through limited educational opportunities; (4) nation-states set policy that relies on the labor of particular racial populations, but deny those same people comparable participation in that nation-state; (5) the stereotypes of racial/ethnic groups in print and popular media denigrate and cause harm; (6) nations or groups profit from geographical and global structures connected to racist beliefs and actions. Influenced by Western theology, Western culture has posited White supremacist ideology and the superiority of White people over against all other races. Concepts such as the elect and people of God, the misuse of the Genesis texts, the Aryan representation of Jesus, and the privatization of Christianity have alienated and excluded many peoples of color and have privileged White races. With the human shadow side, much of the bases of racism exist deep within the subconscious, steeped in fears of anger, guilt, shame, and the unknown. Thus, racism has become normative and occurs because of the injustice that emerges. Injustice manifests amid a distortion in the distribution of power. We must recognize and reject the evil and sin of racial violence, and move toward creating healthier communities and working toward unity as we celebrate differences.[2]

Given that more diversity exists among the genetic profiles within a particular racial group than between them, as well as historical and cross-cultural differences, race seems to be a sociohistorical concept, where the historical context and social relations provide the meaning for the notion of race. Much of the Black-White dichotomy and binary opposition stem from the need for the courts and larger society to decide who could be categorized as White and who could be categorized as Black to maintain the chattel system during slavery and the Jim Crow ethos afterwards. This need led to the scientific quest for racial categorization and classifications in the eighteenth and nineteenth centuries.[3] For those who think race and color do not matter, they should probably read some White supremacist literature, such as the *National Vanguard* that noted "ONLY THE FOOL or the mischief-maker can claim that the same soul dwells in the breast of the Negro, the White, and the Jew. Body and soul are interdependent, and the face more often than not reveals the essence of the inner nature."[4] White supremacists attack race in

---

[2]The Commission on Faith and Order and the Program to Combat Racism, *Racism in Theology; Theology Against Racism* (Geneva: World Council of Churches, 1975), 1–4, 5, 6, 13–15.
[3]Abby L. Ferber, *White Man Falling* (New York: Rowman & Littlefield, 1998), 19, 23.
[4]*National Vanguard*, special issue, in Ferber, *White Man Falling*, 74.

concert with gender and sex, for most of them argue that interracial sex has not only destroyed many civilizations but, as the mongrelization of the White Christian race, is unscientific and immoral.[5]

Racism is not a Black and White issue, even in the United States. During World War II, many Japanese were discriminated against and detained in camps because of virulent, xenophobic, racial prejudice, particularly on the West Coast, against Asians, dubbed the "Yellow Peril." No Italian Americans or German Americans were detained. Although Native Americans helped the first European immigrants, they were betrayed and were on the receiving end of violence and deceit over the land that Native people deemed sacred and White folk deemed property. For their generosity in helping the helpless settlers, Native peoples were murdered, dismembered, and given blankets that spread communicable disease. As racial violence spread to cities such as Boston in the 1750s, vigilantism by upper-class individuals became institutionalized as an excuse to maintain law and order.[6] Racial violence was also cloaked yet perpetuated in patriotic symbols and popular media.

The glorification of the Confederate flag, Thomas Dixon's novels *The Clansman* and *The Leopard's Spots,* and the film based on these two books, *Birth of a Nation,* promoted violence and racism during the early twentieth century. At the same time, the Ku Klux Klan saw a resurgence, broadening its predatory activities beyond lynching and persecution of African Americans to include Catholics, Jews, and new immigrants from eastern and southern Europe. During the New Deal presidency of Franklin D. Roosevelt, organizations such as the Christian Nationalist Crusade promoted Nazi ideology, racial prejudice, and bigotry. Such was the time when Bernard M. Baruch, an adviser to the nation's presidents, was sexist and racist.[7] While today we are more technologically advanced and have more civil rights legislation on the books, the Confederate flag still flies prominently near the state capitol in South Carolina and Black churches and synagogues are still being burned and desecrated. Hate has not gone away. Despite all the documentation, there are still some who decry the Holocaust as a farce. Others have bought into all the stereotypes of all non-White peoples, to the point of acting out their extreme dislike, fear, and ignorance as hate crimes.

---

[5]Ferber, *White Man Falling,* 75, 85.

[6]Bernard Braxton, *Sexual, Racial and Political Faces of Corruption* (Washington, D.C.: Verta Press, 1977), 30, 34–37.

[7]Ibid., 9–12.

The 1992 statistics for the Federal Bureau of Investigation noted that of all reported hate crimes, six of every ten resulted from racial violence and racial bias. Ironically, a country where the majority of persons have immigrant backgrounds, an opportunity for a celebration of difference as harmony, this nation is rife with racial violence. By focusing on the massive racial cleansings and the racial genocide in South Africa, the former Soviet Union, Yugoslavia, and India, we become desensitized to much of the racial violence in the United States. Racial violence exists in the marrow and DNA of the United States soil and persona, and has since the inception of the country. The anti-immigrant sentiments in the United States help fuel increased racial violence and oppression. The increased attacks against Asian Americans have a close correlation with the increasingly tight economic situations in the United States. In the same way that James Byrd was dragged to his death and decapitated in 1998, Vincent Chin was beaten to death with a baseball bat by two automobile workers who had recently been laid off in Detroit, in 1981. Bigotry, hate, and violence traverse class lines notably on our college campuses. The bigotry becomes systemic again when it manifests as environmental and ecological racism, particularly concerning toxic waste dumps, sewage treatment plants, mass transit garages, and landfills. For example, that the stench of the daily processing of 170 million gallons of raw sewage, the pollution of seven of New York City's bus depots, and the marine transfer station that services sanitation trucks from two counties are all located in Harlem is unconscionable. All these facilities are in plain view of a junior high school and a 1,400-unit apartment building complex: environmental racism personified, particularly when the landscape of the rest of Manhattan does not look the same. Such massive garbage has a deleterious effect on everyone, particularly the children. The depths of racism are great and infiltrate all institutions and systems, governmental, business, and retail. Why is it that some minority, impoverished neighborhoods have substandard food in the chain stores in their local grocery stores? And what of the lead and mercury poisoning and contamination that occur frequently in older, more urban communities, communities often populated by non-White people?[8] Some of the racism has involved espionage and intensified fear, scapegoating, and a need to destroy and control.

---

[8]Ginny Gong, "The Pain of Race-Based Violence," *Christian Social Action* 7 (May 1994): 10–12; Vernice Miller, "Self-worth and the Sewage Treatment Plant," *Christian Social Action* 7 (May 1994): 25–27.

From 1938 to 1975, liberal New Deal policies became the context for breeding paranoia and heightened racism, where the House Un-American Activities Committee and the witch-hunting, scare tactics, and blatant lies of Joseph McCarthy and Richard M. Nixon wreaked havoc. These tactics supported character assassinations and ruined people's lives and careers. This paranoia became an American Inquisition that embraced Machiavellian policies of getting away with whatever they could. The institutionalization of racism occurred in government and the church. Bigotry against Jews and African Americans reigned, justified by self-serving, racist biblical hermeneutics. Delusions of grandeur and a sense of racial superiority by the dominant culture afforded and sanctioned these practices. One of the most ludicrous cases, where even sworn testimony of their innocence could not override the hatred of their blackness, was the case of the Scottsboro boys. After the case went to the Supreme Court, the convictions were overthrown because of an improper and inadequate defense. During the next trial, one of the alleged White female rape victims finally came forth as a witness for the defense to state that the boys did not rape the two girls on the train. Despite her testimony and the forensic evidence sustaining her claim, the initial sentence was death for Haywood Patterson and life in prison for the others. Judge James Horton overthrew Patterson's conviction with the defense motion. After four more trials and a sentence of seventy-five years, Patterson managed to escape from prison and left Alabama. All the teens served time in prison, with six years being the least and nineteen years the longest, with parole finally coming for Andrew Wright in 1950.[9] The same pattern of racism appearing in the courts and legal system has pervaded the environs of the church.

There is a history of stark racism throughout the Christian church's history, which involves missionary activity to those alleged savages who need to be civilized and converted, out of a Eurocentric bias. A former director of the Faith and Order Commission of the World Conference of Churches noted that racism is a "theological heresy" with "demonic dimensions."[10] When we view ourselves and those most like us as the center of our reality and our worldview, out of fear we tend to only like and want to be around those made in

---

[9]Braxton, *Sexual, Racial and Political Faces,* 70–94, 109–22, 133–38.
[10]Barbara Rogers, *Race: No Peace without Justice* (Geneva: World Council of Churches, 1980), 2.

our image, thus participating in idolatry and blasphemy. Many churches have strong ties to racist practices and the related ideologies of domination. To shift the dynamics of racist oppression calls for an awareness of entrenched, apartheid-based religious practices and the need to celebrate the unity of the church, along with the specifics of contextuality and history and the impact of privilege and power.[11] Some of these apartheid-based practices have occurred within the purview of missionary activities to two-thirds world peoples and the invasion of Western military engagements and economic pursuits across areas of Asia and Africa in the name of discipleship, interlaced with colonialism (see chapter 3). In the United States, Christian denominations have failed to tap the resources of Indigenous peoples.[12] A few hymns have been translated into Native peoples' languages, but more often than not many of their practices have been exploited and misappropriated under the guise of being inclusive, without understanding the values and ethos of the practices. Such misappropriation is often attached to a price tag: We study those deemed other to then sell what we learn about them without sharing the proceeds. At the end of the day, racism is closely tied to economics. We oppress to limit the competition. We oppress to take, revise, and market what we learn from those deemed other. Thus, we tend to not be bothered by current economic and technological developments, with corporate farms, multinational banks, corporations, and American businesses moving to two-thirds world geographic regions. We go about business as usual, though those deemed other work in modern-day sweatshops for much below what any company would have to pay in the United States in wages and benefits. Racism and racial violence have been and still are a plague upon our nation and upon the world. So often they are rooted in the need to control where the money goes. Granted, interracial and intraracial racism exist, but to understand what is at stake requires that we name the reality of White supremacist hatred and of White privilege, since the arena of Whiteness is the arena of dominant culture the world over.

White supremacist discourse depicts Whites, those of European descent, as under the attack of racial oppression. That sense of oppression is license for the blatant hatred of Jews and all non-Whites.

---

[11]Ibid., 1–7.
[12]Ibid., 9, 13.

Amid this kind of hatred, one needs to investigate the construction of Whiteness, the reality of White privilege, White identity, and how being an oppressor affects those who perpetuate oppression and violence. Just what people perceive about racial oppression has a lot to do with the ideological framework out of which people experience what is going on.[13] The impact of ideological power arises from the power it has to "define what it does and does not make sense to say, the power to define knowledge and reality."[14] Since race is a social, not a biological construct, racialized human beings are not abstract and do not exist in a vacuum, but are themselves discursive effects, elements inherent to the dialogue. White supremacist ideology, then, is a discourse where tracking groups, journalists, scholars, and practitioners all help shape and produce the White supremacist movement and reality. How one handles the concept of Whiteness and White supremacy shapes how one handles racism. Unfortunately, viewing White supremacists as extremist organizations often removes the onus of institutionalized, systemic racism inherent to all of society. Sociologist Abby Ferber argues that not only is White supremacist ideology about efforts to redefine masculinity but that most White supremacist groups do not perform most of the hate crimes. Thus, hate crimes are being perpetrated not by extremists, but by our neighbors next door and down the street. In working to reconstruct masculinity, racist oppression intersects with questions of gender, because understanding the issue of interracial sexuality is germane to understanding White supremacist cosmology. White supremacist discourse can be volatile and, like a chameleon, vary and change "colors" to respond to any situation or issue.[15] Racism and the continuum of ways people express racist thoughts and commit racist actions are complex and multidimensional. Some of these complexities emerge with the review and subsequent analysis of the two stories that will serve as case studies for this chapter: Spike Lee's *Jungle Fever,* and the biblical story of the last judge, Samson, and his lover, Delilah.

The Complexities of Race in Narrative

Set in Harlem, Manhattan, and Bensonhurst, New York, *Jungle Fever* explores the many dynamics concerning contemporary race

---

[13]Ferber, *White Man Falling,* 3–6.
[14]Ibid.,7.
[15]Ibid., 8–13.

relations and interracial romance. A telling feature about what may unfold occurs in the opening dedication, "To Yusef Hawkins," a young African American male murdered in predominantly White, working-class Bensonhurst on the way back from a party. Flipper Purify, an upwardly mobile, Black urban architect with a hopeful future and a devoted family experiences oppression firsthand. Out of sexual curiosity, romantic fantasy, some sense of neglect, and perhaps pain, Purify and Angela (Angie) Tucci, an Italian American secretary who is an office temp, have an affair. Their affair and their telling friends about the affair have major domestic and social repercussions. Flipper and Angie err in telling their friends and expecting them to keep it a secret. Flipper tells his friend Cyrus, who then tells his wife, who proceeds to tell Drew, Flipper's wife. Drew publicly humiliates Flipper by throwing his clothes out of the window and then angrily dismissing him. Angie tells two girlfriends, who tell others, and the story of the affair eventually gets back to Angie's racist father and brothers. Her father violently abuses her and beats her for dating a non-Italian, someone who is outside her neighborhood, her ethnic group, and her race. One of the questions to ponder concerns Angie and Flipper: Is their relationship just about "jungle fever," a momentary curiosity about racial/sexual stereotypes and the taboos for interracial dating, or could it have been something more? In addition to the Tucci and Purify relationship, two other characters are especially critical: Gator and Paulie.[16]

Gator, Flipper's crack-addicted brother, is always hustling for money. He targets his parents and his brother Flipper. Gator keeps returning to his parent's home, ruled over by a puritanical and closed-minded father, the Good Reverend Doctor. The Good Reverend Doctor rails at Flipper for his infidelity and at Gator for his crack addiction and drug dealing. When Gator comes to the house while the Good Reverend Doctor is away to get money from his mother, and she does not have any, Gator starts to get belligerent. The Good Reverend Doctor returns from his walk, finds Gator in his home, after forbidding him to return. He shoots Gator and places the gun on top of his open Bible. In Bensonhurst, Angie's dad has been trying to match her up with Paulie, who runs a newsstand and ice cream shop. For a while, Angie and Paulie dated. But Paulie really likes an African American woman who frequents his newsstand.

---

[16]James Monaco et al., *The Movie Guide: A Comprehensive, Alphabetical Listing of the Most Important Films Ever Made* (New York: Putnam Publishing, 1992), 413.

Paulie, one of the most sympathetic characters in the film, has to deal with an obsessive father on one side and a group of lazy, belligerent neighbors who frequent his store, on the other. Paulie and Angie commisserate about life within and outside their neighborhood. Though his neighbors beat him up, Paulie does go out on a date with the Black woman who frequents his store, the only one who talks to him about his intellectual pursuits. Flipper does return to visit Drew, but the film ends without resolving how their relationship will work out. As he leaves the house telling his daughter it is up to her mother whether or not he returns, Flipper is met by a very young hooker. Flipper holds her and screams, "NO!" No to her violation, no to social injustice, no to his infidelity and stupidity, no to the pain he has caused everyone. In sum, the race matters in *Jungle Fever* include a contrast in Black and White, juxtaposed to each other, and separate, primarily of African and Italian descent. At the end of his story, Samson does not yell no, but does pull down the pillars of the palace.

The beginning of Samson's story parallels other births to barren women. Twice the Angel of the Lord promises the wife of Manoah she will conceive and bear a son. She also learns that the child is to be a Nazirite from birth to death. Samson's life is filled with conflict and tedious decision making, particularly when he tangles with the Philistines and is dealing with covenant obedience. Samson wants a Philistine bride, and his parents encourage him to get a wife from one of his own tribe. Samson and the unnamed Philistine woman from Timnah get married. After Samson has made a wager about a riddle with the Philistines during the wedding feast, his unnamed wife cries and pleads with him for the answer. He tells her, and she tells the Philistines. As Samson tells them that they would not have known the answer if "you had not plowed with my heifer," we encounter an objectification, due to gender and perhaps to race. In that same instance, the Spirit of the Lord comes over him, and he kills thirty men to get their garments to give to the Philistines who answered the riddle. In hot anger, he goes back to his father's house and finds out that his wife has been given to his best man (Judges 13, 14).

Next Samson takes revenge for his wife's being taken from him by burning the fields of the Philistines. When the Philistines raid Judah, the men of Judah leave to bind Samson. Although tied up, Samson escapes when the Spirit of the Lord again comes upon him, and he kills a thousand men. Shortly afterward, Samson wants the

Lord to deliver him of thirst, which God does (Judges 15). Samson then takes up with a harlot, escapes a slaughter at midnight, and falls in love with Delilah.

The Philistine rulers come to Delilah and offer her eleven hundred pieces of silver to help them find out the source of Samson's strength. Three times Delilah inquires about Samson's strength, and three times he tells her the wrong answer. Delilah then asks Samson how he can say he loves her when his heart is not with her. So Samson tells Delilah that he is a Nazirite and that his hair must not be cut or he will lose his strength. He falls asleep, and Delilah has his hair cut. As the Philistines come to seize him, Samson thinks he can get away, not realizing that the Spirit of the Lord has left him. The Philistines grab him, gouge out his eyes, and bring him to Gaza (Judges 16:21, 22). At the celebration to Dagon, the Philistines' god, the Philistines want Samson to make sport for them. Samson calls on God to give him strength once more that he might exact retribution. Samson requests that he be allowed to die with the Philistines. Samson pulls down the pillars that form the support for the house; he dies, and many Philistines die with him. His family comes for him, and he is buried in the tomb of Manoah's father. Samson judged Israel for twenty years (Judges 16). In sum, the race matters of Samson's story deal with the Israelites and the Philistines and their gods. The Israelite God helps them overcome, but in the whole of Judges, the narrator repeats "they did evil in God's sight." Whereas the language of the text does not explicitly call into question the notions of national or racial/ethnic identity, that the two enemies are identified culturally opens the door for exploration.

Dramatis Personae: The Truth beneath the Pain of a Racist Environment

Blatant and subtle issues in *Jungle Fever* hinge on stereotypes, perceptions, and reactions in response to the inherent racism in the United States. At his architectural firm, Flipper has requested an African American assistant and they get him an Italian American temp. When he consults with the managing associates, they claim his request sounds like reverse discrimination. Later, recounting the matter, Flipper tells his best friend, Cyrus, "I'm just a natural Black man trying to survive in a cruel and harsh White corporate America." Flipper's wife, Drew, aware of these sentiments, cautions Flipper that he may not get his pending promotion, even though Flipper asserts that all the company's awards are because of his own work. That color is an issue weaves like a Bach fugue throughout the movie, and it affects everything from Flipper's promotion to all the sociocultural and family dynamics around Flipper and the temp, Angie.

In one of Angie and Flipper's late night conversations at the office, before their relationship becomes sexual, they discuss skin color. After Angie acknowledges that she was thinking about Flipper's skin color, Flipper laughs and says it is amazing what preoccupation people have with skin color. He recounts the litany of names he has been called, every derogatory name for a Black person, and juxtaposes that statement with the reality that White people love a deep, dark tan. One day for lunch Angie and Flipper go to a restaurant and are not being served because the Black server abhors the fact that Angie is White. One of the most powerful scenes in the film, next to the surrealistic crack scene at the "Taj Mahal Crack Den," is the women's "war council," when Drew and her friends talk about men, dating, and color.

There is much confusion, conflict, and pain over issues pertaining to race, sex, dating, stereotypes, and the need to be loved. This group of upwardly mobile, professional Black women talk about good Black men. The conversation is like a variation on the theme of skin color, interracial dating, and all the accompanying pain. The pain is so great for many around the living room because Flipper and Drew were considered the ideal. If they cannot make it, who can? To compensate, one individual counters that Angie is probably low-class White trash who did not finish high school. The level of rage and pain intensifies as someone claims that all Black men, then, are dogs. Consequently, one may as well date White men, since there are not any good Black men. Another says all Black men are dogs: drug addicts, in jail, or homosexuals. The good ones, these women claim, know they are worthless and they have ten babies all over the place.

When asked what the options are, another woman brings up the matter of class and education. As sophisticated, educated Black women, they are looking in all the wrong places by not considering bus drivers, truck drivers, or garbage men. The question is, How many Black men do they know who can deal with a Black woman who makes more money? This is not a war council to only blame Black men, they also blame White women for throwing themselves at Black men. Stereotypically, one woman notes that White women want sex with Black men. When another argues that they are losing their men, another woman calls her on the carpet because she does not date Black men. In response, she says she just wants a man who will be nice to her. Another woman says she is not into rainbow sex, that if necessary, she will go to Africa to find a true Black man. Amid the conversation about reality checks, class, Mandingo-stud stereotypes, and taboos about interracial dating, issues around self-esteem and intraracial racism and male lust emerge.

One participant asks a rhetorical question, "Do you know what it is like to not be liked?" She notes that during high school (they would have probably been in school during the years of segregation) all the boys went after the light-skinned girls, and today they are after the gusto, the White girls. The women seem to be in a catch-22 situation because of their dependence on men for their affirmation while they loathe, almost despise, these same men. Noting that most of the Black men who have made it have a White girl on their arms, one woman argues that most Black men seem to have no race consciousness, no sense of responsibility to "their people"; a fundamental lack of respect. In response, another woman takes the argument out of racial categories to that of sexuality: "I don't know any man who will say no" to sex. Drew ends the conversation, saying, "It don't matter what color she is; my man is gone." Her pain is just as raw around color matters, however, when Flipper visits her at work.

Flipper wants to talk, but Drew is not interested. Back in her office, Drew says that she guesses she is not White enough. She argues that Flipper has a complex about color (the audience is already privy to his feelings). Drew reminds him of how insane that is and how he knows the issues she has had to deal with all of her life: "I've told you how they called me high yellow, White nigger, half-breed, mongrel, octoroon…Don't you know that White people hate Black people because they are not Black. Color has them both messed up. Maybe this is why this hurts me so much. I trusted you and I loved you." Part of the fabric of their own relationship, even prior to Flipper's infidelity, is the stigmatism around color, especially Black and White, and the mixture within the populations of African descent because of miscegenation, because slave masters took great sexual liberties with slave women. The same issues arise about color across town in Bensonhurst, in the neighborhood and at the luncheonette that Paulie runs.

When Angie's Dad learns about her affair with Flipper, he goes ballistic: "I didn't raise you to sleep with a nigger…I raised you to be a good Catholic girl." Her dad calls her a disgrace and beats her so badly that the two brothers have to pull him off her. Later in the luncheonette, her brothers and the other Italian guys who hang around the store engage in a verbal tirade, calling Flipper an eggplant, a spook. They proceed to talk about what Black women they would sleep with and about how Blacks have taken over all the sports. While none of them have ever voted, other than Paulie, the group talks about corrupt Black officials like Marion Berry, and they highlight a Central Park raping incident. These men play the blame game out of their own insecurities and their refusal to take responsibility for their own lives, and they begrudge anyone else who does. As they have begun to speak in stereotypes, it seems as if these stereotypes take on a life of their own. Someone calls the police when Angie and Flipper are sparring on the street.

When the cops come, Flipper tries to downplay their relationship as Angie angrily challenges the cops for stopping them, since they are lovers and are only playing. Flipper tries to deflect the situation and later asks Angie if she was trying to get him killed by telling New York police that he and she were lovers. The power of color prejudice, even between the two of them, emerges yet again when Flipper and Angie talk about their future together. Flipper says, no children; no babies; no octoroon, quadroon, mulatto babies; besides, he is married. Angie asks Flipper, "Don't you have a child with White blood?" Flipper argues that it is hard enough being a Black person; that being of mixed heritage is like being mixed nuts. Although they have dated, they ultimately realize that they both come out of racist environments, and finally Flipper gives up. He says the notion that love can overcome everything is true only in Disney films. He contends that they both were just curious, her about Blackness, him about Whiteness. Whether mere curiosity and fascination about Black male sexual prowess and idealized White female beauty were the only connections between Flipper and Angie remains to be seen, since director Spike Lee did not fully develop these ideas or the attraction with these two principal characters. What is clear is that there is a lot of pain and hurt, anger, distrust, ambiguity, and doubt around color matters in both the Purify and Tucci families, and in the two communal conversations—the Black women's war council, and the Italian luncheonette coarse talk. In toto, the conversations span a continuum, from sorrow and grief, through anger, to humor.[17]

---

[17]Information found on http://www.suntimes.com/ebert/ebert_reviews/1991/06/653818.html in July 2001.

Where *Jungle Fever* clearly names some of the stereotypes, taboos, and pain around matters of race and ultimately power, the story of Samson and Delilah raises questions about power and gender and, I contend, makes room to deal with issues of racial/ethnic identity and violence as well. However, Delilah is not the only biblical woman we can refer to regarding questions of race, judgment, and power.

J. Daniel Hays argues that Miriam and Aaron, Moses' sister and brother, had problems with Moses when he married a Cushite (Black) woman (Numbers 12:1). For speaking, Miriam ends up with a dermatological disease that makes her skin look white, and thus she is banned from her camp for seven days. Some scholars reduce the Cushite woman and Zipporah into one character. Hays notes that the term Cushite specifically pertains to the Black civilization located south of Egypt and that Zipporah was from Northern Arabia. Thus, Miriam's punishment for taking exception to Moses' wife is that she turns White as retribution for her taking a stand against a Black woman: delightful irony.[18] Though this text does not reprimand Aaron, it is fascinating to see the divine response to one who challenges divinely created beauty, divine and human power and authority.

In seeing the story of Delilah and Samson against the base of power relations, we see Samson's phenomenal Yahweh-given physical strength that allows him to do incredible acts of gratuitous violence. Throughout the book of Judges, Yahweh's spirit is the source of power and the only way Israel can escape oppression. Samson's strength and weakness are based in knowledge as power, that is, knowledge about the source of his power. When he loses physical strength, he also loses mental power. Neither Samson nor Delilah fares well at the end. Scholars have called Samson everything from stupid and mentally ill, to an antihero and weak-minded. Many see Delilah as one who whines, deceives, and betrays. Typically, Samson, like other specially gifted persons from an oppressed group, uses his powers, when given the opportunity, to exact gratuitous violence.[19] To pursue the issues of race, we first must see the overarching questions of promise and fulfillment crafted by the Deuteronomist.

This narrative involves a promise-and-fulfillment episode within a larger sequence of a reversal of expectations, where the male

---

[18]Daniel Hays, "Moses: The Private Man Behind the Public Leader," *Bible Review* 16 (August 2000): 16–26, 60–62.

[19]Carol Smith, "Samson and Delilah: A Parable of Power?" *Journal for the Study of the Old Testament* 76 (1997): 51, 55.

characters are usually led by the female characters. Judges 13 begins with a promise, a set of expectations, that are later reversed. Samson's story contrasts power and weakness, high energy and spirits with low ethical praxis, sacred and secular.[20] The backdrop for the lives of all the judges is the deliverance formula motif: a rhetorical framework that forms the common patterns for the stories. Israel does evil in Yahweh's sight as they turn to other gods. Yahweh gives them to be oppressed. Israel cries to Yahweh. Yahweh raises up a judge-deliverer. The deliverer defeats the oppressor. The people are faithful while the deliverer is alive, and the land rests for forty to eighty years, which means peace reigns for that time period. Samson's story also begins without a particularly sociohistorical time or location. The story announces the birth of a son to a barren woman, a son who later becomes a judge, and like Sarah, the unnamed wife of Manoah becomes pregnant during the visitation of Yahweh's messenger or Yahweh. In addition, Samson's beginnings are unique in that he starts with every advantage (born to a pious, married Israelite couple of the tribe of Dan) where other judges have some disadvantage; for example, Deborah was a woman in a patriarchal society, and Ehud's being left-handed was viewed as a deformity. Even though Samson seems captivated by superficial values, Yahweh still uses him as an instrument of deliverance. Given his many shortcomings, Samson falls short of the high level of expectations accorded him: (1) his status as a Nazirite, (2) the annunciation of his birth to his mother, and (3) his reception of Yahweh's spirit in four distinct acts. Samson's story is painfully humorous and full of irony. Along with the uses of wordplay, his strength is foiled by his own hopelessness, and ultimately the reading audience knows more about what is going on than the last judge, Samson himself, knows. He embodies the loss of his tribe's unity and covenant faith[21] amid the many different relationships he has with women. To include the issues around women is not far afield, for even the film *Jungle Fever* cannot make its point about racism and racial violence and the related issues of drugs and poverty without talking about the role and function of the women.

With biblical editors, women who are relationally controlled by men usually stand in the men's shadows and are under patriarchal

---

[20]Lillian R. Klein, *The Triumph of Irony in the Book of Judges* (Sheffield, England: Almond Press, 1988), 109.

[21]Ibid., 109–12, 115, 117, 125, 138, 139.

authority because of male hegemony. Women separated from male authority are often depicted as independent and autonomous. The women divorced from male authority tend to experience economic difficulty: widows and prostitutes. Some scholars see Delilah as exhibiting prostitute-like behavior, because her sexuality is a major factor in attracting Samson and ensuring her own stability by gaining access to the answer to Samson's tremendous strength. The silence around Delilah's background actually forges a sense of independence, because she is not shaped or defined by a relationship with a man. Interestingly, there are many parallels between Delilah's story and that of Samson's Timnite wife. Both women convince Samson to tell them a secret; they both are influenced by the Philistines; both of their stories begin with a particular depicted scene; and it takes both of them several times of interrogating Samson before he divulges the information. The similarities press us to read the stories of these two women as a pair, which also helps us to see the distinctions. Of the four women in the Samson story, however, Delilah is the only named character. The Timnite wife functions within a patriarchal system, and Delilah operates outside of patriarchal authority. Unlike Samson's mother, Manoah's wife; the Timnite wife; and the Gazaite prostitute, Delilah gains power, through learning Samson's secret about his hair.[22]

Some readers view the women in Samson's life as either good women, like his mother, or bad women, like Delilah. Samson's unnamed mother is a good, safe woman because she does not offer any trouble, poses no threat. She demonstrates how her implicit cooperation makes patriarchy possible. Patriarchy relies on women's cooperation as systemically and institutionally it uses fear and force to manipulate and control the women; and the women are complicit in their own oppression, which is one reason that patriarchy is alive and well. These stories also separate the connection between procreation and eroticism. The good woman–bad woman scenario, where the former are respectable and the latter are disreputable, makes gender solidarity just about impossible.[23] We see some of the same tension and disparity in the *Jungle Fever* conversation among

---

[22]Susan Ackerman, *Warrior, Dancer, Seductress, Queen: Women in Judges and Biblical Israel* (New York: Doubleday, 1998), 219, 225, 230, 232–35.

[23]J. Cheryl Exum, "Feminist Criticism: Whose Interests Are Being Served?" in *Judges and Method: New Approaches in Biblical Studies,* ed. Gayle Yee (Minneapolis: Fortress Press, 1990), 78–83.

Drew and her friends. Delilah's issues also relate to identity, but of a different sort.

Delilah's identity is not shaped by a genealogy or skin tones, but by geology, with the name of the region, a place that is rootless in place and time. Lillian Klein notes that, given her availability to men and that she symbolizes a low moral and ethics quotient, Delilah may be a "prostitute betrayer."[24] Her allegiance is to her people, the Philistines, and her own profit margin, over against her lover, Samson.[25] The one named woman in Samson's story, Delilah often gets short shrift and is dubbed a villain who causes Samson's demise. Her wants or desires drive the story, and she is her own woman. She handles matters of love with Samson and matters of business with the Philistines. She does not trick Samson, but asks him outright about the source of his strength. In telling Delilah everything, which was known previously only to his mother and himself, Samson shifts his loyalty from his mother to Delilah, his "substitute lover-mother."[26] Though set in a patriarchal society, the text mentions no father, husband, or brother to care for Delilah, so she fends for herself and ends up with eleven hundred pieces of silver, quite a nest egg, which provides her financial stability. Perhaps Flipper's one-time attraction to Angie mirrors Samson's frequent attraction to Philistine women, because Delilah is the last in a series of foreign women who captivated Samson's attention.[27] Using the verbal and limited physical abuse in *Jungle Fever* related to racism as a lens, one is led to question Samson's violence and wonder what frames his actions, in addition to his self-centered willfulness.

The violence in the Samson story creates a dead hero, not a leader who helps reestablish Israel's autonomous authority. He is also not able to regenerate Israel's vitality amid a seamless narrative that produces an independent, peaceful, well-integrated society. God initiates the violence because of Israel's evil doings. Though it seems Samson is irresponsible and self-centered, Bowman and Swanson argue that the Deuteronomistic narrator indicates that his request to marry a Philistine woman was from the Lord, unbeknownst to his

---

[24]Klein, *Triumph of Irony,* 121.

[25]Ibid., 119.

[26]Danna Nolan Fewell, "Judges," in *The Women's Bible Commentary,* ed. Carol A. Newsom and Sharon H. Ringe (Louisville: Westminster/John Knox, 1992), 74.

[27]Ibid., 73–74.

mother or father (Judges 14:4).[28] Yahweh gets Samson out of scrapes several times, and Samson acknowledges this fact. However, when the Philistines send their Delilah, their "secret agent," to find out the source of his strength, Yahweh does not bail Samson out this time. Samson asks for strength to overcome and asks to die with the Philistines. Earlier the narrator stated that Samson would only be able to begin the process of deliverance for Israel from the Philistines. Although God sanctioned and supported Samson's violence, which results in Samson's demise, God seems to understand that violence leads to death, but God offers no other options.[29] In *Jungle Fever,* Flipper initially appears to be on top of the world and to have it all: success, family, friends. His venture into jungle fever, his affair with a young, inexperienced Italian American woman, and the many ensuing conversations reveal a veneer of success and a depth of pain, insecurity, and hatred for self and for others. Samson seems to experience many of the same emotions. Viewing a Black man from Harlem and a White woman from Bensonhurst dialogically with an Israelite man and a Philistine woman makes for interesting reflection.

In many ways, Flipper and Samson have it all. They have various strengths and the love of their childhood homes. They are gifted in their professions and seem to have some clout. Their personal and professional successes, however, seem to be undermined by their own weaknesses, which both then perpetuate. The insecurities of both Flipper and Samson allow people to recognize them and take advantage of them. The firm takes advantage of Flipper; some women and the Philistines are able to take advantage of Samson. Flipper and Samson both become obsessed with women who ultimately will have a hand in their demise. Flipper clearly walks into the face of all the Black-White taboos. Samson's fascination with foreign women pushes him to lose his life, the thoughts and desires of God notwithstanding. What about the analogy between Angie and Delilah?

Delilah, a complex, fascinating character, is associated not with a particular town, but a region: a flood bed or wadi that cuts through both the fertile coastal range and the harsh Judean hills. Angie is from Bensonhurst. She has brothers and a father, but like Paulie, her mother is dead. Delilah is a Philistine woman without historical

---

[28]Richard G. Bowman and Richard W. Swanson, "Samson and the Son of God or Dead Heroes and Dead Goats: Ethical Readings of Narrative Violence in Judges and Matthew," *Semeia* 77 (1997): 61, 64–65.

[29]Ibid., 68–69, 71–72.

or specific geographical roots and of inconsequential genealogical lines. A woman of independent means, Delilah is an entrepreneur who works with men and uses her sexuality to her benefit. Angie has a high school education and is dependent in that she cannot break free of the codependency of her family. She has become their chief maid and bottle washer, whose place in life is to wait on the men in her family. Delilah's ambiguity in her relationship with Samson makes her out to be the worst of his three women: His spouse's fear causes her to betray Samson, the whore of Gaza does not support or betray her client; and Delilah betrays him for a price despite the fact that Samson loves her. Because Delilah is a Philistine, the narrator of the story entices the reader to judge Delilah by Israelite ethos and mores. Angie's relationship with Flipper is at best a fling wrapped in taboo and curiosity. Angie's ambiguity in her relationship with Flipper is that the relationship lacks depth. Her ambiguity in her relationship with Paulie is that it is not genuine. They want the relationship because their families want the two of them together. Ultimately, they know they cannot be involved. Many see Delilah as a temptress and a prostitute. Drew's friends see Angie as White trash. One can also see Angie as a product of her neighborhood, of a misogynistic, racist mentality, where the forbidden is so utterly desirable, and to go against convention is to defy everyone. Many children delve into premature sexual activities for the same reason: If something is that bad, it must really be good. We can see Delilah, then, as a person who uses Samson's love to help her people. As a foreign woman, Delilah is in an interracial relationship with Samson, which juxtaposes their differences and affects how they understand each other and where their allegiances lie. In Judges, since no father or husband is identified and Delilah must fend for herself, one can see her liaison with Samson as a smart entrepreneurial move. One can see Angie's relationship with Flipper in the same vein. At work, she was valued and not just an extension of her office equipment. Obviously Flipper was smart, so if he advanced, she would too. Unfortunately for Angie and Flipper, their relationship became sexual and never fully developed as friendship. The relationship between Delilah and Samson can be viewed as a ritual process where Delilah and her people want to find out the power behind Samson's strength. She is probably offered eleven hundred pieces of silver for obtaining information about Samson, not for any sexual services or ritual prostitution. In following the men's direction as to how to manipulate Samson, Delilah seems to be following practices of Israelite women who follow this path for obtaining knowledge. Angie is young and naive; Flipper is older but torn: torn about his treatment at the firm, torn about his brother's crack addiction, wondering "Is this all there is?" in all his relationships, and looking for affirmation in some of the wrong places. One could argue that Delilah does not seduce Samson, but speaks directly to him, using three elements: bind/binding, ridicule, and strength. Love and binding stand in opposition for Delilah, but are one and the same thing for Samson. Delilah seems to expose Samson at his weakest, his love for her. At the same time, her act from the Philistine perspective is a politically astute move, often not the purview of ethics.[30] The relationship between Angie and Flipper is a catalyst for surfacing a lot of the Sturm und Drang around the intersection of race and sex.

Because Delilah uses her sexuality to get from Samson what she wants, one could argue that she does seduce him. She nags and bothers him until he tells her what she needs to know. She lies to Samson, and the Philistines manipulate her to be able to overtake Samson. Thus, we may see Delilah as deceitful and a traitor. When Angie pushes Flipper to talk about their future together, he remains committed to his wife and his daughter, Ming. Further, he has such confusion around skin color and race that he adamantly says he will not help bring any mixed children into the world, oblivious to the fact that his daughter's heritage, going back several generations, is undoubtedly mixed. If we focus on Angie's courage to think for herself and not be skewed by her upbringing, then we have to applaud her for being more inclusive, while we chide her for participating in adultery. If we assume Delilah is a Philistine, then she becomes an entrepreneur or resourceful woman who uses her "feminine wiles" to bring Samson down. Without her, the Philistines never could have captured Samson. We may not like her portrayal, but during her time and with her options, she used what was available to her amid a gender-oppressive society. Does received text take this reading because Delilah is a creative woman? Or because she is a foreign woman? Do we see Angie as a tease and slut or as a curious, immature young woman?

---

[30]Lillian R. Klein, "The Book of Judges: Paradigm and Deviation in Images of Women," in *A Feminist Companion to Judges,* ed. Athalya Brenner (Sheffield, England: Sheffield Academic Press, 1993), 61–66.

Critical to one's interpretation about Delilah is the question of whether the author of Judges is concerned about the actual circumstances of women or constructing a polemical point, pro or con, about women's realities. What is Spike Lee ultimately exploring? Lee allows us to see the deep hurt that Drew experiences and the vulnerability and caring side of Paulie. We have an opportunity to ponder some of the Good Reverend Doctor's doctrinaire attitude. We may celebrate Gator's honesty; in one fleeting moment, we see his regrets. We are not so privileged to delve that deeply into Angie or Flipper. That Delilah uses seduction, dishonesty, and her sexual prowess expresses a lot about the mix of power within human relationships. That *Jungle Fever* involves a mutual seduction scene between Flipper and Angie on his office desk, dishonesty, and a curiosity about Black sexuality and the fantasy and drama around Whiteness expresses a magnetism about the mix of denial, power, and need for hope within human relationships, particularly racialized ones.

And there is much ambiguity in both stories. Delilah's social location (prostitute or wife), ethnic/cultural background (Philistine or Israelite), and her power out of weakness stand over against Samson's own agenda and power. That Angie and Flipper are both caught at a vulnerable moment in their lives over against all the pain, unresolved hatred, and low self-esteem in both their communities cries out for healing and wholeness. Carol Smith suggests that we read Judges 13–16 as a narrative about power relationships, the types of power, who has power, and how they use the power: dominant Philistines versus the powerless Israelites; powerless Israelites with a covenantal, retributive justice God; and Yahweh versus Dagon.[31] I strongly suggest we all see *Jungle Fever* many more times and ask the same questions that Carol Smith raises for the Judges text. Part of what we will discover is that the pathological presence of racism has long roots in world history.

Globally or domestically, we still find that many women and non-White persons with the same qualifications and work ethic as White men still do not get the same salaries. Racism, an ideology of violence, and racial violence (the attacks on human beings and nature due to being deemed other) are a cancerous pathology, undergirded by an intricate neurological and alimentary system known as White supremacist propaganda.

---

[31]Smith, "Samson and Delilah," 46–50, 54.

Ugliness: The Contextual Nature of Racism and Some Alternatives

In Toni Morrison's *The Bluest Eye*,[32] the concept of ugliness is the metaphor for all the self-loathing, pain, deceit, hatred, and crippling codependency, rooted in racism, that exists within the Breedlove family. The name in itself is irony, for the family does not breed love, but hate. Longtime rubrics of ugliness and hatred in the United States are the combined pathologies of White privilege, external racism, and intraracial racism: ugliness personified, the ugliness that traps, defiles, and kills Pecola Breedlove psychologically and spiritually.

Pecola Breedlove searches for her self by searching for the beauty she will possess if she acquires blue eyes. This quest, set as a female *Bildungsroman,* results from Pecola's distorted cosmology as a pubescent African American female in America.[33] Her cosmology represents a cultural mutilation that links physical beauty with virtue and notions of love as necessary prerequisites to romance.[34] The symphonic pieces of her world evoke a concerto of blue-eyed blondness. Pecola's answering solo is the wail of an untuned oboe: No orchestra tunes to her pitch or plays her lyric. Her melody is a solo dirge of blue notes. The concerto is Pecola's dysfunctional family and a society that denies her significance, love, health, and well-being before her birth. Pauline, Pecola's mother, creates silent music in a cinematic fantasy world and fashions her *in vitro* daughter to fit her delusions of White beauty represented on the silver screen. Cholly, Pecola's father, creates a free-spirited, dissonant song that kills. Humiliated and unloved in his youth, Cholly loves Pecola enough to touch her, with a caress that violates her spirit, and leads to her lapse into schizophrenic oblivion. The music created by the Breedloves is misunderstood and becomes an "aesthetic of transgression," one that idolizes a single ideal of beauty,[35] that manifests and breeds hate. Their hateful counterpoint denies each family member an opportunity to be a whole person. For example, Pecola's self-actualization embodies the tunes of alienation and annihilation. The family's self-destructive ethos calls out ugliness. The Blackness and poverty surrounding the Breedlove family is

[32]Toni Morrison, *The Bluest Eye* (New York: Penguin/PLUME, 1970).

[33]Phyllis Klotman, "Dick-And-Jane and the Shirley Temple Sensibility in *The Bluest Eye*," *Black American Literature Forum* 13 (1979): 123.

[34]Barbara Christian, "Community and Nature: The Novels of Toni Morrison," *The Journal of Ethnic Studies* 7 (Winter 1980): 69, 73.

[35]Shelley Wong, "Transgression as Poesis in *The Bluest Eye*," *Callaloo* 13 (1990): 474.

common, but their ugliness is unique. Ugliness goes beyond perceived physical description by others and depicts the Breedlove's metaphor for existence: as anthem, their lives of ugliness praise nothingness; as prayer, their ugliness chants "I am victim"; as benediction, their ugliness smothers them and proclaims "Curse." The ugliness embodied by Pecola's family exacerbates their racial and social handicap and offers Pecola no respite or refuge, only rejection.

> No one could have convinced them that they were not relentlessly and aggressively ugly...the father, Cholly['s], ugliness...was behavior, the rest of the family...wore their ugliness, put it on...although it did not belong to them...You looked at them and wondered why they were so ugly; you looked closely and could not find the source. Then you realized that it came from conviction, their conviction.[36]

Their proof of guilt of the sin of ugliness permits Mrs. Breedlove to wear ugliness as martyrdom; son Sammy uses ugliness to cause pain; Pecola's ugliness is a shield that lets her hide from the scrutiny of others.[37] This conviction of ugliness, a catalyst for Pecola's journey of self-actualization, depicts colorism, sexism, and racism as damaging, oppressive factors for Black women. Colorism, sexism, and racism corrupt reality, devalue humanity over the polarities of beauty and ugliness, and foster self-hatred and hopelessness. Addictions to colorism, sexism, racism, and ugliness, together with alcohol or other drug addiction, anesthetize people from their own cultural heritage and drive them to violence and rage. Pecola's parents combine these addictions, which echo the obsessions of the larger society. This sick desire for the unobtainable creates Black and White pain and provokes idolatry at the altar of fictionalized physical perfection. The addicted symphonic voices that orchestrate blonde, blue-eyed sonatas and concertos explode any hope for mutual integration and assimilation posited as crucial for social progress.[38] Pecola's addiction leads to a lone voice singing and playing the blues.

---

[36]Morrison, *Bluest Eye*, 38–39.

[37]Ibid., 39.

[38]Rosalie Baum, "Alcoholism and Family Abuse in *Maggie* and *The Bluest Eye*," *Mosaic* 19 (Summer 1986): 19, 99; Denise Heinze, *The Dilemma of "Double-Consciousness": Toni Morrison's Novels* (Athens: The University of Georgia Press, 1995), 24, 29, 69; Terry Otten, *The Crime of Innocence in the Fiction of Toni Morrison* (Columbia, Mo.: University of Missouri Press, 1989), 12, 13.

Often, Pecola makes no sounds because she cannot speak or breathe. When Cholly attacks and rapes Pecola, silence catches in Pecola's stunned throat.[39] Without breath or a voice, death is imminent. Pecola's annihilation is the genocide of her innocence and the destruction of her personhood: "How can one *Be* when everyone around you declares that you do not exist?" In all of Lorraine, Ohio, the norm for beauty is signified by the idealistic *Dick and Jane* primer: a setting incapable of creating love for Black girls like Pecola.

Pecola wants to know love, but she lives in a pathological milieu where values break down and where love metamorphoses into hatred. Pecola's story is one of insanity, violence, and incest rooted in racism, sexism, and classism at the altar of Eurocentric beauty, where Pecola is the sacrifice, the scapegoat, even for her mother, Pauline. Pauline, wrapped in her own misery and depression, denies Pecola's identity by maintaining maternal distance, and projects that misery onto her daughter. When Pecola visits Pauline at work and accidentally tips over a deep dish cobbler, Pauline pulls Pecola by the arm, slaps her several times, and spews her anger at Pecola. Conversely, she gives only affection to the little White girl in pink whose dress has some berry stains on it and who starts to cry. Pauline gives love to the little White girl and humiliates her own Black child. Pauline's inability to be a nurturer to Pecola results from Pauline's own delusional experiences of her self, husband, home, and marriage. Her inability to step out of her delusions contributes to Pecola's destruction and self-hate, but Pauline's responses to Pecola are also the responses of a victimized woman.[40] The ability to name, define, and perceive reality is power;[41] hence, Pecola is powerless. Pecola knows that she has no worth, no value, no love, and believes she is not lovable. Her mother and other Black and White adults appear to love only White, blue-eyed children, but not Pecola. The ending of Pecola's fractured fairy tale is not a happy one. Her idolatrous worship of Shirley Temple, the icon for blonde hair and blue eyes, brings no blessing or atonement. Pecola and her mother, victimized and made inferior by society because of their Black difference, equate Blackness

---

[39]Morrison, *Bluest Eye,* 87–91, 162.

[40]Gloria Wade-Gayles, "The Truths of Our Mother's Lives: Mother-Daughter Relationships in Black Women's Fiction," *Sage: A Scholarly Journal on Black Women* 1 (1984): 11; Joyce Pettis, "Difficult Survival: Mothers and Daughters in *The Bluest Eye,*" *Sage: A Scholarly Journal on Black Women* 4 (1984): 27, 29.

[41]Cynthia Davis, "Self, Society, and Myth in Toni Morrison's Fiction," in *Toni Morrison, Modern Critical Views,* ed. Harold Bloom (New York: Chelsea House, 1990), 7.

with evil:[42] the unloved, isolated mother begat an isolated, unloved daughter. Both embody the ugliness of victimized sexism, classism, and racism rooted in a response to their Blackness. This ugliness is misbegotten anguish. The related physical, psychological, and philosophical lynchings of one's racial/ethnic group by another is misbegotten anguish: spurious, deceptive discord that bifurcates, violates, and causes death. Such anguish is not unique to the external and internal racism felt by persons of African decent. Such misbegotten anguish, such evil is a global phenomenon. Toni Morrison just illustrates it so well.

For the Black Christian tradition, evil is a historical actuality, not something that is primordial, cosmological, or perpetrated by God, though a few, such as Phyllis Wheatley, an eighteenth-century poet, and Alexander Crummel, a nineteenth-century Episcopal priest, posited divine suffering of African Americans as part of a divine higher calling. Thus, this tradition sees evil as an anthropological issue. God created human beings with the option for choice and in freedom. Consequently, when a human chooses to do bad things, there is no justification to blame for exercising their freedom in this manner, according to slave theology and theodicy. In their exegetical hermeneutics, slaves relied on the exodus and the resurrection as examples of God's victory over suffering, seeing evil historicized and symbolized in Satan. The Black Christian tradition posits a prophetic answer regarding personal and social suffering, where God is Liberator.[43]

In Black communities, and perhaps other oppressed communities throughout the world, intracommunity violence occurs in response to external forces. The need for moral agency and personal and communal responsibility aside, *"Racism and economic exploitation are among the dominant causes of the conditions that have caused the escalation of intracommunity violence among Afrikan Americans."*[44] Thus, White supremacy spawns continuous oppression and violence, which results in humiliation, dehumanization, and subordination. When a group of people are continuously targeted externally, often they begin to embody that prejudice and they start to self-destruct internally,

---

[42]Carole Gerster, "From Film Margin to Novel Center: Toni Morrison's *The Bluest Eye,*" *West Virginia University* 38 (1992): 194–95.

[43]Peter J. Paris, "The Problem of Evil in Black Christian Perspective," in *Justice and the Holy: Essays in Honor of Walter Harrelson,* ed. Douglas A. Knight and Peter Paris (Atlanta: Scholars Press, 1989), 297–309, 300–301, 303, 308–9.

[44]Rufus Burrow, Jr., "Martin Luther King, Jr., Personalism, and Intracommunity Black Violence," *Encounter* 58 (Winter 1997): 46.

embracing mean-spiritedness, hopelessness, lovelessness, and aimlessness. Continuous oppression undermines self-esteem and communal solidarity, which leads to disregard for oneself and for others. Nevertheless, Martin Luther King, Jr., would argue that ultimately every individual is a moral agent, and every moral agent is called to resist participating in anything that destroys one's political and ethical freedom. Moral agency assumes one has the ability and opportunity to act out of freedom—responsibly, reasonably, and with maturity.[45] Some would counter that some oppression is so systemic, so common, so harsh, that many of the oppressed have no real concept of the capacity to be an agent of any kind on their behalf, not to mention being a moral agent. Juxtaposed against internal, Black intraracial violence is the White indifference to ongoing discrimination and morally evil social conditions, including the response by White Bible-believing, Bible-carrying, Bible-reading, churchgoing Christians. To be holy is to be concerned, to be engaged, to end indifference. The problem is not a lack of opportunities to work for social justice, but the paralyzing, dispassionate inertia. Change comes from passion, not from paralysis.[46]

In 1893, at the close of the World Parliament of Religion, one of the organizers proclaimed, "Henceforth the religious of the world will make war not on each other but on the giant evils that afflict [hu]mankind."[47] We can't help but hear those words with a little bit of irony and sadness one hundred years later. And what about the interfaith movement?

> [I]nterfaith cooperation has gotten a good start but interfaith violence has kept pace. The world's religious traditions still manage to provide fuel and symbolic weaponry for the world's strife. The giant evils that afflict humankind have grown as rapidly as our dreams. The chasms between the cultural, racial, and religious families of humankind have oppressed as quickly as the bridge we have built to span them...How quickly we take offense, we escalate offense, we magnify offense, we return offense.[48]

---

[45]Ibid., 46, 47, 51–53.

[46]"The Church After Rodney King: Not Violence, but Indifference to the Evil of Race and Class Is the Persistent Sin of White Christians."Editorial, *Christianity Today* 36 (July 22, 1992): 18–19.

[47]Diana Eck, "Difference Is No Excuse for Hatred," *Christian Social Action* 7 (May 1994): 32.

[48]Ibid., 33.

Finally, what is at stake within personal and institutional racism? We have enough laws, and enough people of conscience have raised the issue time and time again. Sadly, this demonic paroxysm, this misbegotten anguish, is not isolated to one country or to one people. Yes, White supremacy contributes largely to all oppression, but intraracial racism is also a global reality. Why all the civil wars? Why is there division between shanty Irish and lace-curtain Irish? Between Japanese peoples and Koreans? Between Egyptians and Arabs? Between darker-skinned Blacks and blue-vein or first-family Blacks in parts of Virginia specifically, and the rest of the United States as well? Why is it better to be Hispanic or Sicilian than Mexican? Why do the Serbs fight and despise the Croats? How could a Hitler pontificate the absoluteness of Aryanism when he looked nothing like his ideal, but the German masses bought his ideology? Among Whites, why do blond hair, blue eyes, and aquiline noses constitute the ideal? How can we account for the longevity, tenacity, and theology of South African apartheid? As complex as all these questions are, at least part of the answer is also quite simple: economics, power, and control. Misbegotten anguish legislates dominance, avarice, and superiority complexes. Most of the fighting and hatred not attributed to fear and ignorance can be situated within greed. If "we" are dominant, then "they" do not get our jobs; "they" do not pollute our bloodline by marrying our kids. "They" can never be in control over us; "they" will never have the opportunities that we have so that "they" will always be the underdog and can do the work that we despise. Misbegotten anguish is the dogma for a global civil religion that worships at an altar of dysfunctional pathology whose liturgical colors are dictated by pigmentation.

If we are to ever live out Martin Luther King, Jr.'s dream that his children will be judged by the content of their character and not by the color of their skin, we must take stock and claim all the differences. We must see color. A person's skin color cannot become invisible. We must see the color. If Alice Walker is right, "that it pisses God off when we pass by the color purple and don't notice it,"[49] surely it must piss God off if we pass by a person and do not see the color of his or her skin. There are different ways of seeing. We see to register and appreciate. We ought not see to harm, to malign, to defame, or negate. We must see the beautiful different hues of our skin, one of our divine birthrights, and own the colors and love the colors well.

---

[49]Alice Walker, *The Color Purple* (New York: Harcourt Brace Jovanovich, 1982), 167.

Then we must own the pain and the hurt, denial, grief, and degradation. We must name all the pain, dehumanization, schizophrenia, and double messages of dualistic, dichotomous thinking that has developed around skin color and cultural practice. Once we can name all the harm, both interracial and intraracial racism, being fully conscious of how we participate in perpetuating the lies and the stereotypes, then we may be able to begin the journey toward wholeness and healing. Toward being a great salad bowl or smorgasbord of humanity. Surely we never were, never will be, and do not need to try to be a melting pot: Too much gets lost.

Ssh————
No!! Obligato of Wailing
Don't Tell ————
Sshh————
We're not like *those* people.
Don't hurt me!
You made me do it.
But I'm not prejudiced; after all,
I have an Asian friend,
I speak Spanish,
I work with Black people.

You people can't learn;
I don't want no woman telling me what to do!
If they move into our neighborhood, the property values will plummet.
Did you know spare the rod and spoil the child
has nothing to do with spanking?

I hate you!
I hate me!
Cross me, and I will destroy your career!

Don't ask, don't Tell!
You ought to be ashamed.
You never will amount to anything:
Words and deeds.
Capability of daily destruction: immeasurable.
Fatalities: in the billions.
Eroding the sacredness of life.
Using mighty weapons of tongue, currency, denial,
pollutions, firearms, drugs, silence.

Ssh————
Ssh————
The dialect of now;
Is it too simple to love?

Sing: "Simple Song…
for God is the simplest of all."*

---

*Leonard Bernstein, "Simple Song," from *Mass: A Theatre Piece for Singers, Players, and Dancers* (New York: G. Schirmer, 1971).

7

Choosing
Hypocrisy,
Betrayal, and
Miseducation

Our Complicity in Violence

The wounds of oppression were sown in slavery, pampered by Jim Crow, and titillated by the internalized violence of separate and unequal, which vented its anger on others. From these wounds ooze the poisons of pain, self-hatred, self-defeatism, insatiable desire, and rage throughout society, like the afterbirth of Mount Vesuvius. The communities and personal lives of citizens in the United States and the prisons of racism, sexism, classism, ageism, and heterosexism wear different masks. Some *womanist* public intellectuals have begun to address the pathologies that attend such evil in dialogue with the works of bell hooks. Her voice provides a vehicle of sociocultural, critical theory and analysis that helps disrupt those cultural productions that celebrate White supremacy, White privilege, and all hegemonic, oppressive discourse that diminishes, denigrates, and destroys ideas, possibilities, spirits, communities, individuals, and bodies.

Ssh————
Silence; Ssh————
Help me!
Whiteness is not bound by color!

This chapter uses bell hooks' notion of *"killing rage"* as a metaphor of deconstruction to explore individual and communal hypocrisy, betrayal, and miseducation amid our complicity in violence. After analyzing and expanding *"killing rage,"* I then exegete dialogically Lauryn Hill's and Carter G. Woodson's concepts of miseducation. In conjunction with reviewing Mozart's opera *Don Giovanni,* I explore power and authority as weapons of hypocrisy, betrayal, control, violence, oppression, and miseducation, resulting in our callous tongues, our insistence on the blissfulness of ignorance, and the silence of our own killing rage. I use excerpts from various genres of song as response to the call for us to acknowledge our own complicity in the spiral of violence being perpetrated globally.

Prelude to a Curious Moment: Violence and Miseducation

On April 20, 1999, Eric Harris and Dylan Klebold murdered Cassie Bernall, Steven Curnow, Corey DePooter, Kelly Fleming, Matthew Kechter, Daniel Mauser, Daniel Rohrbough, Rachel Scott, Isaiah Shoels, John Tomlin, Lauren Townsend, Kyle Velasquez, and teacher William "Dave" Sanders. Twelve students, one teacher, DEAD, then the killers' suicides, more dead. The deaths at Columbine High sparked serious debate about the complexities of adolescence and the life of high school students, their parents, and their teachers and mentors. Some described these two killers as totally depraved misfits. Their parole officers labeled the two murderers brilliant, most likely to succeed. The Columbine tragedy makes us ask: What does life mean? What are the limits of affluence? What is the role and impact of education and miseducation? What are the power and sting of difference? the reality of death? the deadliness of violence?

Ssh————
I've been 'buked and I've been scorned.
I've been 'buked and I've been scorned, children.
I've been 'buked and I've been scorned.
I've been talked about; sho's you born.[1]

---

[1]"I've Been 'Buked and I've Been Scorned," traditional spiritual.

Few questioned the hypocrisy present in some of the analysis, the levels of betrayal consummated in the murder-suicide, or the level of miseducation in our schools and society that creates the petri dishes for spawning such a virulent outbreak of violence.

Twenty-three-year-old Lauryn Hill, whom *Ebony* magazine touted as "Hip Hop's Hottest Star" in 1999,[2] who balances love, motherhood, and fame, was the first woman to ever win five Grammys, for "The Miseducation of Lauryn Hill." Dr. Carter G. Woodson (1875–1950), an educator, philosopher, mentor to African American scholars, and founder of the African American Historical Association, wrote *The Miseducation of the Negro* in 1933. Hill and Woodson, sixty-six years apart, signify and indict the miseducation of Black children, of all children, of society. Woodson's classic names the problems of racism and demonstrates that the study of African American history would make a better society. Today, much of the miseducation occurs in ways that distort difference and that too often train people for specific tasks and negate the engagement of critical thinking. Despite three and four earned degrees, many of us still do not know how to talk with one another. We do not see our own biases. We lack the chutzpah to work together for change. Many are obsessed with the acquisition of things and lack inner peace. We find little pleasure in life. We spend more, work harder, achieve less, and have more health complications.

Ssh———
Silence is golden.
Silence gives consent.
That's not our problem.
They'll get over it.
Silence fuels contemplation;
Silence lies; and denies;
Silence. Ssh———

These complications, the deafening silence when loud declarations against injustice ought to be resounding, pertain to all age groups, particularly our children. Marian Wright Edelman, president and founder of the Children's Defense Fund, notes that "There is an undeclared war in America's neighborhoods, and children are the casualties. It is shameful that the richest nation in the world, the leading military spender, cannot protect its own children from gun violence. We have to make this a top priority of

---

[2] *Ebony* (May 1999).

our national agenda."[3] The report shows that while the number of children dying from gunfire has declined, 4,205 children and teens lost their lives in 1997, which is equivalent to one child dying every 2 hours, almost 12 children every day, and a classroom full every two days. The report indicates that between 1979 and 1997, nearly 80,000 children and teens were killed in America—more than all the American soldiers killed in the Vietnam War. In addition, homicide is the third leading cause of death among children five to fourteen years old, and the second leading cause of death among young people and adults ages fifteen to twenty-four. The firearm death rate for Black males aged fifteen to twenty-four is nearly three times that of the firearm death rate of White males in the same age group. Suicide is another disturbing trend among Black youths, although six times as many White children commit suicide. The overall suicide rate for Black youths is up more than 100 percent since 1980, and firearm suicides account for 96 percent of this increase. The estimated number of households with guns is as high as 40 percent, and more than half of such households keep their guns in unlocked areas.[4]

With the increased kidnappings of our children, increased suicides, increased prison population, we must ask what is going on. Are the perpetrators all sociopaths and psychopaths? People are not born full of rage, hate, and an ability to murder, to harm, to hurt. What is our responsibility as adults? Do we not have a responsibility to lead a life before all people, young and old, where we model the best behavior? Are we not called to replicate the sacredness imbued within us in every task that we do? Are we not called to illumine responsible living, critical thinking, caring for our neighbor, ourselves, and for the planet?

> This little light of mine, I'm gonna let it shine.
> This little light of mine, I'm gonna let it shine;
> This little light of mine, I'm gonna let it shine.
> Let it shine, let it shine, let it shine.[5]

Letting one's light shine is both a gift of freedom and a responsibility. A womanist epistemology, a way of seeing and

---

[3]Quote found on http://www.childrensdefense.org/release991014.htm in August 2001, as part of a press release on October 14, 1999, entitled "Children's Defense Fund Releases Report on Children Dying from Gunfire in America."

[4]Ibid.

[5]"This Little Light of Mine," traditional African American spiritual.

knowing that juxtaposes suppression and activism, takes seriously the many ways Black women's ontological and existential realities emerge and evolve. To even begin to name the oppression and our own complicity requires being a keen listener who can rigorously see in a way that affords a strenuous critique of self, society, and the various systems that allow us to perpetuate violence. Such a way of seeing and knowing requires a depth of honesty that can afford the weeds and old soil to be replaced by rich loam and fertile earth, the nexus for critical thinking and strategic action.

> So you think you're all that?
> Those people think? Really?
> Not like us; especially those women!
> The stuff they do is not really scholarship.
> They're just wannabees; a Jezebel, mammy, matriarch
> 'Specially those women who we fantasize about
> Those exotic, powerful women:
> Castrate their men.
> Who let them in the front door?
> Ssh————
> If we pretend they're not here,
> Maybe they will just go away!
> Ssh————; Ssh————; Ssh————

Killing Rage: A Metaphor of Transgression

Cultural critic and international scholar bell hooks reminds us that oppression is insidious. If we pretend it does not exist, that we do not see it or know how to change it, then the oppression never has to go away. Change requires a major wake-up call. Denial is not a river in Egypt, but a tool and process that allows us to be complicit in oppression and violence. To transform denial requires "killing rage," militant resistance. Killing rage, the fury and anger that bubbles up amid an experience of violation, is painful. Without an outlet, that rage can evolve into intense grief and destruction. The locus of this rage is a place of aliveness, of immediate presence, "the assertion of subjectivity colonizers do not want to see."[6] Killing rage, a source for metamorphosis and empowerment, helps one to name, unmask, and engage the self and others in profound politicization

---

[6]bell hooks, *Killing Rage: Ending Racism* (New York: Henry Holt, 1995), 12.

and self-recovery. Such rage, a catalyst for courageous action and resistance, helps one grow and change. Pathological, addictive, and dysfunctional behaviors dull the pain and the rage. In those moments, we become complicit with White supremacist patriarchy. Killing rage, a destructive or creative force, gives us the choice to comply or resist, to be pessimistic or hopeful. Because rage can be consuming, it must be tempered "by an engagement with a full range of emotional responses" to employ us in self-determination.[7] Sharing rage spawns communication and facilitates connections. Shutting down rage leads to assimilation and amnesia. The antithesis of engaged rage is victimhood. "To counter the rhetoric of victimhood," we must engage in a dialogue, a discourse of self-determination, as we struggle to end racist, sexist, classist, heterosexist domination.[8] Killing rage is an electrifying tool for change, a catalyst viable for public and private sectors. Killing rage energizes and encourages; titillates, but thwarts violence; instigates, yet incriminates apathy, dominance, misery, and complicit behaviors, thoughts and processes. Killing rage is a healthy "board of education" that affects teaching and learning.

We teach and learn inside and outside the classroom. In either venue, there is a marked difference between the banking concept of teaching that reinforces domination and the experience of "education as the practice of freedom."[9] In the classroom or workplace, many of us wield power and authority, brilliantly or brutally. We use our power and authority to create a living laboratory of thought, experience, and erudition. Some manipulate, castigate, and abrogate: dynamics that undermine the educative process. Students and other learners may be seen as disinterested consumers. We can also see students as vessels of the sacred, a plethora of possibilities who can alter our reality and make a difference in the world. Killing rage allows us to see that both students and the process are sacred. A holistic approach to teaching emphasizes teacher and student well-being, which includes experiencing analytical, critical thinking as liberatory praxis, respect for others, and self-care. Embracing such a pedagogy involves being open to change, to celebrating the opportunity to engage in constructive confrontation and critical interrogation as a freedom quest that expects to expose personal and systemic biases, White privilege, hegemony, and White

---

[7] Ibid., 19.
[8] Ibid., 4, 8, 11, 19, 47, 57, 61.
[9] Ibid., 4.

supremacist tendencies; otherwise, the resulting collective biases distort the educative process. Liberatory praxis expects chaos and healthy intrusion, a practice that is sacred, embracing, affirming, and respecting of all voices. Those same voices feel compelled to be responsible and accountable. Sacredness involves being willing to struggle and shift one's thinking, being, and doing in a nondefensive manner. Giving assent to bourgeois values and competitive one-upmanship thwarts the opportunity for healthy confrontation and conflict in the classroom. Teacher-learner and students need courage to embrace a vision and praxis of wholeness of the self and the community.[10]

> Them that's got shall get; them that's not shall lose;
> so the Bible says, and it still is news;
> Mamma may have; Poppa may have;
> But God bless the child that's got [their] own, that's got [their]
>   own.[11]

Killing rage as a catalyst for such vitality makes it clear that this involved work is not about intellectual masturbation or academic arrogance, but about transformation. Conversely, the move to make theory and praxis public is not about dumbing down information, or engaging in silencing, censoring, anti-intellectualism, or intellectual elitism.[12] Such a liberative dynamic within the halls of education, family life, or other social institutions challenges our need to be right, to be privileged, and to silence another. Experiencing killing rage in the classrooms of life is magical and awesome. Killing rage presses one to go further and deeper amid pathos, poignancy, and seeming powerlessness. Killing rage as praxis toward liberation provides an alternative lifestyle and presses my understanding of womanist theory and theological ethics as radical, revolutionary, righteous, revelatory, rhetorical, realizable, risky, representational, relational, rising, restorative, resilient.

hooks's radical, revolutionary, righteous use of the notion of "killing rage" as persuasive metaphor, is a catalyst, in the words of Katie Cannon, that mines the mother lode of creativity, of life, of total well-being. As we move further into the twenty-first century,

---

[10]bell hooks, *Teaching to Transgress: Education as the Practice of Freedom* (New York: Routledge, 1994), 13–15, 20, 29, 36–37, 55, 178–79.

[11]Billie Holiday and Arthur Herzog, Jr., "God Bless the Child That's Got His Own."

[12]hooks, *Teaching*, 55, 68, 145.

do we have a level of integrity, curiosity, and commitment to transformation that makes us willing to challenge our complicity in miseducated silence?

Lauryn Hill and Carter G. Woodson's Notion of Miseducation

The words of the song "Miseducation of Lauryn Hill" are poignant, poetic, plaintive, prophetic, and propitious. Her rhetorical tone painting through song and instrumentation reveals the process of miseducation and the dynamics of silencing our lambs. Hill sings of trying to be what others want her to be until she realizes that "deep in my heart the answer it was in me."[13]

The performed expression of miseducation exudes a poignancy as it moves and touches the listener to inspect reality, ontologically and spiritually. The poetic rendering of her experience is marked by rhythmical, improvisatory interpolations of sound with a sense of lament, of sadness, about the state of the world and the inner state of the singer/poet. In a way, Hill's "Miseducation" lament joins with other voices that lament the so-called "wretched of the earth."[14] Hill's evocation is as prophetic as it is visionary and farsighted. The protagonist understands that self-deception and a life of needing to acquiesce to others leads to death. Like a lament psalm, Hill's miseducation lays out the woes and the nature of human frailty. Like most psalms, this song ends with a certainty of hearing that the God inside her is vital and empowers her toward wholeness. The lament echoes the speed at which many of us live, too quickly, ignoring the beauty of all of creation, ignoring the beauty and awesomeness of ourselves. In the madness of such Sturm und Drang, one is trapped between internal and external pressures and can easily become a victim of miseducation.

Miseducation, for Hill, is the displaced allegiance to an other outside of self that negates history, denies and silences oneself, involves projection, and sabotages excellence. The steps beyond miseducation begin with an awareness, a conscientization where one knows a visceral, internal God consciousness. Above a pulsating bass and fluid melody, Hill's lyrical, improvisatory, soulful singing

---

[13]Lauryn Hill, "The Miseducation of Lauryn Hill," on *The Miseducation of Lauryn Hill*, RuffHouse Records CD CK69035, 1998.

[14]Cf. Frantz Fanon, *The Wretched of the Earth* (New York: Grove Press, 1963).

embraces the text, which moves from an ontology of awareness to one of critical thinking and engagement. Ecologically, the protagonist senses the larger world and wonders what happened to her passion for life and for things that matter. She also reckons that other moments in the past have been times of maximized potential, where the community exercised an ethic of care. Existentially, the protagonist comes to realize that despite the sense of alienation, there are those in distress with intense pathologies as they denigrate themselves and look for answers external to themselves or to the spirit within. Embracing a womanist rubric, the protagonist presses an epistemology where she knows, sees, and hears contextually as anthropological theology. She knows God is within and that as an individuated self, she must respond and engage in self-actualization. Thus, the answer to miseducation for Hill is the heightened level of awareness and the reality that she indeed can define her own destiny.

One is responsible and accountable for one's situation. Living her own rhetoric, Lauryn Hill says: "In my travels all over the world, I have come to realize that what distinguishes one child from another is not ability but access; access to education, access to opportunity, access to love. Through the Refugee Project, I create social programs for young people to provide access to opportunities that might be unavailable otherwise."[15] She invites others to join her in this effort.

> Did you know that:
> The year you were born
> Hues of your skin
> Width of your nose
> Texture of hair
> Family tree
> Kind of genitalia
> Your address
> Your coat of arms
> Bank account
> Defined and continues to stereotype you?
> Tells me all I need to know about you?
> Silences you? Silences me?[16]

---

[15]Lauryn Hill, liner notes on *The Miseducation of Lauryn Hill*, RuffHouse Records CD CK69035, 1998.
[16]Author's poem.

Carter G. Woodson broke open particular silences as he explored the concept of miseducation by critiquing the 1930s system of education, particularly as it failed to present authentic Black history to African American schoolchildren, despite the material available. Such offense places those in the African diaspora in the categories of nothingness and nobodyness. For Woodson, miseducation, a process of inferior training and disrespect that perpetuates itself, is a pedagogical, political, and socioanthropological strategy created to institutionalize oppression. Through his more than forty years of travel, teaching, research, and writing in multicultural and multiracial settings, Carter G. Woodson debunked numerous myths, critiqued ailing systems, and issued an indictment against a minimalist, that is, a "least common denominator" education for anyone. Woodson's critique illumines an interracial and intraracial tension where those within and those outside loathe the one uneducated. When a group has been oppressed by the dominant culture, those within the group begin to hate others, "the least of these," in their own group, rendering an implosion where those within the nondominant power group are in so much pain that the group often crumbles because of self-destruction. The same educational, political, or economic systemic process that inspires, rewards, and stimulates the oppressor is the catalyst that crushes and destroys the oppressed.[17] Woodson's concept of miseducation involves the prophetic, philosophical, pragmatic, political, and the programmatic.

Woodson's words are prophetic in that he saw the looming disillusionment and cynicism of African Americans amid segregation, minimalized economic support for Black children's education, and the aftermath of the Great Depression, as he pronounced the edict of miseducation that was alive and well then and still exists today. His method is philosophical as he carefully analyzes and constructs his argument, beginning with the roots of the Du Boisian color line. Long before the public intellectual thought of Cornel West, Woodson engaged in pragmatic philosophy. Woodson critiques the sociocultural, economic, and demographic issues that form the basis of miseducation. He indicts unjust segregation, illiterate preachers, the difficulty of serving the masses, and the skewed training that occurs under miseducation, in which Black folk are trained from a Eurocentric perspective but then not hired when they have graduated

---

[17]Carter G. Woodson, *The Miseducation of the Negro* (Washington, D.C.: Associated Publishers, 1933, 1969), vi–xxxiii.

to do the jobs for which that education has prepared them. He bemoans the fact that the genius of Black folk is not mined, even as educated African Americans often decry alleged race consciousness. Woodson celebrates the differences, while at the same time making it clear that difference does not mean inferior.[18] He not only lays blame, but carefully articulates the systemic oppression that occurred to make such a deplorable state of affairs possible. Woodson meticulously critiques political structures, particularly the educational systems, as he talks about the political, the distribution of power and authority. He argues that certain knowledge systems, which embody oppressive rhetoric and the entrenched view of African Americans as inferior, have overwhelmingly skewed socioeconomic and literate reality. Woodson's analysis is programmatic in that he notes what works and what does not work in the Black community. He critiques higher education for causing estrangement from the masses of African Americans. He both critiques the church for only being a shadow of what it could be and applauds it for engaging in public welfare, business, and social uplift. Woodson moves to identify, analyze, and ultimately transform miseducation, using an epistemology of theory, activism, and pragmatism, without romanticizing the situation or providing any sectors with leniency.[19]

> Nobody knows the trouble I've seen;
> Nobody knows my sorrow.
> Nobody knows the trouble I've seen.
> Glory, hallelujah![20]

Woodson names the complicity of all in ongoing systemic oppression and violence. He finds problematic both the educational and religious, that is the church systems, in which conditions allow idolatrous practices and underdeveloped Black citizenry, notably, because the church is the one institution African Americans controlled during the 1930s. Taken together, Hill's and Woodson's understandings of miseducation involve a positive call to freedom and change, an awareness of human foibles, the complexity of socioeconomics and political connections, and the psychological health that is at stake for the individual and the community. Both understandings of miseducation press us to deal with issues of power

---

[18]Ibid., 1–8.
[19]Ibid.
[20]"Nobody Knows the Trouble I've Seen," traditional African American spiritual.

and authority that perpetuate oppression and myths of inferiority and that serve as catalysts to maintain White supremacy. Some oppression as miseducation and misrepresentation unfolds as a systemic problem. Some such evil occurs within individual personalities, where lust and poverty give license to take advantage of others. Such passions unfold in many artistic genres, particularly opera. After providing an overview of the story of *Don Giovanni,* the analysis will explore the opera amid issues of personal and systemic power, authority, miseducation, and complicity around violence.

Callousness, Misrepresentation, and Miseducation Personified: Mozart's *Don Giovanni*

Originally titled *The Rake Punished,* Wolfgang Amadeus Mozart's *Don Giovanni* was first performed October 29, 1787, in "a spirit of levity rather than with the ponderous metaphysical significance in mind that Teutonic critics have pretended to find."[21] The Don Juan legend, emanating from Spain, is the prototype of the remorseless, insensitive libertine. The old Spanish folktale narrates the promiscuous Don Juan's seduction of the daughter of Seville's military commander. Don Juan kills the commander in a duel and then cynically invites the victim's funerary statue to a feast. The statue becomes animated, grabs the contumacious Juan, and drags him down to hell.[22] "Don Juan, as literary personality, artistic figure, and myth, has many characteristics: lover, trickster, joker, anarchist, and archetype,"[23] and has been developed by most eminent sculptors, composers, writers, and painters. The quintessential representation of the Don unfolds in Mozart's operatic treatment in two acts, which assembles several strands of socioeconomic and personal dynamics—class, lust, frivolity, ego, and murder—to effect what some have called one of the greatest operas ever composed.

The overture includes themes that first indicate, in minor keys, the foreboding, anticipatory, dramatic tones of the impending Commendatore's death and reappearance at the end of the opera. Second, these somber tones are followed by energetic, classic, stylistic sounds of the gaiety, sexual flirting, and partying, music in bright major keys that echoes the Don's trysts and liaisons. When act 1

---

[21]Henry W. Simon, *100 Great Operas and Their Stories* (New York: Anchor Books/ Doubleday, 1989), 125.

[22]"Don Juan," Microsoft Encarta Online Encyclopedia 2000 http://encarta.msn.com © 1997–2000 Microsoft Corporation.

[23]Quote found on http://www.don-juan.com/ in July 2001.

begins, we meet Leporello, the Don's servant, who must do the Don's bidding if he is to survive. Leporello complains about how hard it is to work for the Don, and says that he does not want to continue because Don Giovanni has all the advantages and does not have to deal with the consequences of his actions, that consequently, Leporello is often Don Giovanni's scapegoat and alter ego, because he has to hustle for Don Giovanni to earn his keep. Leporello is compromised, caught between a rock and a hard place, without options. Leporello is waiting outside Donna Anna's home when Don Giovanni runs out, followed by an angry Donna Anna. Don Giovanni had pretended to be Don Ottavio, Donna Anna's fiancé. The Commendatore, Donna Anna's father, also follows and challenges Don Giovanni. A fight ensues, and Don Giovanni murders the Commendatore. He then escapes without remorse or guilt. Seeing that her father is dead, Donna Anna is desolate and faints. In a duet, she and Don Ottavio swear to avenge the death of the Commendatore. Meanwhile Leporello and Don Giovanni sing of the Don's many conquests, celebrating his betrayal of women, society, and ultimately himself. In the next scene, Don Giovanni spots Donna Elvira, an old girlfriend whom he abandoned. She has not yet spotted Don Giovanni, but sings that she will burst if her lover does not come back. Leporello wants Giovanni to confess everything and clear up this mess. When Elvira recognizes Don Giovanni, she calls him a monster, criminal, and deceiver, with whom she fell in love. Giovanni manages to get away and leaves Leporello to explain everything. Leporello then sings the famous "Catalogue Aria," which tells of all the women Don Giovanni has seduced and betrayed in every villa, village, and country. The song details how Giovanni goes about exploiting women. His exploits are legion. He has loved 640 women in Italy, 231 in Germany, 100 in France, 91 in Turkey, and 1,003 in Spain. His roster of conquests includes young, old, rich, and poor. Don Giovanni objectifies all women and merely seeks them for his own lustful pleasure. He has no conscience and operates from a perspective of entitlement. Next, Don Giovanni invites himself to the engagement party of Zerlina and Masetto.

With the celebration already underway, Don Giovanni asks about the occasion and when informed, proceeds to flirt with the bride-to-be, Zerlina. Hypocritically, Don Giovanni promises to bestow protection on Zerlina and not only sends Masetto off with the rest of the party but also threatens him. Of course, Masetto is upset. Don Giovanni tries to seduce Zerlina, saying he could not bear that such a sweet thing would be with such a ploughman, a peasant; after all, Don Giovanni is a nobleman. Yet Zerlina begins to see Don Giovanni for what he is, and she protests. Don Giovanni continues to try and persuade Zerlina with his material goods, as together they sing "Là ci darem la mano," a song about innocent love. Donna Elvira enters and breaks up the scene. She tells Zerlina that Don Giovanni lies and deceives and that she does not want Zerlina to be tormented by him as she has been. Don Giovanni tries to pass Donna Elvira off as troubled and claims she is still in love with him. Donna Elvira calls Don Giovanni a traitor and takes Zerlina away, to Don Giovanni's chagrin, as Donna Anna and Don Ottavio arrive.

Don Giovanni tells Donna Anna and Don Ottavio that Donna Elvira is mad and that he was trying to console her. Donna Anna and Don Ottavio are not sure whom to believe. Suddenly, Donna Anna realizes that Don Giovanni may be the one who killed her father. She recalls when Don Giovanni tried to take advantage of her, the horror of the attack, and how she got away. Don Ottavio swears his devotion to Donna Anna's having peace of mind in the beautiful aria "Dalla sua pace." Outside Don Giovanni's palace, Zerlina makes up with Masetto, singing "Batti, batti." Don Giovanni still tries to pursue Zerlina, but Masetto stops him. From the balcony, Leporello sees three masked figures (Donna Anna, Donna Elvira, and Don Ottavio) approaching, and he invites them in. The three sing to heaven asking for help in bringing the despicable Don Giovanni to justice. As the last scene comes to an end, Don Giovanni has once more propositioned Zerlina. She screams for help, and all his enemies come after Don Giovanni, but he draws his sword and escapes.

When the curtain rises on act 2, Don Giovanni is still in hot pursuit of his female conquests. He convinces Leporello to trade places with him so that Don Giovanni can seduce Donna Elvira's maid. Yet Donna Elvira comes out to be serenaded, and Leporello, disguised as Don Giovanni, makes love to her and goes off with her. Dressed as Leporello, Giovanni sings. But Masetto, with a group of friends, interrupts him, looking to attack the Don. They mistake him for Leporello, and the Don sends Masetto's friends off on a wild goose chase and then beats up Masetto. Zerlina finds Masetto and comforts him, singing "Vedrai carino." Then three couples enter the garden where the Commendatore lived: Donna Elvira and Leporello (disguised as Don Giovanni), Donna Anna and Don Ottavio, and Zerlina and Masetto. Leporello reveals his disguise and escapes. Don Ottavio, convinced that Don Giovanni is the villain, sings "Il mio tesoro," and then sets off to contact the police.

Giovanni and Leporello meet near an equestrian statue of the Commendatore in the churchyard about 2 a.m. The two discuss whether Giovanni has made love to Leporello's wife, but are interrupted by a ghostly voice emanating from the Commendatore's statue declaring that soon Giovanni's joking will come to an end. (Giovanni has been adulterous with the wife of Leporello, who now has also participated in adultery by seducing Donna Elvira while impersonating Giovanni.) Leporello reads the writing on the base of the statue that says, "Here I await vengeance on the impious man who killed me." Shaken but cocky, Giovanni tells Leporello to invite the statue to dinner. The statue accepts twice. Giovanni mutters that this is all most strange. Don Ottavio then tries to convince Donna Anna that justice will prevail and that she should marry him. Donna Anna says she loves Ottavio, but she sings "Non mi dir," telling him that she is still grieving the death of her father and cannot possibly think of marriage at this juncture.

The last scene opens in a festive way, finding Don Giovanni having a lavish meal by himself as Leporello names the various tunes the orchestra plays for the dinner meal. Donna Elvira comes and pleads with Giovanni to change his lifestyle. Giovanni ignores her. When a knock at the door interrupts them, Donna Elvira hides behind the door, frightened. Giovanni orders Leporello to open the door, but he refuses. The Don goes to the door and sees the stone statue waiting at the door, having come to dinner. The statue grabs Giovanni, and when he refuses to repent, the Don and his palace all disappear in a supernatural fire. The Don is now dead, presumably in hell, and all the other characters tell of their future plans, having learned a lesson from the Don's escapades. The opera ends on a joyful note: Zerlina and Masetto will marry soon; Donna Anna and Don Ottavio will marry toward the year's end; Elvira will go to a convent; and Leporello will look for a better master.[24] Much of the hypocrisy, betrayal, and miseducation unfold through the acts of Don Giovanni, but the systemic nature of his ills affects everyone he comes in contact with.

The hypocrisy, the double standards, are in place because the women are expected to be faithful, but characters like Don Giovanni

---

[24]See Wolfgang Amadeus Mozart, *Don Giovanni* (New York: Schirmer, 1961); and Simon, *100 Great Operas,* 126–30.

have free reign, at least up to a point. That the Don Juan character is so popular in many media is indicative of society's lust for the quest of female prey. Giovanni traps Leporello into his schemes and pollutes Leporello's character, ultimately reinventing Giovanni within Leporello, where Leporello ends up committing similar acts of betrayal on behalf of Giovanni. To his credit, Leporello does encourage Giovanni to cease his escapades and to atone for his violations of personal trust, boundaries, and propriety. As a servant, Leporello has severely limited choices. That Donna Elvira continues involvement with the Don shows how one can ultimately become complicit in his or her own violation. Donna Elvira knows of Don Giovanni's reputation, yet she continues to be around him. To her credit, she does protect Zerlina from being betrayed and compromised. Women did not have a lot of authority, so in one respect, the authority of self that Donna Elvira did have was compromised by her ongoing entanglement with the Don. That Masetto has to yield, at least initially, to nobility regarding his fiancée indicates some compromise, fear, helplessness, and class distinctions. That Giovanni's cavalier attitude allows him to see no wrong in having: (1) seduced and slept with 2,065 women; (2) murdered the Commendatore; (3) compromised Leporello on numerous occasions; and (4) wanted to break up the engagement of Zerlina and Masetto indicts him for betrayal and hypocrisy. Further, his acts ultimately make him complicit in his own death; a death related to his perception of his inherent power and authority.

Power and Authority: Tools of Oppression and Violence

Power yes; power no.
Makes me lie; makes me high;
Makes one want to go and fly:
Through ivory towers,
Cathedrals of deceit;
Wall Street, Disneyland
Cyberspace
Ignoring you
Bastardizing myself,
Scruples be damned![25]

Power is one of those words like love: We use it often, uncertain, unsure about what we mean. I define power as having control and

---

[25]Author's poem.

influence, taking seriously the Greek terms *dynamis,* the ability to perform, and a modified definition of *exousia. Exousia* means power as the gift of freedom from any inward restraint in the exercise of that ability. I shift to define power as the gift of freedom to listen or not to listen to oneself, God, and others in making decisions; authority is to be invested with the privilege of decision making. Thus, power is the gift, the freedom of being in charge, in control, of having influence. Authority is the institutional investiture, sanction, and privilege of making decisions.

> To this we've come
> That we withhold the world from them;
> No ship nor shore
> To them that die at sea;
> No home nor grave to them that die on land.
> To this we've come
> That we be born a stranger upon God's earth
> That we be chosen without a chance for harm
> That we be hunted without the hope of refuge;
> To this we've come
> To this we've come.
> And you, you too shall weep.[26]

Womanist theological ethics, as the foundation of a constructive praxis, exposes the evils, the oppressions of betrayal, compromise, and complicity toward change, balance, and promise. A womanist emancipatory hermeneutic prompts a logic of care, compassion, and responsibility as it builds on the notion that all humankind has an essential goodness and that nurture for self and community requires a commitment to justice, respect, and mutuality. Womanist theories want us to focus on the complex, pathological institutions and communities that are ailing and wounded: empowerment instead of denial, destruction, and silence.

First, womanist thought provokes honest conversation and ethically based research to expose evils and to empower an ethics of accountability and sensible praxis, toward possible solutions that benefit "the least of these." The reality of oppression and silencing indicts all of us and presses us to explore who has the power, to question whether it is being used judiciously, and to consider the creative ways that we can share it.

---

[26]Gian Carlo Menotti, "To This We've Come," in *The Consul* (New York: Schirmer, 1952).

Second, womanist theories celebrate life as gift, which means that all of the living are responsible for making a difference and for empowering people, not merely fixing them. Often those of us who claim to be liberal are actually Stalinist. We have a fixed way we want to relate to *those* people and we dare *them* to trespass on our turf or to even think about challenging our authority base.

Third, womanist theory moves us to acceptance and letting go of as it invites us to not be ashamed of our bodies, wants, and needs and challenges us to identify and give witness to the sacred within humanity. We are to use language carefully and to enjoy a realized, eschatological, holistic life. If life itself is a privilege, then we cannot take anything for granted. We should not take more than we give back, and must avoid worshiping a God or Spirit or discipline that cannot love us. We must avoid any practices that cause us harm. We need to name the oppression that we see on a daily basis, accounting for our own actions. We must query ourselves in profound ways to determine whether we have acted in a just manner. We must never silence someone because of our own ignorance, shame, or guilt, or because we did not, cannot, will not see.

> Sometimes I feel like a motherless child;
> Sometimes I feel like a fatherless child;
> Sometimes I feel like an unloved child,
> A long way from home; a long way from home.[27]

But for time or different circumstances, we might be the statistics of Jonestown, Rwanda, Afghanistan, Bosnia-Herzegovenia, Uganda. We might have known the horrors of middle passage, the Trail of Tears, the Holocaust, the Japanese internment camps in the United States. In reality, we are the children of that terror. We have inherited the legacy of global violence. And in the process of life itself, we contribute to oppression as we humiliate, ignore, or dismiss those we teach, hire, supervise, and with whom we are intimate. Most of us do not own uzis or AK-47s, but daily we use our tongues to lie, defame, intimidate, manipulate, and disrespect those we have a need to control.

Fourth, we affirm stewardship and become responsible and accountable as we hold our lives and our blessings in trust, as part of our religious life. As a country, we have not been the best stewards of our human or natural resources. We believe stereotypes about people before we come to know them. In some states, we have voted

---

[27]"Sometimes I Feel Like a Motherless Child," traditional African American spiritual.

to try children as adults. We work to anesthetize those same children with things, withholding our love because we often do not love ourselves. We have unprecedented pollution and ecological toxicity. Perhaps we need a year, a decade, of global, national, local mourning and atonement for us to begin to see the systemic sexism, classism, racism, ageism, and homophobia in society, in our faith communities, and in our schools. Why do so many women still get less money for the same job? How many Don Giovannis are running around loose, preying on innocent men and women, with institutional sanctions and power? Why was the United States so adamant about welfare reform in the 1990s, when welfare concerned less than 10 percent of the national budget? We gossip and manipulate facts to suit our best interests, like the Moynihan report and the bell curve. We often fear embracing difference because we will have to deal with learning about how many other lies we have believed.

Recently we numbered 6 billion persons on the planet. Increased numbers mean a greater potential for violence. Approximately 200 million people were murdered by global government activity in this century alone. Daily, teachers around the world kill off that many human spirits out of fear, ignorance, deception, and a need to control. The absence of the vitality of killing rage clearly fosters complicit behavior. The misinterpretation and fear of killing rage causes us to experience intimidation, and we cannot know pleasure in the classroom or anywhere else. The absence of empowering killing rage means that patriarchy remains alive and well. Miscommunication, miseducation, and marginalization arise out of domination. Instead of loving the whole people and dealing with the sacrality and preciousness of people's lives, we continue to play the games of oppression, creating bifurcated, schizophrenic modes of being that lead to increased hypertension, migraines, depression, cancer, and premature deaths.

Many of us would balk with outrage and claim that we do not engage in White supremacist behavior. We claim to be law-abiding citizens, upstanding members of faith communities, and persons who work hard to make the places where we work comfortable and appealing. We fail to see the Don Juan, the trickster within our own characters. The problem is that there is so much historical violence and oppression that we often deny, that we cannot begin to see our levels of complicity until we seriously analyze the ways in which power and authority have been manipulated and misused for centuries. In these moments, we do not take seriously Hill's or Woodson's notions of miseducation. We like to pretend that we do not enjoy the privileges that we do. We like to pretend that class distinctions are not a reality in the United States. We often are so complicit in the violence that surrounds us that we become our own victims. We stifle our killing rage and are unable to go further and deeper amid pathos, poignancy, and seeming powerlessness.

Our complicity in violence takes the shape of working ourselves to death. We are so wedded to our curriculums and business profiles that we do not see the walking time bombs that sit in our classes, offices, and congregations. While teen violence to other people and property is down, teen suicide is escalating. We confer more degrees while many cannot get work. Many in this country can afford more palatial homes, but these homes must have burglar bars and alarm systems. Drug, tobacco, and alcohol use is ravaging the poor and the rich. Too many babies are born addicted. Too many professionals are substance abusers. Together, systemic or institutional violence and our own compulsions to individually destroy ourselves set up a chain reaction like nuclear fission, causing some of us to slowly self-destruct, like Don Giovanni, and some of us to go quickly, like Columbine's Harris and Klebold. We use computers instead of black trench coats. We belong to various social and professional organizations, commensurate to some degree with Goth culture. At some levels of elitism, we engage in ritual acts of social and political murder, where we undermine colleagues and keep *those* people, the undesirables, from being a part of *our* organizations. In the academy, professors get different treatment, from tenured professors, to those on tenure track, to those who are ABD (all but dissertation), to those who are lecturers and adjunct professors. Since the money sometimes feels negligible in higher education (except for those in graduate/ research programs in law, medicine, and the other sciences) and the demands and time-consuming projects are so large, many of us in the academy give ourselves carte blanche to behave like boors. We make sure those in more servile positions appreciate our status and venerate our particular levels of power. Cooperative, supportive, collaborative faculty teams are often in smaller numbers than we would like to imagine.

When it is all said and done, many of us are just like the Don, Klebold, and Harris. Many of us, however, do not have the chutzpah to self-destruct so publicly or so quickly. We do have displaced allegiances to forces outside of ourselves. In the process, those allegiances force us to negate history and our own stories, we deny and silence ourselves, we project our own neuroses on everyone, and we allow other persons and circumstances to sabotage our potential for excellence. We have allowed knowledge systems and organizational cultures of oppression to exist that find women and people of non-European descent to be inferior. We live in an overwhelmingly skewed socioeconomic and literate reality, where people live in poverty in the wealthiest nation in the world. We have world-class institutions of higher education and yet manage to graduate students from high school and college who cannot read or write. Each day we spend more on prisons than on elementary education. We now have privatized jails, producing a new form of slave labor, so that the next telemarketing call you get will probably originate from a jail cell—the quantum collection of killing rage deferred.

Killing rage, as a source for metamorphosis and empowerment, helps us name, unmask, and engage the self and others in profound politicization and self-recovery. Such rage, a catalyst for courageous action and resistance, helps one grow and change. Pathological, addictive, and dysfunctional behaviors dull the pain and the rage. In those moments, we become complicit with oppression and violence. We know that change can occur with new kinds of mentoring, teaching, preaching, writing, and living in an exemplary manner, cognizant of who we are and why we are here, and seeing and respecting our lives and our universe as gift. If we are open to seeing and embracing action for justice, to according simple dignity and respect in all living spaces, we can halt nihilistic praxis, and become progenitors of possibility and hope.

We must listen well to the philosophies of hooks, Hill, and Woodson. We must teach by word and example to transgress static norms that lead to death. We cannot afford for one more child or adult to engage in miseducation. Such violence is horrific, in that it is so subtle. Such violence does not create visible scars that the naked eye can identify. Miseducation creates a violence of long standing that systematically rips the soul apart, deadens the mind, and quenches the hope that did not have to die. To miseducate is to deny the rage that implodes on us because it is not polite to be angry, or because we are in so much denial that we have no idea of the amount of rage that coexists in our bodies. Critical, analytical thinking requires the same kind of compassionate action. We can no longer afford to be limited by our Enlightenment mentalities of *cogito ergo sum.* We must be and act in a manner commensurate with peace, where we see the aesthetic and awesome potential for a new way of being, doing, and growing that we might bask in the silence of contemplation, but never the silence of violence.

PART IV

Prophetic Promises

Wistfully, the days of our lives blow
Like leaves in fall
Snowflakes in winter
Rainfall in spring
Grains of sand in summer.

Fleetingly, we are here on the planet,
But a moment.
Can we afford to violate our time?
The gift of our lives?
The sacred spaces we inhabit?

How can we yet betray ourselves and the God within?
How can we dance to the music of hypocrisy
Laugh to the jokes of cynicism
Betray through deceit and miseducation
Divest ourselves of honesty
Violate that which ought to be inviolable?

In but a moment
We have an invitation to choose:
Justice and mercy, or prejudice and domination
Love and hope, or hate and despair
Death and annihilation, or Life and sanctuary
And all of the continuums in between,
Within the cathedrals of our minds
The sanctuary of our souls
The temples of our bodies
Options to dwell within
A cornucopia of blessedness
Dignity unfurled.

8

Changing
Creation

*A Prolegomenon to a Theology
and Ethics of Violence*

In Blythe, California, crime investigators, child protective services, parents, and the district attorney asked themselves, Is it a crime when a 5- and 6-year-old suffocate a 3-year-old? The stuff of television whodunits and drama series? No. Damion Stiffler was smothered with a pillow, and he fought for his life. The two girls had to be terribly angry to suffocate Damion as he fought, but he was not strong enough. The district attorney stated that the girls were too young to be tried or punished. Children must be conscious that they are doing wrong when they commit the crime for them to be tried. There must be intent and there must be a motive. Was this a case of child endangerment, since the parents have minor drug convictions and there have been domestic problems? Damion was buried the week of August 28, 2000, and child protective services was trying to determine a course of therapy and care that would benefit the other Stiffler children.[1] This story is all too real and makes

---

[1]Andrew Murr and Karen Springen, "Death at a Very Early Age," *Newsweek* (August 28, 2000): 32.

us wonder about the serial killers, the psychopaths, and sociopaths: When does the undeniable urge to do harm take root? Is it genetic? And what about the rest of us? What does it take to push someone over the edge?

Through this text, we have explored various manifestations of violence on the personal and systemic level. The picture has been rather horrible, the pain suffocating, the need to control and manipulate disgusting. Every day some other travesty of justice, some other heinous crime, some other devastating loss of human life occurs. Every day, embodied misbegotten anguish saps the life out of our world and out of us. This chapter explores the dynamics of a theology and ethics of violence. After offering a confession of guilt for global, corporate betrayal, I then explore the schematics of God and humanity within the categories of oppression discussed throughout the text, and conclude on a celebratory note that gives testimony for transformative options.

Misbegotten Anguish: Betrayal as Manifest Destiny

The history of the twentieth century and of the other nineteen centuries before paints an awfully grim picture about how we have lived together. The exponential acts of violence surely must grieve God's heart. Human beings have betrayed each other in massive and subtle ways. To betray is to expose one to treachery, to fail to uphold a trust. To betray involves acts of deceit, seduction, dishonesty, and hypocrisy. To betray means to disclose in violation of confidence. Every act of betrayal is an act of violence. Every act of violence names the criteria of misbegotten anguish.

On the levels of socioeconomics and politics or intimate friends, we sabotage one another. We undermine and distort reality. Many times within family systems, people are cold and hurtful. The divorce courts, battered women's centers, the hundreds of abandoned children indicate that as much unfaithfulness, abuse of power, and breaking of covenant happens in our homes as in our governments. We often react out of fear, and we violate out of need. We rob others of joy, hope, and possibility. We do not know how to parent and have not created educational systems in schools or in faith communities that will begin to help us learn to communicate, to love, to agree to disagree. Much of the pain projected outward emerges from the pain stuffed within. Sometimes this pain materializes as self-centeredness, superiority complexes, or massive dysfunctional families. The staggering numbers of practicing alcoholics, drug addicts (on street or prescription drugs), workaholics, gamblers, adulterers, and child abusers indicate we are in trouble. The escalating numbers of prison inmates and the persons who then marry or have partnerships with these inmates clearly states an epidemic of spiritual and psychological malnutrition. People are hurting, and they are hurting badly. The prevalence of addiction signals the personal hurt that shapes all relationships and becomes a societal hurt. There is nothing redeeming about this level of pain.

So many hurting people are the living dead. Suffocating with rage, they lead miserable lives and have little hope. Their pathologies cause them to create relationships with others who are just as sick, if not sicker. When so many people who are spiritually, mentally, and emotionally sick continue to surround themselves with other sick people, their plight becomes a self-fulfilling one. They believe they are not good. Their psyches are convulsive with pain, so the venom spews out like hot lava, destroying, or at best crippling, those in its path. With such levels of disaster comes loss of hope, dishonesty, lack of trust, and more self-destructive behavior. Such pain does not know boundaries. This scenario is not focused singularly on poor or oppressed people, so class does not protect one from this level of affliction. An education from the best universities in the world does not make one immune from the experience of desolation, of fear, of unworthiness. Being male does not protect one from deep levels of betrayal. Unfortunately, we tend to socialize our boys as toddlers to believe they are men and thus have no feelings, have no right to express those feelings, and have to forever prove they are men based upon a patriarchal, often maniacal set of do's and don'ts. Having a deep religious faith will not shield one from doubts, loss, and confusion. Playing by all the rules does not mean that one is always safe and will always get what one works for. Life is much more fragile than that. People hurt themselves, and in a quest for empathy or vengeance, or a need for human attention, will hurt others. Misbegotten anguish rests like a giant tent cloaking many aspects of our lives and our world. Violence, whether born of pain, dominance, or curiosity, still destroys. To see the destruction is to inquire about the acts of God and of humanity.

Confession: The Acts of God and Us

When reviewing the contexts of scapegoating, war and colonialism, sexism, classism, racism, and the daily complicity of ordinary people in the perpetration of violence, the God we see and hear largely concerns our own situation, belief systems, level of cynicism, or level of hope. The scapegoat presents a most precarious position for those deemed other in any given society.

As the narrative of history, literature, or opera unfolds, it seems that God rewards the crafty servant or cannot be involved. Sometimes it appears that the hiddenness of God cannot possibly be transcended when one individual or group is sacrificed for the many. Those with the power seem to deny God the ability to speak. Others would argue that God suffers with the victim. How could any god demand sacrifice of a being whom that god claims to love, to have created, to have invited into an alleged relationship. The arguments for theodicy for freedom and soul-making notwithstanding, the one scapegoated is still the sacrifice. These arguments are incomplete and unsatisfying to those who suffer or who watch loved ones suffer. That much is left in mystery is also not satisfactory. Some choose a humanistic argument, but for the theist, this argument is not too helpful, for why would a good god allow the kind of freedom that gives some individuals the sanction to do gross harm to another? Since God created both the oppressed and the oppressor, since God knows everything, why would God allow such pain to be inflicted, particularly on innocent persons? God, of course, is not in this scenario alone; we must deal with the human factor.

The human participants involved in scapegoating fall across a spectrum of those who are deceitful to those who are so gullible they refuse to believe that someone might take advantage of them. Scapegoating fosters a false sense of piety. Some of those in the crowd may be weak and caught up in the mob mentality. Some have experienced so much pain that they have become callous and unfeeling. They lose the sense of what it truly means to be human and to value the lives and well-being of others. What surfaces in a scapegoating module is the dis-ease within the group that claims power, the need to objectify another, to be in denial, and to blame others. Those being scapegoated are those easily identifiable, who make good targets, whom those in power deem dispensable. The deaths of Madame Butterfly and the unnamed, secondary wife cannot be justified. Without Theophus Smith's notion of mimetic intimacy, where the sacrificial system can be subverted by love and respect with a practice such as the *Imitatio Christi,* the reality of scapegoating seems to be necessary, particularly for students of history. When cornered, desperate, or in deep depression, many would rather blame someone else than engage in critical thinking to assess any and all options before engaging in reactionary violence. Some do not have the capacity to rationalize when they are chemically depressed or have other genetic disorders. Scapegoating allows for an unconscious escalation of violence in subtle and sophisticated ways. Given the many acts of violence perpetrated in the name of religion and faith, one cannot move too quickly to any kind of solution. Modern-day war and colonialism are equally devastating.

War and colonialism produce global violence and international civil religion run amuck. The battle call often echoes with the beliefs and prayers that "God is on our side." We are right; therefore, as we are the dominant culture, God champions our causes. Perhaps in times of war, God allows all sides free will as a concerned parent. If we are all God's children, then we are learning to discern. Conversely, if God is on our side, then God may enact divine violence to shield us, "to prepare a table for us in the presence of our enemies." As we become triumphant and remain obedient, we have the status of favored nation. Such sentiments clearly are a part of the Deuteronomists' agenda in the Hebrew Bible. Whatever God's actions, human beings ensconced in war and colonialism are often able to rationalize their positions, if they have not relegated their view to fate, chance, or luck.

During war, many a nation-state, parent, and soldier is clear that the war is being fought for some higher good, although beneath the rhetoric, the higher good is often an economic issue. Amid notions of patriotism, domestic safety, and the sense of manifest destiny or our right to conquer, jaded individuals and highly trained soldiers have to believe that life is expendable. War games allow one to focus issues of jealousy, rage, and control. In certain cultures, war becomes a ritual to celebrate their status as *ubermensch*, as a super race. The drama of war is also about a chess game of honor. On a segment of "JAG: Judge Advocate General," a soldier intentionally stepped in front of a fellow officer's gun during a military exercise, because he could not face his father with the truth that he was gay and had AIDS. He needed to die a noble death. Militarism—the pageantry and celebrations before, during, and after war—are powerful adrenaline stimulants. But whose side is God on? Is God on any side? And what of the plight of the civilians? What of the 200 million dead from war and governmental sanctions? Surely God is not pleased. Surely a loving God would not authorize such massive crucifixion of the *imago Dei* within all those persons. What happens to individuals who are trained assassins? Do they lose a bit of their humanity so that they can objectify other people to the extent that they can kill them? How can war ever be holy? And what of the families left behind? Who has the right to make decisions about war conquest? Would Private Ryan ever believe that Captain Miller's squadron and General Marshall did the right thing in launching a rescue mission on his behalf, on behalf of his family, even given that his three brothers were already dead? How can one justify the war against Jezebel and the Baal prophets? What was at stake, and why must she then die such a heinous death? As brutal as these accounts of war are the acts of gender violence.

Gender violence cheats, defames, and abuses all of society, directly and indirectly. As in all situations of violence, the target of the violence is never the only one affected by the evil. Everyone related to, or who comes in contact with, the person/group will experience the ramifications of the violation. Theologically, some identify God with the victim as the God of the oppressed, the Compassionate One who created the victim and who thus will sustain and be with the victim at all times. From a patriarchal view, God is the warrior who puts those inferior in their place. God is powerful. Because God gives the man "dominion" over the woman, the man then has the right to control, manipulate, and even abuse her, especially if she misbehaves. Others will see the divine as enabling or absent, that the oppressor has pushed God away. Some victims may experience God as distant or unknowable and have more of an agnostic view of God. Neither *Seven Brides for Seven Brothers* nor *The Women* focuses on the place of the divine. *Seven Brides* does include Milly's reading the Bible, a birth, and marriage, thus a focus on religious ritual, but not necessarily a strong divine presence. The Dinah/Shechem story places the power in the hands of the brothers and brings up many issues related to the roles socialization and tradition play in gender violence.

With the onset of gender violence emerges dysfunctional family systems driven by fear. Time and time again, the fear relates to warped understandings about gender identity, that is, what does it mean to be male and what does it mean to be female? Amid patriarchal mores, the questions of power and authority are never far from the surface. Who controls the household? Who makes the decisions, and who controls the finances? What kind of reputation does the family have, and how does that play out on an economic level? Within dysfunctional family units, the denial is so great that even when the physical evidence is unmistakable, the abused party often remains. The physical abuse is usually accompanied by mental and emotional cruelty, neglect, and exploitation, sometimes in the name of love. The cyclical abuse relies on fear and disrupts any healthy understanding of sexuality and sensuality. The abuse that metes out gender oppression causes harm that tends to be generational, for the children in such situations will pick up on the behavior and in turn become perpetrators themselves unless they are able to get help and healing at strategic points in their lives. The physical, spiritual, and emotional selves of all persons involved are out of sync and are problematic. Too often the victim does not realize that there are options. When poverty, low self-esteem, and neediness are central, the victim stands a greater chance of remaining in a valley of sexism, where seduction is used as a ploy to set the stage for domestic violence. Not only do many of us not really know what it means to be male or female, beyond the roles to which we have been socialized, we have no clue to what it means to be fully human. Gender violence is pernicious as it obliterates an individual, a family, and a home and taints all the relationships. In some families, gender oppression continues because classism or elitism affords a shield from persecution.

Classism/elitism is designer oppression. The lines are drawn to effect a separation that reads as distinct, desirable, and special. Classism affords an isolation from the lives of everyday working people. The economics and clout that come with a certain level of affluence often provide a false sense of reality and a mind-set that most things have a price, that the right phone call, the right political connection, the perfect timing, and superior grooming will bring about the desired answer. As in all instances of violence, classism trades on power. Some persons have become so sheltered that their own sense of reality is but a collage of images and impressions. Depending on the particular level of access, there are more or fewer options. The more options, the less tendency to rely on God or Spirit. With certain levels of power and clout, some people begin to think they are invincible, that the rules do not apply to them. Theologically, God may take on the role of deist, as creator who maintains a distance, or that of crisis manager, there when needed, mildly tolerated otherwise. This is not to say that all upper-class people are heels and all lower-class people are saints. People are people. Material provisions often allow one to get a better picture of who the people really are. The unjust steward reminds us that the issue of classism may force people to be more clever. In some instances, classism might tend to have some people outsmart themselves. Certainly a key issue that gets distorted with classism is access to resources. In *Cry, the Beloved Country*, neither poverty nor affluence shields the fathers from losing their sons prematurely. Clearly, poverty makes people uncomfortable. Success also makes some people uncomfortable, including those who have been able to attain excellence. The murky sensibilities around class often spill over into racism. In fact, sometimes issues identified as racism are really issues about class.

Racism corrupts the magnificent rainbow of humanity created by God. Racism kills the differences natural to color. Many of the civil wars around the globe have ostensibly arisen out of racial conflict. When connected with holy wars, some believe that God favors one experience of color and culture. Some have taken their dominant culture status to signify that in reality God is White, and thus, only people who look like them (White), talk like them, and act like them can be redeemed. All others are bound for hell. Such sensibilities makes God racial and gender specific. This kind of divine construction shifts depending on one's race and faith persuasion. Since race is a part of one's humanity, then the question of being made in God's image becomes even more crucial. In addition, the question of what it means to be human must again take center stage.

Some human beings are so riveted by fear that they are quite gullible about racist propaganda. If one believes in God, and that God created all people as good, then to be racist is to take exception to an inclusive doctrine of creation born of love. Racists become more absorbed with genetics and race and keeping the blood lines pure, for people deemed other pose a major threat to their survival. Others are so fraught with ignorance that they cannot begin to unpack all the misconceptions and stereotypes that they have assumed to be gospel. Racism also allows cruelty and elitism on one side, but can allow for the glorification of victimhood if situated in a particular manner. Some oppressed people will stay that way, regardless of the dominant governing practices, because they have a sense of entitlement and have allowed themselves to be brainwashed into believing they are inferior. Ultimately, racism harms the entire body politic if for no other reason than that those who dominate with power today may become the oppressed tomorrow. When oppressed and oppressor buy into the same lies that allow for institutional racism, they will continue to nurture dysfunctional behavior and will always be too traumatized to make a difference. One could highlight the role of the Philistines in the Samson and Delilah story and make it a question about race. One can also see that the racist pathology in *Jungle Fever* was so overwhelming that everyone suffered, and the oppressed became oppressors. From scapegoating to issues of colonialism or gender oppression, we are complicit with such violence in major and minor ways on a daily basis.

When we choose to operate from a perspective of hypocrisy or betrayal, we participate in miseducation. We miseducate because we make wrong assumptions. We miseducate because we either would rather not know or we know in ways that could be hurtful to someone else. We can be complicit in so many ways as to overwhelm us to the point of a manic or catatonic state. Much of the ordinary person's complicit violence occurs at an unconscious level. During such excursions, we tend to give lip service to "Hear no evil, see no evil, speak no evil," even as evil is unfolding right before us. Feigning ignorance is no excuse. Our complicity often skews our sense of God, so we may not be able to discern who or what God is, and how God is working on our particular behalf. Yet one who engages in violence may think God is on his or her side, because he or she has not yet gotten caught. The operative word here is yet. When the unexplainable happens and a well-intentioned, but misinformed person says, "It must have been God's will," he or she has made God complicit in evil. Why would a good God want an innocent child killed by a drive-by, a gun going off accidentally, or in a car collision with a drunk driver? Part of the problem is that we make God anthropomorphic and try to reason away awful quandaries by attributing them to God. Perhaps we are asking the wrong questions. Perhaps we are looking for the wrong answers. Our ignorance and confusion can never be a justification for our own participation in acts of violence, from slandering someone's character, to taking advantage of someone who entrusts their well-being to us, to committing premeditated murder. Along with outlining the criteria and the confession, one must find the hope. And in the hope comes the celebration.

Changing Creation: Celebrating Prophetic Promises

The process of writing and living with *Misbegotten Anguish* has been a journey over several seasons. Many voices have been part of my celestial chorus, my muses, my inspiration sparked by the divine. Being torn by and at points even stunned by the level of complicity, of hurt, of deadly pain, I knew that an awareness of the statistics and the stories would open the conversation, but would not finally open a door to the journey toward wholeness. This part of the journey emerged on a three-mile run in the farmlands of Wisconsin, north of Milwaukee. A framework for transformation lies in the context of celebrating the beautiful and the sacred from a perspective of stewardship, with the content of acknowledgment, attitude, and action.

For violence to shift requires that we first understand the true nobility and fragility of beauty in all of the world, in all of the people. There is a magnificence and artistry inherent in the construction of the human body, mind, and spirit. Each individual is a cathedral, a place of worship as our bodies echo the image of God. There is beauty in the synchronization of the most minute bodily functions. There is a rhythm that affects our temperature, heartbeat, blood pressure, so that when all the systems are in balance, we know health. There is beauty in the symmetry of hands and feet, of eyes and ears. There is beauty in the complex mechanisms that allow our bodies to ingest fuel efficiently and to rid ourselves of wastes and toxins. The beauty that comes with sexual intercourse and sensual intimacy toward a oneness of two beings is celestial. When such communion results in the gift of birth, beauty has multiplied exponentially. This beauty is not one of superficiality, crafted by makeup artists or marketing groups. We need to grasp the incredible depths of the beauty of the human body, mind, and spirit to be able to exorcise the many demons of ugliness that function to cripple, disappoint, and defeat. To begin to lessen the impact of misbegotten anguish, we must tap into the genuine beauty in the body called human. This is a beauty that emerges from the very essence of our beings; a beautiful balance, an exquisite rendering of the sacred.

That which is sacred is holy, is in union with God. The sacred is that to which we accord dignity and respect. Holiness is blessedness and transcendence. Holiness is powerful. That human beings are made in God's image entitles them to respect. God created us to be in relationship, to be holy, to love and be loved. We consecrate buildings for the worship of God. We dedicate houses and homes so that all who dwell within may be safe. We place cornerstones on buildings to commemorate the work of particular persons. Human beings are created on the cornerstone of God's love, for God's work with the people of God. If we can consecrate a building and then respect it by not desecrating it or using it irresponsibly, how is it that we are incapable of appreciating the sacred within ourselves and each other? To begin to even fully hear one another, and then to discern who and what we are and why we are here, requires that we accord humanity and creation itself a reverence of the sacred. This is not a practice of idolatry, but simply an appreciation of the fullness of God in the world. With an understanding of the theological import of the beauty and the sacred within each of us, within the world, we can move to involve the praxis, the ethics that will move us toward wellness and wholeness, the practice of stewardship.

Stewardship means to become responsible and accountable as we hold our lives and our blessings in trust as part of our religious life. In the Hebrew Bible, a *steward* is one who rules, oversees, governs, is worthy, is appointed to the position, and is meant to be in relationship. In the New Testament, the term *steward* expresses the role of one who is involved with religious economy, a domestic manager, guardian, tutor. A steward needs to exercise clearly demonstrated piety, that is, grace, devoutness, allegiance, godliness, holiness. Stewardship concerns the use of all resources given us in trust by God, toward the right use of power as we accord dignity to ourselves and others. As we relate to ourselves and to nature with sensitivity, we are clear that our motivation for life is one of love and justice.

To live in loving relationship with God means to have a radical, revolutionary relationship of stewardship with our bodies, minds, and spirits. God created us for ultimate intimacy, out of love, to think, to grow, to learn, to be, to share. Speaking biblically, in the first creation story, God speaks; something exists; and God calls that thing good. On the sixth day, God speaks human beings into existence and calls us good. Our minds, bodies, spirits, thoughts, sensuality, and sexuality have all been pronounced good by God. To function as a steward, in a balanced, loving capacity, requires that we know who we are. We are sacred beings, and we live in a sacred world. Health, spirituality, and ecology must be priorities. As ethical praxis, stewardship of bodies, minds, and spirits means a daily, living commitment to a healthy lifestyle. We need to understand how to use our bodies; how to strengthen our minds; how to gird up our spirits: how to eat, exercise, think, pray, meditate, and discern; how to choose not to violate or be violated. Stewardship requires that we set boundaries as we put God first, ourselves second, all others third. Radical, revolutionary stewardship calls us to tithe with our whole sacredness, to respect our whole selves. Violence via language or physical or psychological force is unacceptable.

The Earth cries out, our children act out, our own bodies cry out for mercy, for love, justice and balance. If we can grasp the rubric of BS^2–beauty, sacrality, and stewardship–as the context for our lives, central to balance, health, and wholeness, we can then work on the content, A^3–acknowledgment, attitude, and action.

Before the global, national, and local violence can be dissipated, we need to acknowledge their existence. We have to be willing to tell the truth, to confess historical and contemporary wrongs. Confession is an opportunity to begin the process of righting wrongs. We have to admit our participation in violence, regardless of how large or small. And we have to be willing to be wrong; to have someone help us engage in critical reflection to assess our lives and activities in a way that we can admit that we made a mistake. Sometimes pride precludes any growth because with the stubbornness that comes of having been oppressed, or made wrong, or made unique, may come the feeling of having been betrayed. In actuality, to admit being wrong can be most freeing. When we are willing to admit that we were or are wrong, we can then be willing to be answerable to a higher ethic. Then all of life ceases to be solely on me, but can open to others. Yet one is always at a point of choice. With freedom comes a great deal of responsibility. In reference to the violence that occurred in only the last decade, think of how many people would be alive if governments could have sat down together and placed the health and well-being of the world first and the issues of needing to control and to be right second. Perhaps we need a time of mourning and atonement to begin to see the problems all around us. We cannot change the devastating realities of destruction, cruelty, exploitation, dehumanization, and violence until we admit our own shortcomings and opportunities. The choice to react positively and to acknowledge areas of growth is the choice to live in the wake of paradox. We can be powerful and impotent, safe and in danger, using a language of survival where one can create a power base without harming others and without losing oneself. In the process of acknowledgment, we begin to regain ourselves. The freedom of acknowledgment is the gift of being able to change our attitudes.

An attitude is a posture, a mental position regarding a fact or state of being, an organic state of readiness to respond in a characteristic way to a stimulus–an object, concept, or situation. An attitude adjustment is central to produce any change, any healing. A healthy attitude affords us the room to mourn the tremendous acts of violence, loss, and death in the world. An open attitude fosters growth and learning and gives one an appreciation for history. A healthy attitude gives us the permission and the authority to sometimes be and not always need to do. With an attitude of gratitude, one can face the music to admit to wrongs and then prayerfully search for alternative models of building a healthy, relational life. One then has the room to explore and tap into what a healthy notion of atonement, of being at-one with God really calls for. The acknowledgment and the attitude shift are preparatory for taking action.

Action is embodied praxis, that is, taking one's theological commitments and focusing them into transformed, lived behaviors. In studying behavior, one is able to assess value systems. Action allows room for change, which sometimes may feel like a criticism, and sometimes it is. Action, though, has to be on the level of in-house and beyond. How can I teach what I do not know? In thinking through the individual and communal values, one can then choose values that are consistent with health, wholeness, and liberation. Action need not be violent or crisis-driven. The actions are shaped by behavior and initiative. Individuals and communities need visions coupled with mission statements—confessional adages that daily let them know who they are and whose they are. The role of action filters throughout our entire lives and can be for the benefit of ourselves and others. Good action steps call for inclusive, critical, investigative planning, planning that includes connecting with God and loving ourselves well. Contextually, beauty, sacrality, and stewardship create a frame that thwarts the complacency and deadliness of misbegotten anguish. When the light of God radiates from within and from without, there is a connectedness that is unstoppable. The love of God illumines the soul and makes a way for new conversations to begin, which can reconnect with new conversation partners, building relationships and moving toward transformation. The content of acknowledgment, attitude, and action shifts one from the stagnation of misbegotten anguish to the revolutionary possibility of living together in a world of global communities with deep regard, respect, and a commitment for renewal.

As Secretary-General [Kofi Annan] has begun to thrust the U.N. into new realms of global life, in internationalist circles, his vision of a moral world order is debated with ferocity.

What Annan proposes is nothing less than a world filled with dignified people. A world where Sierra Leonean rebels would have enough innate dignity to not chop off the arms of infant girls. A planet where India and Pakistan would be dignified enough not to blow up each other, where the indignities of chemical weapons would be a thing of the past, where the world's rich would be, yes, dignified enough to worry about the millions of Africans who will die of AIDS in the next two decades. This is the kind of world Annan imagines. It is the sort of world his very presence—serene, quiet, intent—suggests.[2]

This is the kind of world that we need to leave as a legacy for our children. This is the kind of world we deserve for our living. Only when we deal with all of our misbegotten anguish will we be able to live with such dignity and nobility that we can glimpse the sacred in each other. Then the need for scapegoating and all the *-isms* and their exponential entrees into grief will cease. "And we'll study war no more."

---

[2]Joshua Cooper Ramo, "The Five Virtues of Kofi Annan," *Time* 156 (September 4, 2000): 37.

Index

A

Aaron 167
Abraham 74
Absalom 46, 137–41, 147–48
abuse, sexual 89, 100, 108, 110, 118, 119
agape 23
Agent Orange 65
Ahab 72–76, 87, 91
Alexander VI, Pope 81
Ambrose, Stephen E. 71–72
anguish, misbegotten 3, 5, 27, 32, 58, 60–62, 77, 90, 123, 124, 148, 178, 180, 208, 209, 215, 216, 219, 220
Annan, Kofi 220
anomie 61
apartheid 82, 84, 136, 137, 140, 146, 147, 148, 159, 180
Aquinas, Thomas 129
Aristotle 22, 84, 128, 129
Augustine 6, 18

B

Baal 73, 74, 76, 87, 91
Bailie, Gil 34
Bartmann, Sarah 59
Baruch, Bernard M. 156
batterer 101, 102, 110
Beatitudes 127
behavior 10, 11, 20, 29, 30, 31, 36, 44, 49, 57, 61, 62, 66, 76, 88, 89, 95, 96, 98, 100, 101, 107–11, 118, 119, 123, 143, 203, 212
Belasco, David 30
Bible 5, 8, 11, 32, 46, 48, 56, 73, 74, 86, 87, 92, 121, 122, 128, 136, 147, 161, 167
bind *See* double bind
Birth of a Nation 44, 156
bisexual 112, 113
"Bless Your Beautiful Hide" 103, 104
Bluest Eye, The 176–78
Bobos 132–33
Bourdieu, Pierre 131

Brown, Robert MacAfee 17
Brunner, Emil 22
Butterfly. *See Madama Butterfly*
Byrd, James 40, 157

C

Camara, Dom Helder 17
Center for Women and Religion, Graduate Theological Union, Berkeley 153
Children's Defense Fund 185, 186
Chin, Vincent 157
Christ 13, 45, 113, 114
Christianity 12, 13, 17, 30, 43, 75, 77, 79
chutzpah, sociopolitical 107
Civil Rights Movement 146
Clansman, The 156
classism 110, 141–49, 188, 213–14
clergy sexual misconduct 118
cogito ergo sum 203
Colonialization 79, 80, 82, 84, 85
Colonizer and the Colonized, The 77
Columbine 20, 184, 202
Comstock, David 112, 113
concubine. *See* wife, secondary
Condillac, Etienne Bonnot de 130
confessional 13, 219
Crummel, Alexander 178
Cry, the Beloved Country 127, 136–41, 146, 214
Cui Bono 66
Cushite 167

D

Dahmer, Jeffrey 32
Das Kapital 130
D Day 67–71
Delilah 56, 154, 160, 167, 169–74, 215
Descartes, Rene 84
Deuteronomist 33, 47, 59, 60, 66, 73, 76, 167, 170, 211
dialogical 5, 13, 153, 171, 184
Dick and Jane 177

Dinah 96, 106–7, 121–22, 212
divorce 19, 31, 48, 52, 56, 105, 116, 120, 121, 208
Dixon, Thomas 156
Don Giovanni 194–98, 201, 202
Don Juan. *See Don Giovanni*
double bind 43
Durkheim, Emile 50

E
ecology 12
economy, market 78
ecumenical 13, 14
Edelman, Marian Wright 185
Elijah 66, 69, 72–76, 90, 91
Elisha 73–75, 91
elitism 114, 127, 133, 189, 202, 213, 214
Ephraim 32, 33, 47, 59, 147
epistemology 34, 102, 186, 191, 193
Etsinger, Shirley 116
exousia 199

F
Fanon, Frantz 190
feminine 12, 61, 90, 113, 173
feminist patriarchy. *See* patriarchy
Freud, Sigmund 39, 109

G
Gandhi 84, 87
gay 41, 42, 44, 112, 113, 211
geisha 30, 49, 52, 53, 55, 56
Genesis 32, 56, 87, 106, 107, 121, 122, 155
genital mutilation 99
genocide 65, 78, 79, 81, 86, 87, 91, 157, 177
Girard, Rene 34–39, 43, 45
globalization 78
"Going Courtin'" 105
Greider, Kathleen 17
Gulf War 66

H
Hagar 16
hanging. *See* lynching
harlot 48, 122, 163

Hays, J. Daniel 167
Helvétius, Claude-Adren 130
Hemings, Sally 97
hemoclysm 67, 69
Hill, Lauryn 184, 185, 190–91
Hitler, Adolf 68, 98, 99, 180
Holmes, Sherlock 27
hooks, bell 186, 187, 190, 192

I
ideology 68, 87, 99, 155, 156, 160, 174, 180
Imago Dei 10, 12, 13, 211
integrity 4, 11, 119, 122, 190
Isaiah 14
Israel 33, 46–48, 56, 57, 73–75, 121, 147, 163, 167–69, 171, 172

J
Jacob 106, 121, 122
Jefferson, Thomas 97
Jehu 74–76, 87, 91
Jepthah's daughter 57
Jeroboam 73, 74
Jesus 16, 19, 45, 50, 114, 127, 135, 155
Jezebel 66, 69, 72–77, 87, 90, 91, 212
Jim Crow 146, 155, 183
Johnson, Raynard 40
Judges 30, 32, 33, 46–49, 55–57, 60, 154, 162, 163, 167–74
Jungle Fever 154, 160–62, 167, 170–74, 215

K
Kant, Immanuel 24
karyukai 53
Kennedy, Jacqueline 96
kenshin. See suicide
killing rage 184, 187–90, 201–3
King, Jr., Martin Luther 87, 179, 180
Kings 72–75, 87
Koran 128
Krafft-Ebing, Richard von 98

L
Leah 106
Lee, Spike 154, 160, 166, 174

Leopard's Spots, The 156
lesbian 44, 112, 113
liturgical 13
Livingstone, David 83, 84
Locke, John 24, 130
Lorde, Audre 14
Lord's Prayer, The 17
Lot 87
Luke 128, 136, 137, 145
lynching 8, 35, 42, 43, 156, 178

M
Maafa 83
Madama Butterfly 30, 32, 33, 46, 56, 57
Malamuth, Neil 108
male dominance. *See* patriarchy
male superiority. *See* patriarchy
Mandela, Nelson 136, 146
manifest destiny 66, 77, 82, 91, 110, 154, 208, 211
Manson, Charles 99
Marshall, George C. 70, 71, 91
Martin, Joan M. 131
Marx, Karl 26, 127, 129, 130
masculine 12, 90, 96, 107, 110, 113
Matthew 127, 171
Memmi, Albert 77
Mengele, Dr. Josef 99
mimetic, mimesis 29, 34–36, 38–40, 45, 149, 210
minister 98, 116, 144
Miriam 169
miseducation 184, 185, 186, 190–94, 197, 201, 203, 206, 215
Miseducation of the Negro, The 185, 192
misogynistic 48, 49, 107, 172
Mitchum, Robert 4, 5
Morrison, Toni 175–78
Mozart, Wolfgang Amadeus 184, 194, 197

N
Niebuhr, Reinhold 18, 22
Night of the Hunter, The 4, 5, 7, 8, 15
Niland, Fritz 71
nonviolence 92
Nozick, Robert 24, 25

O
Obadiah 73, 76
Omaha Beach 69, 72, 91
Onassis, Aristotle 96

P
papal 81
Pascal, Blaise 26
patriarchs. *See* patriarchy
patriarchy 3, 48, 57, 59, 90, 107, 108, 111, 113, 114, 121, 123, 169, 188, 201
peacemaking 87, 88
pedagogical 13, 14
Philistine 162, 163, 169–74, 215
pilegesh 46, 55
Pinkerton. *See Madama Butterfly*
Plato 128
Poling, James 19
praxis 11, 13, 15, 23, 27, 33, 168, 188, 189, 199, 203, 217, 219
preacher 5–8, 103
priest 58, 73, 75, 129, 136, 137, 140–42, 148, 178
prostitute, prostitution 5, 7, 19, 48, 52, 89, 137, 147, 169–72, 174
Puccini, Giacomo 30, 32, 50, 51, 53, 60

R
Rake Punished, The. See Don Giovanni
rape, rapists 16, 19, 33, 48, 56–59, 65, 82, 85, 89, 97, 99, 100, 101, 103–9, 112, 114, 117–19, 121, 158, 177
Rape of the Sabine Women, The 103, 114, 122
Rawls, John 24
Resurrection 45, 46
Roodt, Darrell J. 136
Roosevelt, Franklin D. 156
Rosen, David 132, 133
Rousseau, Jean Jacques 24, 130

S
Sabine 103, 105, 114, 115, 122. *See also The Rape of the Sabine Women*
Sacher-Masoch, Leopold von 98

sacrality 11, 16, 37, 201, 218, 219
Sade, Marquis de 98
Saint Simon 130, 131
Samson 57, 154, 160, 162–63, 167–74
sati (widow burning) 99
Saul 46, 56, 59
Saving Private Ryan 27, 66, 69, 71, 72, 77, 90, 91
Seeger, Pete 65
seppuku. See suicide
servant, suffering 14
Seven Brides for Seven Brothers 103–5, 106, 122, 212
Shechem 96, 106, 121, 122
Shepherd, Matt 40
Shiloh 47
Simon says 38, 120
slavery 81–83, 97, 99, 128, 155, 183
Smith, Adam 129, 130
sociocultural 61, 66, 78, 89, 101, 107, 114, 164, 183, 192
socioeconomic 16, 19, 130, 148, 154, 193, 194, 203, 208
sociotheological 96
South Africa 84, 89, 136–38, 148, 157, 180
Stalinist 4, 200
steward, unjust 127, 134–36, 146, 148, 213
stewardship 12, 14, 18, 77, 200, 216, 217–19
Suchocki, Marjorie 18, 19
suffering servant 14
suicide 30, 31, 40–42, 50, 52, 55, 57, 186, 202
supremacist patriarchy. *See* patriarchy

T
Tamar 56, 123, 147
Theology, Womanist 10–14
Till, Emmett 43, 44
transgender 112, 113
Trible, Phyllis 76

U
umfundisi 136–41, 147, 148

United Nations Convention on the Elimination of All Forms of Discrimination Against Women 114

V
Vedic 128
violence, domestic 19, 21, 60, 90, 95, 96, 99, 107, 108, 113
violence, gender 96, 99, 122, 212, 213
violence, male 48, 57, 100–102, 107, 108, 117
violence, sexual 17, 19, 97–100, 102, 108–9, 116–18
visibility 11, 15, 34, 99

W
Walker, Alice 9, 13, 153, 180
Walzer, Michael 24, 25
Warren, Jr., Arthur Carl "J.R." 41, 42
West, Cornell 192
Wheatley, Phyllis 178
When Work Disappears 145
"When You're in Love" 104, 105
wife, secondary 30, 32, 33, 38, 46–48, 55, 60, 210
Williams, Delores 13, 16
Wilson, William Julius 145
Wink, Walter 92
Womanist, Womanist Theory 3, 5, 9–16, 153, 183, 186, 189, 191, 199–200
Womanist, Christian 10–12
women, battered 19, 95, 113, 114, 208
women, "invisible" 99
Women, The 48, 89, 105, 106, 119–21, 212
Woodson, Carter G. 184, 185, 190, 192, 193, 201, 203
World War I 70, 83
World War II 36, 50, 67, 69, 72, 79, 84, 112, 156
"wretched of the earth, the" 190

Y
Yahweh 56, 73, 75, 76, 87, 167–69, 171, 174